D0900620

Printed in the United States of America
First Printing, 2012
ISBN 978-1-938800-02-3
The Autistic Press
Washington, DC

Dedicated to

*Tracy Latimer, 12 years old, gassed by her father, 1993 * Scarlett Chen, 4, drowned by her mother, July 2004 * Tiffany Pinckney, 23, locked in a basement and starved to death by her sister and brother-in-law, 2005 * Katie McCarron, 3, suffocated by her mother, May 2006 * Marcus Fiesel, 4, wrapped in heavy blankets by his step-parents and left in a closet to suffocate while they went out of town, August, 2006 * Francecca Hardwick, 18, locked in a burning car with her mother, October 2007 * Naomi Hill, 4, drowned by her mother, November 2007 * Calista Springer, 16, chained to a bed and abandoned in a fire by her entire family, February, 2008 * Tom Inglis, 22, died after his mother administered an overdose of heroin to him, November 2008 * Jeremy Fraser, 9 years old, died of recurrent leukemia after his mother withheld the medication that would have saved his life, March 2009 * Peter Eitzen, 16, stabbed by his mother, July 2009 * Jeremy Bostick, 11, gassed by his father, September 2009 * Tony Khor, 15, strangled by his mother, October 2009 * Betty Anne Gagnon, 48, tortured to death by her sister and brother-in-law, November 2009 * Walter Knox Hildebrand Jr., 20, died of a seizure induced by his brother's physical abuse, November 2009 * Laura Cummings, 23, tortured to death by her mother and brother, January 2010 *Ajit Singh, 12, forced to drink bleach by his mother, February 2010 * Gerren Isgrigg, 6, died of exposure after his grandmother abandoned him in a remote area, April 2010 * Leosha Barnett, 17, starved to death by her mother and sister, May 2010 * Glen Freaney, 11, strangled by his mother, May 2010 * Payton Ettinger, 4, starved by his mother, May 2010 * Christopher Melton, 18, gassed by his mother, June 2010 * Rylan Rochester, 6 months old, suffocated by his mother because she believed him to be autistic, June 2010 * Kenneth Holmes, 12, shot by his mother, July 2010 *Zain Akhter, 5, and Faryaal Akhter, 2, strangled by their mother, July 2010 * Rohit Singh, 7, beaten to death by his father, September 2010 * Zahra Baker, 10, murdered and dismembered by her stepmother and perhaps her father, October 2010 * Chase Ogden, 13, shot by his mother along with his sister Olivia, October 2010 * Kyle Snyder, 9, shot by grandmother. October 2010 * Karandeep Arora, 18, suffocated by his parents, October 2010 * Julie Cirella, 8, poisoned by her mother, July 2011 * Noe Medina Jr., 7 months, thrown 4 stories by his mother, August 2011 * Benjamin Barnhard, 13, shot by his mother, August 2011 * Jori Lirette, 7, decapitated by his father, August 2011 * George Hodgins, 22, shot by his mother, March 2012 * Daniel Corby, 4, drowned by his mother, April 2012 * And all of the names we may never know*

Rest in peace.

Table of Contents

Authors

Acknowledgements

Foreword

Someone should have warned me how difficult writing the foreword for this anthology was going to be.

Michel Foucault once asked, "If you knew when you began a book what you would say at the end, do you think that you would have the courage to write it?" The varied contributors for this anthology are some of the toughest, bravest people I know; none of us knew, when we started, what The Loud Hands Project was going to become. Not even me.

When we started less than a year ago, plans were vague and needs were looming. Action happened in tiny flurries and eddies, here and there in the corner of people's lives, for months. I drove four terrifying hours to access the closest thing to a physical Autistic community I could find and spent a whirlwind twenty-four hours filming a promotional video. Back on the internet, where the Autistic community has its roots and liminal spaces, people sent in clips filmed on iPhones and webcams: ten-to-fifteen seconds of themselves holding signs, smiling at the camera, stimming, telling the world they were *fine*. I sat at my kitchen table and learned how to use iMovie, coaxed my sister into filming me, my brother into holding signs. One friend transcribed and captioned the video; everyone agreed to keep quiet and wait, while the other preparations were put in place. I spent hours agonizing over emails, making plans, refining logistics, bullying ephemeral dreams into concrete objectives.

I was asked, *how are you going to do this*. Bit by bit, I made the answer.

Most dreams stay dreams: escapes, nightmares, obsessions, fantasies. To make The Loud Hands Project cross from dream to reality, we needed the basic ingredients of any project: an identified community need, a meaningful solution, and the resources to provide that solution. Armies can't march on prayers; in order to do what our community needed, we needed money. So on midnight, December 26th, with bits of wrapping paper still scattered across the house and a piece of cold apple pie on a plate, we made our indiegogo page public, sent out an announcement, and waited.

Twenty four hours later, we'd raised over $3,000.

Our original fundraising goal was $10,000. After four days, we here halfway there; after nineteen days of fundraising, we met and surpassed our goal. After 80 days, several interviews, too many tumblr posts, an ambitious blog carnival, hundreds of shared facebook updates and tweets, thousands of emails to families, friends, coworkers, and arch-nemeses, and a constant, concerted effort by the Autistic community to keep the momentum rolling and the energy building, fundraising for The Loud Hand Project's first anthology and website ended at 11:59 pm PST with $15,610 from 224 separate donations.

We hadn't known.

When we first started exploring the concept that would grow into The Loud Hands Project, we knew a few basic things. We knew that the autistic community is comprised of terrifyingly brave and resilient people; that the autistic community has many things to say and is perfectly capable of saying them in our own ways with our own voices; and that there is something beautiful and powerful about a community of people who are routinely silenced, abused, neglected, and murdered, yet who continue to survive, finding and nurturing one another and growing in strength and sense of purpose, year after year.

We knew that there was a need to honor this collective and individual strength, beauty, and voice, and project it out further into the world to reach those who didn't yet know that other people like them existed, and tell them that they were *fine*.

That the community was so hungry for a formal project like The Loud Hands Project should not, perhaps, have come as such a surprise after all.

Our initial campaign could not have succeeded if it hadn't struck a chord with so many community members who spent hours promoting it to anyone who would listen, and quite a few who would not. The broad-based, enthusiastic support we received even in our earliest days is indicative of a founding, driving principle of the project: The Loud Hands Project is community-based, community directed, and community driven. Rather than being top-down, we ask the community what their priorities as a whole are, and give individual and collective community voices a platform.

Many people responded with particular, focused joy to the name of the project itself: *loud hands*. Abuse and silencing is a constant, pervasive theme in the lives of autistic people, and for many people it is best expressed by that old, familiar phrase from special education: *quiet hands! Loud hands* means resisting. *Loud Hands* means speaking, however we do, *anyway*--and doing so in a way that can be very obviously Autistic. It means finding ways to talk and think about ourselves on our own terms. The Loud Hands Project is a start in that direction.

One of the cruelest tricks our culture plays on autistic people is that it makes us strangers to ourselves. We grow up knowing we're different, but that difference is defined for us in terms of an absence of neurotypicality, not as the presence of another equally valid way of being. We wind up internalizing a lot of hateful, damaging, and inaccurate things about ourselves, and that makes it harder to know who we really are or what we really can and cannot do.

If no one ever acknowledges that we have a voice, we can forget how to use it. We might even decide not to.

The Loud Hands Project seeks to consolidate the power of the autistic community by centering and projecting our voices, however they manifest, to provide an authentic alternative to all of this noise. We have an overarching commitment to undoing the cultural processes and ghettoization that make autistic people strangers to ourselves and spectators in our own stories--but we are not, at our core, reactionaries. Autistic people exist in an unsafe and actively abusive world, but we're more than what happens to us. The autistic community needs to be heard, speaking in our own ways on our own terms about the items on *our* agenda, on an unprecedented scale, reaching a much broader audience than we ever have been able to before.

Which brings us back to this anthology.

The Loud Hands Project is a transmedia project, which means we use multiple forms of content--written words, videos, visual art, the internet, and more. We have numerous projects in development now, which you'll be able to read about in more detail towards the end of this anthology. But we decided to start with a book, because every good project needs a founding document.

So we asked you to help us make one.

Over the last several months, we've gathered contributions from a wide variety of sources, more than we could ever afford to print. Some were sent in, unsolicited. Others were pulled from the earliest chapters of the autistic community, with authors kind enough to grant us permission to reprint. Others came from blogs, and still others were solicited from people responding to the following focus paragraph:

The anthology is structured around twin themes of *simplicity* and *voice*. *Simplicity* because autism, for all its diversity, isn't *complicated* or scary or hard--it just is. *Voice* because autistic people have voices, otherwise we wouldn't be silenced. These two concepts go hand in hand. Autistic brains are different from non-autistic brains--not better or worse, just different. Autistic voices, similarly, can take different forms or styles or express different things through different means than non-autistic voices. These facts are simple and neutral, but regularly obscured and overridden by cultural scripts and fallacies demanding broken, voiceless not-people stranded by huge chasms from the rest of the world in place of everyday autistics. *Simplicity* and *voice* are routinely sacrificed for dehumanization and spectacle. That's not our baggage, but when it's used to silence our voices and complicated our realities, it becomes our business. The Loud Hands Project is designed as a counter to that, and this anthology is to be our guiding, founding document.

The diversity of voices here is truly incredible. People of all ages, genders, backgrounds, and abilities responded with grace, passion, and clarity, articulating brutally honest accounts of the world as it is and shining visions of what we can make it into. It starts with the basic, foundational idea that *there is nothing wrong with us*. We are fine. We are complete, complex, human beings leading rich and meaningful existences and deserving dignity, respect, human rights, and the primary voice in the conversation about us. We can have loud hands. To say that flapping can be communication, that autistic people have voices regardless of whether or not we speak orally, and that our obviously autistic communication and thoughts have intrinsic worth is an inherently revolutionary thing. This anthology, and The Loud Hands Project as a whole, serves to document and explore that.

Bit by bit, piece by piece, we're rewriting the world into one where our voices are heard.

Thank you for reading. Thank you for writing. Thank you for speaking, and thank you for believing in us when we started to wonder, many months ago, what this book might have to say.

Julia Bascom
Project founder and organizer
The Loud Hands Project

Historical Foundations

Don't Mourn For Us

by Jim Sinclair

[This article was published in the Autism Network International newsletter, Our Voice, Volume 1, Number 3, 1993. It is an outline of the presentation Jim gave at the 1993 International Conference on Autism in Toronto, and is addressed primarily to parents.]

Parents often report that learning their child is autistic was the most traumatic thing that ever happened to them. Non-autistic people see autism as a great tragedy, and parents experience continuing disappointment and grief at all stages of the child's and family's life cycle.

But this grief does not stem from the child's autism in itself. It is grief over the loss of the normal child the parents had hoped and expected to have. Parents' attitudes and expectations, and the discrepancies between what parents expect of children at a particular age and their own child's actual development, cause more stress and anguish than the practical complexities of life with an autistic person.

Some amount of grief is natural as parents adjust to the fact that an event and a relationship they've been looking forward to isn't going to materialize. But this grief over a fantasized normal child needs to be separated from the parents' perceptions of the child they *do* have: the autistic child who needs the support of adult caretakers and who *can* form very meaningful relationships with those caretakers if given the opportunity. Continuing focus on the child's autism as a source of grief is damaging for both the parents and the child, and precludes the development of an accepting and authentic relationship between them. For their own sake and for the sake of their children, I urge parents to make radical changes in their perceptions of what autism means.

I invite you to look at our autism, and look at your grief, from our perspective:

Autism is not an appendage

Autism isn't something a person *has*, or a "shell" that a person is trapped inside. There's no normal child hidden behind the autism. Autism is a way of being. It is *pervasive*; it colors every experience, every sensation, perception, thought, emotion, and encounter, every aspect of existence. It is not possible to separate the autism from the person--and if it were possible, the person you'd have left would not be the same person you started with.

This is important, so take a moment to consider it: Autism is a way of being. It is not possible to separate the person from the autism.

Therefore, when parents say,

> I wish my child did not have autism,

what they're really saying is,

> I wish the autistic child I have did not exist, and I had a different (non-autistic) child instead.

Read that again. This is what we hear when you mourn over our existence. This is what we hear when you pray for a cure. This is what we know, when you tell us of your fondest hopes and dreams for us:

---

that your greatest wish is that one day we will cease to be, and strangers you can love will move in behind our faces.

Autism is not an impenetrable wall

You try to relate to your autistic child, and the child doesn't respond. He doesn't see you; you can't reach her; there's no getting through. That's the hardest thing to deal with, isn't it? The only thing is, it isn't true.

Look at it again: You try to relate as parent to child, using your own understanding of normal children, your own feelings about parenthood, your own experiences and intuitions about relationships. And the child doesn't respond in any way you can recognize as being part of that system.

That does not mean the child is incapable of relating *at all*. It only means you're assuming a shared system, a shared understanding of signals and meanings, that the child in fact does not share. It's as if you tried to have an intimate conversation with someone who has no comprehension of your language. Of course the person won't understand what you're talking about, won't respond in the way you expect, and may well find the whole interaction confusing and unpleasant.

It takes more work to communicate with someone whose native language isn't the same as yours. And autism goes deeper than language and culture; autistic people are "foreigners" in any society. You're going to have to give up your assumptions about shared meanings. You're going to have to learn to back up to levels more basic than you've probably thought about before, to translate, and to check to make sure your translations are understood. You're going to have to give up the certainty that comes of being on your own familiar territory, of knowing you're in charge, and let your child teach you a little of her language, guide you a little way into his world.

And the outcome, if you succeed, still will not be a normal parent-child relationship. Your autistic child may learn to talk, may attend regular classes in school, may go to college, drive a car, live independently, have a career--but will never relate to you as other children relate to their parents. Or your autistic child may never speak, may graduate from a self-contained special education classroom to a sheltered activity program or a residential facility, may need lifelong full-time care and supervision--but is not completely beyond your reach. The ways we relate are *different*. Push for the things your expectations tell you are normal, and you'll find frustration, disappointment, resentment, maybe even rage and hatred. Approach respectfully, without preconceptions, and with openness to learning new things, and you'll find a world you could never have imagined.

Yes, that takes more work than relating to a non-autistic person. But it *can* be done--unless non-autistic people are far more limited than we are in their capacity to relate. We spend our entire lives doing it. Each of us who does learn to talk to you, each of us who manages to function at all in your society, each of us who manages to reach out and make a connection with you, is operating in alien territory, making contact with alien beings. We spend our entire lives doing this. And then you tell us that we can't relate.

Autism is not death

Granted, autism isn't what most parents expect or look forward to when they anticipate the arrival of a child. What they expect is a child who will be like them, who will share their world and relate to them without requiring intensive on-the-job training in alien contact. Even if their child has some disability other than autism, parents expect to be able to relate to that child on the terms that seem normal to them; and in most cases, even allowing for the limitations of various disabilities, it is possible to form the kind of bond the parents had been looking forward to.

But not when the child is autistic. Much of the grieving parents do is over the non-occurrence of the expected relationship with an expected normal child. This grief is very real, and it needs to be expected and worked through so people can get on with their lives—
but it has *nothing* to do with autism.

What it comes down to is that you expected something that was tremendously important to you, and you looked forward to it with great joy and excitement, and maybe for a while you thought you actually had it--and then, perhaps gradually, perhaps abruptly, you had to recognize that the thing you looked forward to hasn't happened. It isn't going to happen. No matter how many other, normal children you have, nothing will change the fact that *this* time, the child you waited and hoped and planned and dreamed for didn't arrive.

This is the same thing that parents experience when a child is stillborn, or when they have their baby to hold for a short time, only to have it die in infancy. It isn't about autism, it's about shattered expectations. I suggest that the best place to address these issues is not in organizations devoted to autism, but in parental bereavement counseling and support groups. In those settings parents learn to come to terms with their loss--not to forget about it, but to let it be in the past, where the grief doesn't hit them in the face every waking moment of their lives. They learn to accept that their child *is* gone, forever, and won't be coming back. Most importantly, they learn *not to take out their grief for the lost child on their surviving children*. This is of critical importance when one of those surviving children arrived at t time the child being mourned for died.

You didn't lose a child to autism. You lost a child because the child you waited for never came into existence. That isn't the fault of the autistic child who does exist, and it shouldn't be our burden. We need and deserve families who can see us and value us for ourselves, not families whose vision of us is obscured by the ghosts of children who never lived. Grieve if you must, for your own lost dreams. But don't mourn for *us*. We are alive. We are real. And we're here waiting for you.

This is what I think autism societies should be about: not mourning for what never was, but exploration of what is. We need you. We need your help and your understanding. Your world is not very open to us, and we won't make it without your strong support. Yes, there is tragedy that comes with autism: not because of what we are, but because of the things that happen to us. Be sad about that, if you want to be sad about something. Better than being sad about it, though, get mad about it--and then *do* something about it. The tragedy is not that we're here, but that your world has no place for us to be. How can it be otherwise, as long as our own parents are still grieving over having brought us into the world?

Take a look at your autistic child sometime, and take a moment to tell yourself who that child is not. Think to yourself: "This is not my child that I expected and planned for. This is not the child I waited for through all those months of pregnancy and all those hours of labor. This is not the child I made all those plans to share all those experiences with. That child never came. This is not that child." Then go do whatever grieving you have to do--*away* from the autistic child-- and start learning to let go.

After you've started that letting go, come back and look at your autistic child again, and say to yourself: "This is not my child that I expected and planned for. This is an alien child who landed in my life by accident. I don't know who this child is or what it will become. But I know it's a child, stranded in an alien world, without parents of its own kind to care for it. It needs someone to care for it, to teach it, to interpret and to advocate for it. And because this alien child happened to drop into my life, that job is mine if I want it."

If that prospect excites you, then come join us, in strength and determination, in hope and in joy. The adventure of a lifetime is ahead of you.

(A version of this essay appeared previously on jimsinclair.org.)

Autism Network International: The Development Of A Community And Its Culture

by Jim Sinclair

The American Heritage® Dictionary of the English Language (2000) defines "community" in part as: A group of people having common interests," "A group viewed as forming a distinct segment of society," "Similarity or identity," and "Sharing, participation, and fellowship." Its entries for "culture" include "The totality of socially transmitted behavior patterns, arts, beliefs, institutions, and all other products of human work and thought," "These patterns, traits, and products considered as the expression of a particular period, class, community, or population," and "The predominating attitudes and behavior that characterize the functioning of a group or organization."

Nearly all the operative terms in those definitions would seem to be at odds with the traditional view of autism as profound impairment in social functioning. Autistic people are seen as lacking the ability to share common interests with others, disconnected from social participation and fellowship, and inaccessible to social transmission of behaviors and attitudes. How, then, can we speak of autistic community and autistic culture?

This article will describe how one particular group of autistic people joined together on the basis of common interests, and grew into a community. Along the way I will tell you a bit about the culture that has developed within that community. It is my hope that through this introduction to my community, you will begin to reconsider many of the assumptions you may have about autistic social characteristics. Is it always correct to view differences between the behavior of autistics and NTs as "symptoms" of some "disorder" in autistic people? Is it necessarily helpful to respond to such differences by trying to teach autistic people to emulate NT social behaviors so they can "fit in" with NT culture? What alternatives might there be for addressing social difficulties between autistic and NT people? These are some questions you should ask yourself as you read this article.

A disclaimer: I can only report about the culture that has developed within the Autism Network International community. Other autistic communities may have very different cultures. To the best of my knowledge, ANI was the first autistic community to be created naturalistically by autistic people, and it remains the largest autistic-run organization to have regular physical gatherings of autistic people.

FIRST ENCOUNTERS

Autism Network International was created by a handful of verbal autistic people who had made contact with each other via a penpal list maintained by a parent-run organization. A few of us had also met each other in person at autism conferences. But typical autism conferences, run by and for NT parents and professionals, do not tend to be very good places for autistic people to connect meaningfully with each other. There's simply too much going on--too many people, too much movement, too much noise, often fluorescent lights, and above all, the overwhelming onslaught of speakers and articles and exhibits all stressing that there's something terribly *wrong*with us, that we're a horribly defective type of human, and that our very existence is a source of never-ending grief for our families.

Some of us came to autism conferences anyway, because we had no other way to meet others like ourselves. But even if we did happen to find other autistic people there, the environment was very hostile from both a sensory and an emotional standpoint. At best, meeting at conferences gave us a chance to find out about the existence of someone we might want to get to know better, and to exchange contact information so we could follow up later, usually by means of writing letters. Not many of us were on the Internet at the time.

In February 1992 Donna Williams came to the U.S. to promote her first book, *Nobody Nowhere*. During her trip, she took a few days away from the book tour to visit with Kathy Lissner (now Kathy Grant) and me, two of the autistic people she had been corresponding with through the penpal list. I drove to St. Louis, Missouri, where Kathy lived, and we all stayed together in Kathy's apartment.

Donna's description of that visit can be found on pages 184-187 of her second book, *Somebody Somewhere*. We spent two or three days together, in a place where *everyone* was autistic, and where there were only three of us instead of a large crowd. We were all somewhat familiar with each other through our written correspondence; Kathy and I had also met briefly in person at a conference or two. The combination of these factors produced a new kind of autistic encounter that was vastly different from meeting other autistic people at NT conferences. Donna's description of the experience reads in part:

> Despite thousands of miles, our 'our world' concepts, strategies, and experiences even came down to having created the same made-up words to describe them. Together we felt like a lost tribe. 'Normal' is to be in the company of one like one's self.

> We all had a sense of belonging, of being understood, of being normal . . . all the things we could not get from others in general. It was so sad to have to leave. 'Why can't we alllive together?' we had each asked at some point or other.   (p. 186)

My own recollection of this meeting is of feeling that, after a life spent among aliens, I had met someone who came from the same planet as me. We understood each other. At one point I overheard Donna talking on the phone to someone associated with her book tour. Apparently the caller had asked her something about how the visit was going. I heard Donna's answer: "We don't get a lot of cooking done, but we speak the same language."

It was an amazing and powerful experience to be able to communicate with someone in my own language. I had sometimes been able to establish meaningful communication with people before, but it always involved my having to learn the other person's language and do constant laborious translating. (Sinclair, 1988) Here, with people who shared my language, meaning flowed freely and easily.

Autistic socializing

We talked a lot during those two days, and laughed a lot, and played around with each other's fixations, and sat on the floor stimming a lot. The first time I had met other autistic people, at a conference nearly three years earlier, I had observed the phenomenon of autistic people using their fixations as a bridge to make connections with other people. Now, with Kathy and Donna, I experienced another form of natural autistic social behavior--interactive stimming:

> Even before I met Donna in person I had recognized that she must have some visual fixations, because she would always enclose some shiny or brightly-colored object in each of her letters. When I was going to meet her, I thought of bringing something shiny as a gift, but I didn't have enough of a feel for it to know what would be appropriate. Then during the time I spent with her, I watched her go into fits of ecstasy while arranging colorful objects and looking at them through a kaleidoscope...And while she was engaging in this activity of arranging objects and looking at them through her scope, *she kept insisting that Kathy and I look at them too.* Of course, being

autistic I'm not supposed to understand things like this, but to me that looked suspiciously like a person wanting to share a pleasurable activity with her friends. And for my part, having seen her reach the peak of rapture over an empty Coke can, and having heard her say that metallic red was her favorite visual stimulus, I knew what would be an appropriate gift for her. I got a red sequins-covered belt from Kmart and sent it to her: pretty tacky from a fashion perspective, but just right for someone with her sensory responses.   (Sinclair, 1992)

In the years since that first meeting, I have seen this kind of spontaneous sharing of pleasure in fixations and stimming occur again and again among autistic people. It is an aspect of the autistic culture that has evolved within this autistic community.

Besides communication and fun, we also began to glimpse the possibilities of autistic peer support. It's true, as Donna said, that we didn't get a lot of cooking done; but what did get done was usually a result of our reminding each other that it was time to eat or that the soup someone had put in the microwave was ready. All of us had significant difficulties managing the tasks of everyday life. But between the three of us, someone was generally able to remember and to remind about the really necessary things.

We speculated that if we could all live near each other, we could divide up the activities of daily living so that each of us would only need to remember and organize 1/3 of the tasks. We could share the responsibility for reminding each other when it was time to cook, eat, bathe, etc.

Thirteen years later this idea of a permanent physical community, where autistic people could live together and support each other, still gets discussed from time to time on the ANI-L email list and at Autreat conferences. Maybe someday we'll have the material resources needed to try to make it happen.

Autistic adults as a resource for parents

Another dynamic of autistic community--or of autistic subcommunity within a larger NT community--emerged during that first meeting: interactions between verbally proficient autistic adults and parents of less-communicative autistic people. Each of us individually had a lot of experience interacting with parents of autistic children. What was new this time was the opportunity to interact meaningfully with other autistic people, and the distinction between that and our interactions with parents.

In this case the parents, Rita and Doyle, were actually foster parents. They were knowingly and voluntarily becoming parents of an autistic child, taking into their family a teenager who was completely nonverbal, not toilet trained, not able to feed herself, and was sometimes self-injurious. Some time earlier, Doyle had posted a query on an Internet forum I was on, asking for advice about teaching his foster daughter to chew solid food. I had noticed that he lived in St. Louis, and had referred him to Kathy because she lived in the same city. Now, with Donna and me coming to town for this visit, he had asked if he could come over and meet us. We agreed to spend a couple of hours with him one evening.

The dynamic of our first meeting with Doyle and Rita was similar to that of many interactions between autistic adults and parents of autistic children within NT-dominated autism organizations (including online forums): They saw us as a valuable resource, and hoped that we would be able to give them first-hand information that would allow them to understand and help the autistic person in their lives.

We were willing to help them if we could, because we did care about the welfare of their autistic child who couldn't communicate for herself. The NT world might call her "low-functioning" and us "high-functioning," but we saw her as part of our world. Donna talked to Rita on the phone during the afternoon, and in the evening Doyle came to Kathy's apartment to meet with us in person. (We did not meet the autistic foster daughter during that visit, but Kathy and I met her at many of our later gatherings.)

As it turned out, this particular set of parents respected us and liked us for ourselves, not merely as tools to help them understand their child. Kathy and I both formed lasting friendships with them, and in the coming years they often opened their home and gave their support to other gatherings of autistic people. When Doyle and Rita, and many other parents, became our friends, we became comfortable sharing our space with them. They even became important parts of our community. But on that first evening, during our first creation of "autistic space," we knew them only as non-autistic people wanting to use us as a resource to help them with their child. And we responded with what has continued to be a characteristic feature of the autistic community that has grown from that first meeting: We set boundaries between the time we gave to them and the time we reserved for ourselves. We agreed to spend some time answering questions about our experiences of autism, but we set limits on how much time. The non-autistic parent came over, we talked with him for a while, and then he went home and we had our own autistic space again.

MAKING IT HAPPEN: THE NEXT STEPS

So--we spent a couple of days together, and we communicated, and had fun, and helped each other, and we talked to parents in the hope that our experiences might help them help their child. And we decided that autistic space was a good thing for autistic people to have. We decided to start our own organization, rather than continue to be dependent on NT-run organizations to help us find each other and to provide the only places where we could meet.

Since Kathy and I lived about 300 miles apart, and Donna lived on another continent, we had to settle for distance communication: a printed newsletter, and a penpal list for private person-to-person communication. This was modeled after the parent-oriented organization whose penpal list had enabled us to make contact with each other. But our newsletter would be written by and for autistic people, not just another "parent" newsletter. I volunteered to edit it. That's how I became coordinator of Autism Network International.

We called it a "network," not a "community." At that time, I really didn't believe "community" would be a meaningful concept for autistic people. We don't tend to function very well in groups, let alone *as* groups. Autistic connections seem to be made on a person-to-person basis, one person at a time. In our new autistic network, as we envisioned it, the newsletter would be the vehicle for information-sharing among the group as a whole, while the penpal list would allow for contact among people who wished to have person-to-person contact.

Defining membership: Who are "we"?

Right away we had to make some decisions about who could be included in our organization: Autistic people only, or would parents and professionals also be allowed to join? "High-functioning" autistic people only, or all autistic people?

At that time it was still generally believed that "high-functioning" autistic people were a rarity. The term "Asperger syndrome" was just beginning to be introduced in the United States. Autistic people who could speak fluently, who could read and write, who could demonstrate self-awareness and insight into their own experiences, who could participate in higher education, have jobs, and live independently--these were still viewed as novelties, exceptions to the general rule that autistic people are severely learning disabled. (The fact that while many of us are capable of doing *some* of those "high-functioning" things, very few of us are actually capable of doing *all* of them, is still not widely recognized. The tendency is to assume that those of us with a high degree of verbal ability are "high-functioning" in all other areas as well. The reality is quite different.)

Kathy and Donna and I had found each other through a penpal list maintained by an organization of parents of "high-functioning" or "more able" autistic people. We all communicated using language (both oral and written). We all had university degrees. We all lived on our own. Notwithstanding our various difficulties with sensory processing, social comprehension, emotional modulation, employment, adequate self-care, household management, and assorted other life skills, we were all considered to be "high-functioning." We could have kept our focus only on other autistic people who were also "high-functioning."

But we had all fit descriptions of "low-functioning" autistic people when we were younger. We all recognized commonalities between ourselves and autistic people who were still considered "low-functioning." We also recognized abilities and strengths in many autistic people who just didn't happen to share our skills in using language.

We decided that our mission was to advocate for civil rights and self-determination for *all* autistic people, regardless of whether they were labeled "high-" or "low-functioning," and regardless of whether they were able to participate independently in our language-based network. To that end, we understood that we really had to make our newsletter available to parents and professionals, because educating parents and professionals was the only way we could hope to affect the lives of autistic people who weren't able to participate on their own. But we decided that the penpal list was to be confidential, for autistic people only. Once again, we set boundaries between our public activity and willingness to serve as a resource for non-autistic people, and our private autistic connections.

Spreading the word

Kathy immediately began mailing announcements about ANI to all the (NT-run) autism organizations she could find in the U.S. Donna worked on spreading the word internationally during her book tours. And I, the only one of us who had Internet access at the time, posted announcements online. I was a member of a new online autism mailing list, and for a while I was the only autistic person in that forum. Most of the other members of the mailing list were parents of young autistic children; a few were professionals who worked with autistic people. As usual for an autistic person trying to participate in an NT-oriented autism forum, most of my participation consisted of describing my personal experiences of autism, and trying to answer parents' questions about whether my experiences might shed light on their children's behavior. It was an autism forum, but it was definitely not "autistic space."

I printed the first issue of "Our Voice," the ANI newsletter, in November 1992. We had about fifteen subscribers, most of whom were non-autistic parents of autistic children. It was hard to find other autistic people. In terms of numbers, the initial response was discouraging. Hostile responses from established (NT-run) autism organizations were also unexpected and upsetting.

ENCOUNTERING OPPOSITION

When I had first started seeking to communicate with other autistic people in the late 1980s, I had approached autism organizations and professionals who worked with autistic people, in the naïve belief that they and I, and other verbal autistic people, had some common purpose. My purposes in seeking to form a mutual aid-self help group for autistic people were to share first-hand experiences to counter the uniformly gloomy and pessimistic (and often offensive and insulting) portrayals of autism in the existing literature; and to advocate for improved support services for autistic people. (At the time I began my search, I had lost my job and was homeless, but I was unable to qualify for any assistance because I was considered "too bright to be disabled.") It seemed to me that these goals ought to be shared by people who were interested in learning about autism or in helping autistic people. But most of the responses ranged from total indifference to empty encouraging words that were not backed up with any action--people would say it sounded like a good idea, but would not run announcements about the project in their newsletters or put other verbal autistic people in contact with me. The only two exceptions to this pattern were the organization for parents of "more able" autistic people, which occasionally printed letters from autistic people and maintained the penpal directory through which I eventually contacted Kathy and Donna; and an autism professional who arranged a scholarship for me to attend a conference (the first autism conference I ever attended, in fact), and set aside a room during one of the conference sessions for any autistic people who wanted to meet. No other newsletters were printing our letters, no other conferences were facilitating contact among autistic people, and no one else was offering any practical support whatsoever to autistic peer contact. (A few professionals, though, did take advantage of my meetings with them to ask me personal questions about my experience of autism.)

Even worse, it seemed that when we did manage to find each other and work together to further our goals, responses from the "autism establishment" escalated from indifference to active subterfuge. By the summer of 1991, several of us had made contact with each other via the penpal directory, and the 1991 Autism Society of America national conference was the first conference I attended where I met autistic people whom I already knew. Several of us made a point of asking questions or making comments during the question-and-answer portions of as many presentations as possible, always identifying ourselves as autistic people. The presenters seemed pleased with our contributions, and a great many audience members sought us out afterward to talk to us and ask us questions.

Our visible presence at the 1991 conference, and the obvious interest many parents had in meeting us, drew the attention of the ASA Board of Directors. Two of us were approached by a Board member and some other parents, and asked if we would like the Board to help us form a committee that would be advisory to the Board and would have some input into ASA and its future conferences. We accepted on the spot. We were told that our committee would be allowed to have a representative present at ASA Board meetings; would have some input into planning the 1992 national conference (both in the organization of facilities to be accessible to autistic people, and in the selection of presentations); and would be given space in the ASA newsletter. In addition, when we told them that we were already working on forming an organization of our own, they offered us some unspecified amount of financial and/or administrative support for creating our own autistic self-advocacy organization.

None of these promises was honored. The only mention the ASA newsletter carried of our attempts at autistic self-advocacy was an item in the précis of the July 1991 Board meeting, authorizing one of the Board members to *take charge of* organizing an advisory committee of autistic people--and we never heard from them again about that committee, despite several follow-up phone calls I made. One of the ASA Board members later confirmed my suspicion that these offers were merely empty gestures by a Board that wanted to impress parents of autistic people--who hold most of the voting power in ASA--but who didn't expect to have to follow through because they never expected autistic people to be capable of organizing ourselves.

When, contrary to expectations, we *did* begin organizing ourselves and announced the establishment of ANI, ASA continued to ignore the announcements we repeatedly submitted for inclusion in the newsletter. But now there did begin to be some acknowledgment of the existence of autistic people trying to self-advocate, in the form of rumors started by some ASA Board members to the effect that I was not really autistic. (This despite of the fact that my records had been reviewed by two psychologists who were members of the ASA professional advisory board, and both had stated--one of them under oath at a rehabilitation services hearing--that I am indeed autistic.) In a clear attempt to undermine our group cohesion, Kathy and some other autistic adults were directly "warned" that I was not what I claimed to be. Meanwhile, Donna was encountering similar denunciations as her book began to receive international attention.

Contexts and politics of opposition to self-advocacy

At the time all this was happening, it took me completely by surprise. Nearly all of us who were involved in the earliest period of ANI had met many parents of autistic children, at conferences and local parent support groups. Almost invariably, the parents were pleased and excited to hear from us. True, their primary interest was in using us as resources for their children rather than supporting us in our own goals; but still, they were not *hostile* toward us. It seems that one autistic person at a time--and preferably a passive one--might be welcomed as an interesting novelty or an amusing diversion or possibly even a valuable source of information and insight. But autistic people organizing together, autistic people pursuing our own interests rather than furthering the interests of parents and professionals-- suddenly we were perceived as a threat.

Only several years later, while researching the history of self-advocacy by disabled people (Sinclair, 1996), did I learn of the long history of similar opposition to attempts at self-advocacy and self-determination by people with a variety of disabilities (Kugelmass, 1951; Putnam, 1979; Williams & Shoultz, 1982; Van Cleve & Crouch, 1989; Lane, 1992; Shapiro, 1993; Christiansen & Barnartt, 1995; Dybwad & Bersani, 1996; Kennedy, 1996). Any attempt by a group of disempowered people to challenge the status quo--to dispute the presumption of their incompetence, to redefine themselves as equals of the empowered class, to assert independence and self- determination--has been met by remarkably similar efforts to discredit them. The discrediting tactics used most frequently are:

1) If at all possible, to deny that the persons mounting the challenge are really members of the group to which they claim membership. This tactic has been used against disability activists with learning disabilities and psychiatric disabilities as well as against autistic people. As people with these disabilities often look "normal" and the disabilities are all defined in terms of behavior rather than empirically

measurable physical differences, many of us have been told that the very fact that we are able to express ourselves, object to the ways our freedom has been restricted or our rights violated, and demand change proves that we cannot truly be autistic, or learning disabled, or psychiatrically impaired.

2) If there is incontrovertible evidence that the activists are members of the affected group, to aver that they are rare exceptions who are so unlike typical members of the affected group that what they have to say is irrelevant to the group as a whole. Michael Kennedy, who obviously and indisputably has cerebral palsy, explains the destructive impact of this tactic:

> When people tell me that I am "higher functioning" than the people they are talking about, I feel like they are telling me that I don't have anything in common with other people with disabilities. It's like they are putting me in a whole different category and saying that I don't have any right to speak. It upsets me because I take it that they don't want to give anyone else the opportunities I have been given, and that what I say can be ignored because they see me as more capable. It is a way of dividing us and putting down those who have more severe disabilities or who haven't had the opportunities to experience different situations in life.   (Kennedy, 1996)

3) If it is not possible to deny that the activists are authentic representatives of the affected group, to appeal to the very prejudices and stereotypes the activists are seeking to overturn, and use those prejudices and stereotypes to claim that the activists are incapable of fully understanding their situations and knowing what is best for them. Often this approach incorporates the belief that disabled people need to have their freedom restricted for their own good, to protect them from coming to harm through their inability to act in their own best interests.

These strategies to undermine credibility are not new, nor are they limited to situations involving disability. Frederick Douglass was a nineteenth-century African American who escaped from slavery in 1838 and became a well-known abolitionist writer and speaker. In his 1855 autobiography *My Bondage and My Freedom*, he recalled that at the beginning of his career speaking to white audiences about the evils of slavery, he was presented as something of a curiosity. Most anti-slavery lecturers where white; lecturers who were themselves fugitive slaves were a rarity. As the novelty wore off, people began to doubt that he had ever been a slave. He was suspected of being an impostor because he was too educated and too well-spoken to fit prevailing stereotypes about the ignorance of slaves. He also expressed frustration with white abolitionists' demand that he confine his speeches to simply recounting his personal experiences of slavery, and allow white people to elaborate on what they meant: "Give us the facts, we will take care of the philosophy." Eventually Douglass stopped working for white abolitionists and started his own anti-slavery publication.

BECOMING A GROUP, ONE PERSON AT A TIME

In the spring of 1993 I received a telephone call from Katherine, a woman who had just been diagnosed with Asperger syndrome after years of being labeled with an assortment of other "disorders" and "disturbances." The clinician who diagnosed her had also given her contact information about ANI. That in itself was a very encouraging development: A newly-diagnosed autistic person had immediately been referred to a network of autistic peers, instead of being given the usual clinical information about all the things that were "wrong" with her. Having finally found out why she had spent her entire life being, in her words, "an alien," she was interested in meeting other autistic people.

It happened that I was going to be traveling through St. Louis in the near future, so I suggested another meeting there. Katherine came to

St. Louis and met with Kathy and me, as well as Kathy's fiancé Ray, Doyle, Rita, and their family. She wrote of the experience:

> For me, this day will become an anniversary that I will celebrate with great joy. It marks the beginning of not being an alien. It will be a day of validation. A day to set aside and remember.
>
> That night [first night after arriving] in my journal I wrote that if nothing else of significance happened during this trip that one experience of being understood was worth all the timeand expense of coming to St. Louis. I went to sleep feeling I belonged.
>
> My visit to St. Louis literally changed my life. I now know that there is a group of people I can spend time with who do not expect me to be any certain way. Not many things surprise them, nor do many things offend them. They do not try to make me like them. They accept my interests and don't try to change them. I believe all persons with Autism need the opportunity to become friends with other Autistic people. Without this contact we feel alien to this world. We feel lonely. Feeling like an alien is a slow death. It's sadness, self-hate, it's continuously striving to be someone we're not. It's waking up each day and functioning in falsehood.   (French, 1993)

Katherine's experience mirrored that of Kathy and Donna and myself when we had first met and created an autistic space. This experience was repeated with more people as ANI expanded. While we were not successful in reaching large numbers of autistic people via announcements in established autism publications, autistic people began to find us, one by one.

(As an aside, I felt a great deal of personal pleasure and satisfaction in watching Katherine have the same kind of magical "first contact" experience that I had had the year before. At a later gathering where we welcomed two additional autistic people for their autistic first contact, Katherine expressed to me that she was happy to be part of creating that experience for them. Facilitating these kinds of first contact and homecoming experiences for autistic people continues to be one of the most rewarding parts of my work as coordinator of ANI; this sentiment has often been expressed by other ANI members about welcoming newcomers. Where is the famed autistic lack of empathy?)

Looking back at this period of ANI's history, I think it's best that it happened the way it did. A large influx of new members all at once might have made for a larger and (perhaps) more organized political force; but it probably would have precluded our coming together as we did, one person at a time, building the personal connections that allowed us to learn how to share our lives with each other. *Organizations* may be built upon goal-oriented or idea-oriented networks. But as ANI has developed, contrary to my own expectations, into a true *community*, I have come to understand that community is built on intersecting networks of interpersonal relationships. Autistic people have characteristic difficulties with person-to-group relationships, but many of us are quite capable of establishing and maintaining person-to-person relationships.

Routes to ingathering

During the early years there were two main avenues by which new autistic members made contact with us: online, in the parent-oriented autism forum mentioned earlier; and at conferences.

Online parents' forum

Sola Shelly (2003) describes the way a typical online contact would begin:

> As the only public forum about autism at that time, it was the first place that newly diagnosed HFAs (adults and adolescents) turned to for support. It was neat to watch this: Someone would appear, and either tell about recently being diagnosed, or just learning about autism and finding out how "things fall

into place" when many of his or her difficulties and otherwise abnormal characteristics could be accounted for by autism. Then the person would get replies from other HFAs, comparing notes, offering support. In many cases, the person would express a feeling of finally finding his own kind, as if he or she was an alien who had been stranded on this planet, and now has found other aliens who were from the same planet.

As had been the case when I was the only autistic person there, forum participation by autistic people consisted mostly of posting narrative descriptions about our lives and being questioned by parents seeking to understand their autistic children. But as more autistic people began participating, an increasing number of forum messages began to consist of peer communication between autistic people. Private email correspondences also developed among autistic people who had initially made contact on the forum.

Among the autistic people who learned about ANI and began communicating with other autistics via the Internet forum, a few established personal relationships and eventually became interested in meeting their online friends in person. Kathy and I, and Rita and Doyle and their children, continued to meet occasionally in St. Louis. After I moved to Syracuse, New York, in 1994, my house became another location for autistic visits. These gatherings were sometimes the occasions for first meetings with new online friends. Kathy and Ray's wedding in 1994 featured both the presence of a contingent of autistic friends among the many non-autistic family and community members, and autistic cultural influences on some of the wedding customs: Kathy's fixation with flags was incorporated into part of the ceremony itself, and several of her autistic friends presented her with decidedly non-traditional gifts (such as a used book in Russian that had been discarded by a library) relating to her special interests and fixations.

Becoming a presence at autism conferences

A growing number of us were attending NT-run autism conferences. Some of us were even being invited to speak at conferences. But now we weren't just isolated individuals lost in the chaos of the conference. More of us were already acquainted with each other before attending a conference, and were able to plan in advance to get together at the conference.

At the group level, ANI began to exhibit at conferences. Being a conference exhibitor meant that we had an assigned booth or table in the exhibit hall, where we could set up displays and hand out information about ANI. The ANI exhibit became a kind of home base for autistic people during the conference. While the exhibit halls were usually noisy and crowded, there was space behind the table (and also under the table) where a few people could sit and not be jostled by the crowd. Despite the difficult sensory conditions and the pervasive negativity of the rest of the conference content, autistic people would gather at the ANI exhibit to talk, laugh, stim, and revel in each other's company.

We also found places to gather after hours. While NT conference participants were attending banquet dinners or entertainment performances or other large-group activities, autistic people in pairs and small groups were finding quiet spots in hallways and cloakrooms and parking lots. Most of us couldn't afford rooms at the expensive hotels where the conferences were held (I often slept in my car while attending conferences), but if someone did have a hotel room, that became another enclave of autistic space.

Finding "home"--or creating it

This kind of live contact was not something that was of interest to every autistic person we encountered online. Obviously if someone wasn't interested, he or she did not choose to come to in-person gatherings. But for those of us who did come to them, often driving hundreds of miles and sleeping in our vehicles or on the floors of other people's rooms, there was a powerful shared will to make contact with others like ourselves. Our autistic contacts came to be a very important part of our lives. Many of us had never had friends before, and had difficult relationships with our families. Finding people who actually understood us and liked us, and whom we understood and liked in return, was a life-changing experience.

ANI had an exhibit table at one particular conference in St. Louis in early 1994. Doyle was able to arrange for a group of us to camp indoors on an empty upper floor of a large office building near the downtown conference center. All the interior walls on that floor had been knocked out for a not-yet-completed renovation process (except, fortunately, a restroom remained intact with walls and a door). Naked support beams were exposed throughout the space. Bits of crumbled plaster and other building materials were everywhere. Piles of debris lurked in corners and against walls. There was no furniture; we brought our own mats and sleeping bags, as well as a couple of floor lamps, and some empty refrigerator boxes for anyone who wanted to sleep in one or needed to retreat alone to a dark enclosed space for a while.

In this huge, dim, dusty, cavernous space, eight adults, along with Doyle and Rita's young son (who was not disabled), spent the weekend. During the days we went to the conference, took turns staffing the ANI exhibit and talking to curious parents, and listened to presenters talk about all the tragedies of our lives. In the evenings we returned to our "cave," which, like a legendary faerie hill, was transformed into a magical place of celebration.

During our second day of camping out in this building, Doyle pointed out the window at a radio tower and mentioned that it was for sale. He jokingly asked me if I thought we should buy it. I asked what possible use we might have for a radio tower. Then I looked around the room and, in keeping with our frequently shared experience of having always felt like aliens on Earth, I remarked that we could use the radio tower to send a message to the "mother ship" (a common reference in science fiction stories), telling it that we were all together now and it could come retrieve us and take us home.

But I'm glad there was no spaceship to come get us back then. We've found so many more of our people since that day, and there are still many more wishing and searching for a community to come home to. We've come a long way toward creating a home for ourselves right here on Earth.

REALITY CHECK

Autistic people, like any other group of people, are not all alike. We don't all have the same needs and desires for social interaction. Some of us don't get along with others of us. There have been misunderstandings and disagreements among us, hurt feelings, lost friendships, and worse. One extremely persistent autistic predator has harassed and terrorized enough members of our community that we stopped publishing our penpal list, developed security procedures to verify the identities of people applying to join our Internet forum, and established a policy of not publicizing the location of our gatherings. Less dramatically, some autistic people have made contact with some aspect of our community, decided they weren't interested or didn't like it, and gone away.

ANI is no longer the only autistic community in existence, and it's not what every autistic person needs or wants. Some autistic people may find other organizations or communities more to their liking. Some autistic people may not be interested in autistic organizations or communities at all. The characteristics of our particular autistic community result from the characteristics of the particular people who have become active participants in it. Some of these characteristics are:

- Probably the most central shared value of the ANI community is that it's okay to be autistic--it's not "wrong" for us to be the way we are, and it's not our goal to become (or to learn to emulate) NTs. Autistic people who value "passing for normal," or who do not want to be associated with people and with behaviors considered to represent "low-functioning" autism, are likely to be uncomfortable with the range of members and the openly, unashamedly autistic behaviors that are welcome in ANI.

- We are not as politically intense as some autistic activist organizations (mostly because we aren't organized enough to engage in much political activity as a community), but we are firmly aligned with the disability rights movement. Both autistic people who want more organized political activism than ANI engages in, and autistic people who prefer to avoid any political controversy at all, are likely to be unhappy about ANI's level of involvement with disability politics.

- We have a lot of members who have sensory sensitivities, and who want community norms that protect them from overstimulation. While we have tried hard to accommodate the needs of as many autistic people as possible, those who are very loud, are prone to touching people without invitation, or have other behaviors that create sensory distress for sensitive people may feel uncomfortably constrained by our requests for self-restraint and consideration for the sensitivities of others.

- We are not a separatist community. Autistic people who want contact *only* with other autistic people, and want no contact at all with NT people (this attitude is usually a reaction to a lifetime of coerced contact and pressure to behave like and socialize with NTs), are likely to be unhappy about the involvement in the ANI community of many NT family members and friends of autistic people.

- We are an autistic-run community. Non-autistic people may participate, but decision-making power and organizational leadership are held by autistic people. Given the nature of autism and the prevalence of difficulties with executive functioning, we are often less organized and less efficient than NT organizations. Despite our best efforts, there's a certain amount of disorganization and unpredictability that we have not been able to overcome. Autistic people who can't deal with that are likely to find ANI events very frustrating. (As a matter of fact, *I* find ANI events very frustrating, because they overtax my organizational skills. But I put up with the inevitable frustrations, because the rewards of participating in this community make it worthwhile to me.)

- Those amazing and powerful experiences of finding kindred spirits, while common, are not universal. When they do happen, they seem to happen to people who were not expecting them. People who come to ANI seeking information about autism so they can better understand themselves, or help with practical solutions to everyday challenges, or simple affirmation that being autistic means more than just having a collection of deficits, tend to be the most satisfied with what they find. If they also happen to find personal friendships or a feeling of belonging in the group, these are most likely to come as surprises.

- In terms of social motivation, we have members who are outgoing and effusive, and members who are reserved and withdrawn, and members who are everywhere in between. As with sensory sensitivities, the community norms that have developed within ANI have mostly been concerned with protecting the more sensitive members from unwanted social pressures. While many people have been fortunate enough to form rewarding friendships with other ANI members, we do not recognize any social *obligation* on the part of any person to have a personal relationship with any other person. People are likely to be disappointed if they join ANI expecting that all the other members will automatically like them and befriend them and want to socialize with them, or will automatically agree with all their opinions and have the same life experiences they've had.

If an autistic person's needs and expectations are not compatible with what ANI has to offer, then the person might be disappointed in ANI. There are also reasons why ANI might ban some autistic people from participation (e.g., the person who harassed so many of our members). Autistic people as a group are not all innocent and perfect. ANI as a community is not ideal for every autistic person. It has become the community that it is, in consequence of the people who have come together and stayed together to create it. Over the years, some people have left and others have arrived. Some long-time members have changed their perspectives or their priorities. These changes have been reflected in the evolution of community customs and the availability of community resources.

FROM "NETWORK" TO "COMMUNITY"

During 1993 and 1994 several critical events occurred in ANI's development from a network of personal acquaintances into a community. The International Conference on Autism, a joint conference of the Autism Society of America and Autism Society Canada held in July 1993 in Toronto, was the springboard for these events.

In many ways this conference was similar to other autism conferences that our small group of friends had been involved with. Several of us who had met before, plus a few people who were coming to meet ANI members for the first time, arranged to drive together or to meet at the conference. A group of us stayed together at a campground on the outskirts of the city, and carpooled daily to the conference hotel. One of our NT-parent members offered the use of her hotel room as a gathering place for evening discussions among autistic people. ANI had a booth in the exhibit hall. All this had become fairly routine to us by now.

"Don't Mourn For Us"

The first thing that made this conference different from earlier ones was my presentation. I had spoken at conferences before; usually I had been asked to simply describe some aspect of "what it's like to be autistic" and then answer questions from parents. This time I had a message of my own that I wanted to present. I had submitted it the previous year for the national Autism Society of America conference, but the ASA president had taken the unusual step of personally instructing the conference planning committee not to accept it. I submitted it again for the international conference in 1993, and the Canadian host organization accepted it. And so it was at this conference that I presented "Don't Mourn For Us" (Sinclair, 1993), directly challenging the "autism as tragedy" paradigm upon which the conference--and its sponsoring organizations--were based. This presentation drew a lot of interest to ANI. While some people strongly disagreed with it (I still get occasional hate mail about it even now), the more common response was (and still is) positive.

Strangers and cousins

The increased attention generated by my presentation drew more people to come to the ANI exhibit for information about us, and many of them became members. We were reaching the point at which our members no longer all knew each other; individual ANI members could be strangers to each other. For ANI to continue as a meaningful social entity, it had to be an entity that provided a common "home" even for people who did not have personal relationships with each other. I think it is this sense of being a "home"--a context for people's lives as a whole--that distinguishes a community from a simple organization.

Another development during the 1993 conference was the recognition of a new segment of the ANI community, and the adoption of a new term to refer to it. One of the people who had been corresponding with ANI members online, and was attending this conference to meet with us in person for the first time, was not autistic. He had hydrocephalus, another congenital neurological abnormality. In our online discussions he had been noticing many similarities between his experiences and characteristics as a person with hydrocephalus, and the experiences and characteristics of autistic people. At the conference he met Kathy, who was not online at the time and did not know who he was. He introduced himself to her, explaining that he was interested in exploring similarities between himself and autistic people. He briefly summarized the effects of hydrocephalus in his life. Kathy considered this for a moment, and then warmly exclaimed "Cousin!" (Cousins, 1993). From that time on, the term "cousin" has been used within ANI to refer to a non-autistic person who has some other significant social and communication abnormalities that render him or her significantly "autistic-like." The broader term "AC," meaning "autistics and cousins," emerged soon afterward.

Snore Wars

A further consequence of the 1993 conference was a huge spike in autistic conversation on the Internet autism forum after the conference was over. By this time there were enough autistic people on the forum that when we all started posting at once, the NT parents (who were still the great majority) noticed a dramatic increase in the amount of message traffic. And this barrage of new messages was from autistic people (and one cousin), excited from having been together at the conference, missing each other now that the conference was over, communicating with each other in some very autistic ways: lots of perseveration on details of things that had happened at the conference, lots of echoing each other's messages, lots of autistic humor that few of the non-autistic people could understand or appreciate. Before long, even autistic forum members who had not attended the conference were participating in the post-conference message explosion.

Some of the NT members began to post irate replies demanding that we stop "wasting bandwidth" with messages that were not of interest to them. We replied that our conversations were of interest to *us*, and we were members of the forum too, and autistic people ought to be allowed to communicate with other autistic people on an autism forum. Several parents supported us. But other parents countered with angry accusations, attributing a variety of sinister motives to our autistic conversations. Some of us responded with angry accusations of our own, expressing frustration that these parents were happy to have us participate in the forum when we served *their*purposes (i.e., when we answered their questions and allowed them to use us as resources), but were not willing to respect *our* wish to engage with each other on the forum. The ensuing flame wars became known in ANI as the Snore Wars, because some of the autistic messages the parents first began complaining about were playful perseverative discussions about someone's snoring at the conference.

A series of similar flame wars occurred over the next year or so: Any time autistic people became particularly active on the forum, or affirmed the sentiment that autism is something other than a devastating tragedy, there would be accusations and attacks from parents. This left most of the autistic members feeling that the forum was now a hostile place for us. We decided that we wanted our own Internet forum. After having experienced coming together physically to create autistic space, we were now ready to create an autistic cyberspace.

ANI-L

At that time there were not yet any public Internet sites such as yahoogroups to host email forums. We had to use a listserv on an academic server. One of our autistic members set up ANI-L, the Autism Network International listserv, on a server at his university. We launched our new forum in the fall of 1994. In 1996 our member's university announced that it was going to discontinue the server, and we moved ANI-L to its current home on the Syracuse University server under the sponsorship of a university faculty member. (That move represented the first time ANI had ever accepted any kind of sponsorship from a non-autistic source. "By autistics for autistics" has always been a core value of ANI. We do as much as we can for ourselves, and rely as little as possible on non-autistic people to take care of ANI business for us.)

In many ways, starting our online forum was similar to starting our newsletter in 1992. We had a strong commitment to the concept of autistic space, where content would be determined by the interests of autistic people. We needed to decide once again who would be eligible for membership. This time, due to the vicious attacks we'd been subjected to by some of the parents on the public autism forum, there were a number of autistic people who felt strongly that our forum should be for autistic people only. But ANI had always allowed parents to participate in its activities, and some of us felt that it was important to remain open to those parents who supported our values and our goals.

Rules and divisions

In the end, we settled on a decision to allow NT people to join, but only after securing their agreement to abide by a set of forum policies designed to ensure that ANI-L would remain an *autistic* forum (www.ani.ac/ani-l-info.html). These detailed rules were developed from within our community to address members' concerns and to prevent the occurrence in ANI-L of many negative experiences we had had in the NT-dominated public forum. *All* new members, NT or AC, are required to read them and agree to honor them.

As further compromise, we opened the forum with just autistic people and cousins at first. NT people were allowed to start joining a little later, after the AC members had settled in and gotten some conversations underway. When NT people began joining, we appointed two parents and a professional whom we trusted to be parent moderators. It was their job to make sure parents understood the forum rules, and to respond to parents who got out of line (e.g., by insulting autistic communication styles) so the AC listowners would not have to deal with hostile parents.

Shortly after ANI-L started we instituted another safeguard for the comfort of autistic people who were concerned about dynamics between autistic adults and NT parents of autistic children. We subdivided the forum into an "AC" section for messages of interest to autistic people and cousins, and a "Parents' Auxiliary" (PA) section for messages about parenting (or otherwise providing care and support for) autistic people. Another set of rules was developed for determining what messages belong in each section (www.ani.ac/ani-l-PA.html). These sections are not meant to segregate *people* according to their status as AC or NT. Any forum member is permitted to post messages in either section. The sections are to indicate message *content*:

- Some autistic people are willing to talk with parents about the parents' concerns regarding their autistic children. Those autistic people who choose to read messages about parenting, and possibly to respond to them, can participate in the Parents' Auxiliary section. But other autistic people find it very disturbing to be treated as a parent resource when they enter a forum for the purpose of having peer contact with other autistics. This was a particularly sensitive issue at the beginning, because of the recent clashes with parents on the public forum. Those people who do not want to read messages about parenting can stick to the AC section.

- Similarly, some parents and professionals are happy to read, and perhaps participate in, autistic people's discussions about whatever might happen to interest us. They are welcome to participate in the AC section, where they relate to us as friends. Others do not have the time or the interest to read our sometimes meandering, sometimes perseverative, sometimes just plain weird autistic conversations, but they are interested in talking to other parents (and any autistic people who choose to participate) about raising autistic children in an accepting and supportive manner. They can stick to the PA section.

Sorting the messages by topic allows each member to choose which subset(s) of messages he or she wants to receive. Since the initial decision to subdivide the forum, we have added three more sections: a Disability Rights section for discussion about rights and disability politics; a Conference section for discussions and planning regarding physical gatherings; and a Virtual Party section (which is not used much anymore) for special occasions when a lot of playful messages would get posted in a short period. Virtual parties were a way for us to communicate in near-realtime, before online chat became widely available. We would set a time, and everyone wanting to attend the virtual party would go online at that time and start posting email messages to the virtual party section. Since we were all online at the same time, we could respond to each other's emails very quickly.

Space and healing

When we first introduced the division into sections, there was a lot of anxiety especially among parents, some of whom thought they were only allowed to post messages in the PA section even if they were replying to messages posted in the AC section. There was vigilant turf protection by autistic people, who were quick (though usually not aggressive) to correct parents who posted parenting-related messages in the AC section. There were sometimes complaints by autistic people about feeling uncomfortable with the content of some messages by parents or professionals.

These issues became the subjects of sometimes intense discussion, not just by the listowners and parent moderators, but by the ANI-L membership as a whole. For the most part, our NT members have been respectful of the concept of, and eager to learn how to behave as guests in, autistic space. For the most part, our AC members have been patient with each other and with NT members, and have tried to be helpful when anyone was confused or uncomfortable. As the listowner who has been most active in responding to policy questions and interpersonal conflicts on ANI-L, I quickly came to appreciate the wonderful way our members have of working things out together. Very often if someone asks a question about the forum policies, or if someone flagrantly violates forum policies, or if people start having a disagreement that escalates beyond the bounds of civility, other members have already stepped in and started dealing with it by the time I read my email and find out there's been a problem.

Over time, the use of the AC and PA sections has changed. There is much less concern expressed now about messages being posted in the wrong section. While there are still some messages that clearly belong only in one section and not the other, for the most part the AC and PA sections now function together as the "social" component of the forum, and members very often post conversations about their personal lives and personal interests to *both* sections. We introduced the AC/PA division as a way to allow space for some wounds to heal. I think the preponderance of messages now posted to both AC and PA is an indication that healing has taken place.

ANI-L quickly replaced the printed newsletter as the primary vehicle for communication among ANI members. Private correspondences, personal friendships, and visits in person have continued to occur among people who meet first on ANI-L.

For several years after ANI-L was established, some members continued to participate in the parent-dominated public forum, or to monitor it for new autistic arrivals. Many autistic people continued to join the public forum seeking information. ANI-L members would tell them about the existence of ANI-L, and often they would join, especially after becoming disillusioned with the hostile climate on the public forum. A number of parents of autistic children also came to ANI-L through this route, finding our philosophy more to their liking than the grief-wallowing and cure-seeking that characterized the public forum. It was not uncommon to see posts in which one ANI-L member referred to another member's having "rescued" him or her from the public forum.

Today, there are many different online autism forums, some primarily for parents and some for autistic people. There is no longer a single forum that most people find first when seeking information about autism.

A NEW LEVEL OF CONFERENCE INVOLVEMENT

In November 1995, an organization for parents of "high-functioning" autistics held its first conference. During the early stages of planning for that conference, the president of the organization contacted me and asked if I would arrange a separate strand of conference sessions that would be of interest to autistic people. I made this an ANI project, and planning the ANI strand for the conference became another topic of discussion on ANI-L.

We put together a program of sessions, nearly all of them presented by autistic people. The topics of our sessions included school issues for autistic children, autistic family relationships, approaches to supported living (including both ways autistic people can receive support, and ways autistic people can provide support to others), autistic community, political implications of medical research, asexuality, and a panel discussion about what our autism means to us.

Innovations for autistic accessibility

We spent a lot of time planning ways to make this conference more autistic-friendly than most autism conference we had attended. Three things we did for that conference, that have remained parts of our own Autreat conferences, are:

> 1) We requested that the conference organizers provide a room for autistic people to retreat to during the conference, to take a break from sensory overload and from NT social pressures. We

placed a lamp with an incandescent bulb in the room, and kept the overhead fluorescent lights turned off. We put some refrigerator boxes in the room. We originally called this room the "Quiet Room," but subsequently some ANI members who had experienced institutionalization pointed out that in many psychiatric institutions, "Quiet Room" is a euphemism for a room people are locked into for involuntary seclusion. We now call our Autreat break room the "crash room."

After we introduced the use of a crash room at this conference in 1995, we were pleased to start noticing that some other autism conferences also began providing crash rooms for autistic attendees.

2) Even verbal autistic people are likely to have difficulty being verbal *all the time*, especially under conditions of sensory overload such as are likely to occur at a conference. Many of us had found ourselves struggling with speech shutdown at conferences. Non-autistic people would want to talk to us, when we needed to be left alone for a while. Of course we could always leave and go off somewhere by ourselves; but sometimes we were still interested in listening to presentations or being around our friends, even when we weren't up to having interactions. After discussing these situations on ANI-L, we created color-coded interaction signal badges. These were plastic name badge holders, with a piece of red paper on one side, and a piece of yellow paper on the other side. People needing to restrict interaction could wear a badge with the red side facing out to signify "Nobody should try to interact with me," or with the yellow side facing out to signify "Only people I already know should interact with me, not strangers."

The interaction signal badges were easy for autistic people to use, and easy for both autistic and non-autistic people to understand. We still use them at Autreat. In 1997 we added a third color to the badges, in response to a concern expressed by an autistic person who was planning to attend her first Autreat, and said she sometimes*wanted* to interact with other people but had trouble initiating an interaction. We added a piece of green paper to signify, "I want to interact but am having trouble initiating, so please initiate an interaction with me."

3) Many of us had had very stressful encounters with non-autistic people at autism conferences. We compared notes, and came up with a list of common unpleasant behaviors that included sensory assaults, persistent and intrusive questioning (some of us who were frequent conference presenters had been followed to our hotel rooms or phoned in our rooms by parents wanting to ask us questions; one person reported having been followed into the restroom by a parent who refused to stop demanding answers to questions), demands for NT-style social interactions, and treating us as parent resource material instead of as people. (I eventually coined the term "self-narrating zoo exhibit" to describe the role we are often expected to play in NT-centered autism forums and conferences.) We drafted a list of guidelines for NTs at the conference, detailing how we wanted them to interact with us. Our guidelines were printed in the conference program book, and we also had copies of them at the ANI exhibit at the conference. These guidelines have since evolved into guidelines for *everyone* to treat each other considerately at Autreat.

Good news and bad news

It was empowering for us to work together on ways to make the conference experience better for autistic people. It was refreshing to be given an opportunity to decide what topics we wanted to see presentations about, and to have autistic presenters speaking on substantive issues rather than being put on display as self-narrating zoo exhibits. It was exciting to plan for a larger live gathering of ANI members than had ever occurred before (including attendance by at least a couple of people from outside North America).

But this was not "our" conference. A parent-centered organization and a university department were in control of the event. When the organizers first contacted me, they had indicated that ANI would be a full partner with them in conference planning. That was just the first of many promises they failed to honor. During the months of conference planning, they consistently excluded ANI from planning meetings, even from those aspects of planning that directly affected our strand of sessions. Their behavior toward us ranged from condescending to controlling to outright dishonest.

At one point during the conference planning one of the organizers told me that the conference was only for "high-functioning" autistic people and their families, and that I should instruct "low-functioning" ANI members and their families not to attend. I am proud to report that I disregarded this instruction. At least one non-speaking ANI member did come to the conference with his parents. They attended the sessions in the ANI strand, and they later became regular participants at Autreat as well.

Difficulties with the conference organizers continued during the conference. Several of our members were treated rudely or condescendingly by conference organizers. There was more attempted interference with peer support among our members: As usual when ANI members used conferences as occasions to get together, some people who came had very little money, could not afford hotel rooms, and could not afford the high prices of meals in the hotel restaurant. And as has been the case since the founding of ANI, members of our community did their best to look out for each other. Some of our less-impoverished members had donated a supply of crackers, peanut butter, pasta cups, and microwaveable soup cups to make sure nobody starved. The hotel management had no objections to our keeping this box of food behind the ANI exhibit for low-income autistic people to take as needed. But the university conference coordinator (who did *not* work for the hotel, but for one of the conference co-sponsors) tried to forbid us to give food to hungry people. At one point she was screaming at me that we had to remove the food immediately because the hotel wouldn't allow it, even as hotel employees were bringing us an extra table to put the food on.

After the conference, the organizers barely acknowledged ANI's contributions, even though our sessions were well attended and well received (by many parents as well as autistic people). An unhappy discussion occurred on ANI-L. Interestingly, it was mostly parents who expressed indignation over the lack of acknowledgment of ANI. Those autistic people who had been heavily involved in planning our part of the conference had other complaints, about the disrespectful and paternalistic ways we had been treated.

One day the president of the conference organization phoned an ANI member and verbally abused her for sending a post to ANI-L expressing disappointment about how the conference organizers had treated ANI. ANI-L is a private forum. Every member agrees to a confidentiality policy. The conference organizers were not members of ANI-L. We never did find out who leaked the posts, but the entire ANI-L community experienced a loss of trust in the security of our online home.

In many ways our participation in this conference was a horribly unpleasant ordeal. There was no question of our ever agreeing to work with that organization and its conferences again! And yet--the time we got to spend with each other was precious, as always. The presentations in the ANI strand were stimulating, meaningful, and valuable to many people. Our panel presentation on autistic self-understanding drew a standing-room-only crowd. It was one of the most powerful autistic presentations I've ever seen--and so many people came and saw it! People took it seriously and let it touch them. Half the audience--and also half the panel--was in tears by the time it was over. The panelists talked about many things that we really wanted parents to understand; and there the parents were, willing and eager to let us teach them. We could be so much more than self-narrating zoo exhibits.

We've come a long way

There was one very significant difference between our online community's reaction to the problems with the conference organizers, and the reaction to the online Snore Wars at the time ANI-L was founded less than two years earlier. The Snore Wars--bitter conflict between autistic people and non-autistic parents and professionals occurring in an NT-dominated forum--had a polarizing effect within ANI. A significant number of the autistic people involved reacted with resentment and distrust toward non-autistic people in general. They argued that the new ANI-L forum would not feel safe to them if NT parents and professionals were allowed to join. This became a source of conflict between autistic people who wanted an autistic-only forum, and those who wanted a more inclusive one. We worked together to respond to those concerns by developing the detailed ANI-L forum rules, thus managing to keep our community from being torn apart by the conflict.

In the negative fallout from the 1995 conference, there was once again bitter conflict and mutual resentment between some autistic people and cousins (ANI members who felt we had been treated badly by the conference organizers) and some non-autistic parents and professionals (conference organizers who were offended by our demands to be respected as equals). But this conflict did *not* result in an anti-NT backlash among ANI members--most likely because by this time, a number of NT parents and professionals were accepted members of ANI-L. Our NT members supported us, commiserated with us on ANI-L, wrote letters in our support to the conference organizers, tried to comfort the person who received the abusive phone call, and expressed their own feelings of dismay and betrayal at the violation of forum confidentiality. Sometime during our first year online, our NT members had stopped being "guests" and had become part of our community.

Ever onward...

There was also a very significant parallel between our response to the Snore Wars and our response to the conference conflict. The Snore Wars occurred because our community had discovered and embraced online mailing lists as a vehicle for making connections, but our ways of connecting were not accepted by the NT-dominated online forum where we were trying to do it. So we created an AC-dominated online forum, giving ourselves our own place to connect in our own ways. The conflicts surrounding the conference occurred because our community was discovering and embracing the possibilities of being active participants in autism conferences, of adapting conference environments and procedures to suit our own needs, of producing conference presentations that addressed our own interests--but our initiatives were not accepted by the organizers of the NT-dominated conference where we tried to advance them. And so we decided that the time had come to create our own autistic conference.

AUTREAT: COMMUNITY IN PHYSICAL SPACE

Finding a space

The idea of "autistic space" remained a guiding theme as we prepared for this new step in autistic community development. We searched for a place that we could have to ourselves, without being surrounded by distracting NT activity. We wanted autistic children to be able to come and meet autistic adults. We liked the idea of complete immersion: having conference activities, meals, and lodging all in the same venue, rather than having to move back and forth every day between our autistic space and the NT world. In the course of our discussions, some members pointed out the importance of having not just a building, but also outdoor space where people could move around. It had to be considerably less expensive than a traditional hotel venue. The concept of an autistic retreat began to take shape: Autreat.

After much searching, we found a children's summer camp that was available for rentals after the end of the summer season. It was in a rural area, several miles from the nearest city. There were hiking trails and woods, a pond, and a pool for swimming. Staff from the camp provided child care.

The first Autreat took place in late August, 1996, beginning on a Sunday afternoon and lasting two days. About fifty people attended: autistic adults (some on their own, some with family members or caregivers), autistic children with their families, parents of autistic people of all ages, and a professional or two. We met at that same camp every year through 2000. There was no Autreat in 2001 (due to organizational difficulties in the transition from one or two people doing all the work to having a functioning Autreat planning committee). In 2002 and 2003 we met at a different camp, still with features similar to the first camp (rural, rustic, self-contained), but with better physical accessibility for people with mobility impairments. In 2004 we moved again, this time to a university campus that still provides a degree of seclusion from the outside world, and has outdoor space for roaming, but has more comfortable indoor spaces (including residence hall rooms shared by two to four people, instead of cabins for six or more people) and better food service. In response to people's requests for Autreat to be longer, we added a third day in 1997 and are planning to add a fourth day in 2005.

People who attend

While the majority of Autreat attendees live in the United States or Canada, people have also come to Autreat (some of them year after year) from countries including Australia, Finland, Israel, Japan, New Zealand, Norway, and others. Most Autreat attendees are verbal, though a significant number do not use speech. Wally Wojtowicz Sr., the father of a non-speaking autistic adult, said of the first Autreat in 1996:

> Here people who could paint and draw equally shared experiences with those who can't hold a pencil or a brush.

People who are very articulate equally shared experiences and understood those who could only jump or clap their hands or point to letters on a letter board or picture board to respond to a question. (Personal communication)

Presentations

The first year, other than a workshop introducing concepts of self-advocacy to non-autistic parents (Johnston & Sinclair, 1996), all sessions were presented by non-autistic people. I think this decision was an instance of backlash against the "self-narrating zoo exhibit" phenomenon--the pervasive use of autistic people at conferences as resources to be used for the benefit of parents, and as sources of raw data the meaning of which was to be determined by NTs. ("Give us the facts, we will take care of the philosophy.") This time, at *our* conference, we invited non-autistic presenters to provide information for the benefit of autistic people. At subsequent Autreats 50% or more of the presenters have been autistic people. Topics have included disability politics, practical issues in autistic people's lives, and social/interpersonal issues. The Autreat call for proposals (http://ani.autistics.us/aut05cfp.html) details differences between the kinds of presentations that are accepted at Autreat and the kinds of presentations that are offered at typical parent- and professional-oriented autism conferences:

- Autistic people are the primary audience at Autreat. We expect presenters to be speaking *to* us, not to speaking to non-autistic people *about* us.

- We are interested in workshops about positive ways of living with autism, about functioning as autistic people in a neurotypical world, and about the disability movement and its significance for autistic people. We are *not* interested in workshops about how to cure, prevent, or overcome autism. We do *not* appreciate having non-autistic people come into our space to talk to each other about how difficult we are to deal with, or how heroic they are for putting up with us.

- We are not interested in "self-narrating zoo exhibit" presentations. Presentations about the presenters' personal stories are not considered, unless the presenter is able to use his or her story in a way that will help other people share and understand their own experiences in a new way.

Social rules and norms

Every year since its beginning, Autreat has been attended by some people who have been together in person before, some who are acquainted via online contact but have never met in person, and some who have had no prior contact with ANI. Each year we hold an orientation session on the first afternoon, to introduce newcomers to the social features of Autreat; and a written summary of the orientation information is included in the Autreat program book. Orientation information addresses use of the interaction signal badges; other badges to signal that a person does not want to be photographed; accommodating sensory sensitivities (perfume and scented personal care products are not allowed; flash photography is allowed only with permission of everyone who is close enough to be affected by the flash); prosopagnosia (name badges are worn throughout Autreat to help people recognize each other); and acceptable behavior:

> We do not expect you to "act normal" or to behave like a neurotypical person at Autreat. It is perfectly acceptable at Autreat to rock, stim, echo, perseverate, and engage in other "autistic" behaviors. The only behaviors that are *not* acceptable are actions that infringe on the rights of others: by violating their personal boundaries or their property boundaries, or by preventing them from participating in Autreat activities, or by causing undue distress through physical, verbal, or sensory assault. (Autreat orientation materials)

Also included in the live orientation session is information about options in the use of the Autreat space: location of the crash room; warnings about sensory hazards of the space (at both camp venues we had to endure tests of the fire alarm system, so we told people when that would happen and suggested places to go to be as far as possible from the alarm when it went off; in the university residence hall the room doors will slam loudly if not handled carefully, and the halls carry a lot of sound and echoes, so we ask people to be careful with the doors and to be quiet in the halls); options for people who do not want to eat in the dining hall (people may take their meal trays and eat somewhere else, provided they return all trays and utensils to the dining hall).

A basic principle of Autreat social conventions is that social interactions are only desirable if they are voluntary:

> For some ANI members, meeting other autistic people and having a chance to socialize with others like ourselves is an exciting and wonderful experience. Others are not interested in social contacts and may come to this event just for the workshops. Some of us are interested in socializing some, but need to be able to take time out from interacting. Autreat is meant to provide opportunity, but not pressure, for social interactions. (ANI web site, www.ani.ac/autreat.html)

"Opportunity but not pressure" is a core principle for *all* Autreat activities: attendance at presentations, informal discussions that are held in the evenings, swimming and other recreational activities, socializing, meals (people who prefer to make their own meal arrangements are able to register for Autreat without paying for Autreat meals), on-site lodging (people who prefer to stay at an off-site hotel can register for Autreat at a commuter rate)—all participation is purely voluntary.

Freedom from pressures and expectations

For some autistic people attending Autreat, the sudden absence of pressures and expectations to behave in certain ways can be quite disorienting at first. NT people are often disoriented as well, and may experience culture shock. One NT attendee described feeling unsure of how to behave and how to relate to people, confused about how to interpret other people's behavior, and anxious that he might offend people without realizing it (personal communication). In other words, he was able to experience at Autreat some of the same social confusion and discomfort that autistic people frequently experience in NT society. While this can be somewhat disturbing, a number of NT people have reported that it was a valuable experience that helped them to better understand what autistic people go through on a daily basis.

Many (but, again, not all) autistic people have felt the same sense of homecoming at Autreat that characterized the early meetings of ANI members in small groups. At the first Autreat in 1996, JohnAlexis Viereck stated, "I feel as if I'm home, among my own people, for the first time. I never knew what this was until now" (personal communication). This sentiment is so widespread among regular Autreat attendees that it was addressed in an Autreat workshop comparing the autism community to a diaspora (Schwarz, 1999).

The absence of any expectation or pressure to socialize, and the knowledge that they're free to withdraw at any time, seem to free many autistic people to *want* to socialize. People spontaneously get together for hikes or tours of local sites of interest. Sleep deprivation is a common experience at Autreat, as conversations and informal discussion groups go on late into the night. One morning I watched with interest as people came into the dining hall for breakfast. The dining hall was furnished with small tables, about six or eight chairs per table, and was large enough to seat about 200 people. Our group was small, and some people were eating outside to avoid the noise and crowding in the dining hall. There were plenty of empty tables. But at least half the people in the room were clustered around just a few of the tables. As I watched, more and more people brought their trays to tables that already had people sitting at them. As the tables filled up, some people took chairs from unoccupied tables and brought them to squeeze around one of the full ones. In similar settings in NT society, autistic people would be more likely to *avoid* the occupied tables and to seek out the empty ones.

DECOMPRESSION AND RE-ENTRY

Some of the same phenomena that had occurred in small gatherings of autistic people, and on ANI-L, have also been observed at Autreat. While none of these experiences is universal for all autistic people, these are some of the things that do occur with some frequency in the ANI community:

- Many autistic people need to know ahead of time what they will encounter and what will be expected of them. It's important to have an opportunity for people to ask questions. I have had extensive email correspondences with online friends about what it would be like to visit my house. People planning to attend Autreat often have a lot of questions about anything from general social conditions to minutiae about the physical space. The detailed rules for ANI-L, and the Autreat orientation information, grew out of both a desire to avoid reoccurrence of past negative experiences, *and* out of the common need for autistic people to have clear structure in order to feel comfortable. Most early ANI members had this need for structure and for clear explanations of boundaries and expectations. As ANI has grown, we have been joined by more people who have different responses to rules, including some people who resent the concept of having any rules at all. Balancing the needs of different autistic people remains an ongoing challenge.

- While many autistic people do have an immediate positive reaction to being in autistic space, occasionally (at Autreat, approximately one person every year or two) someone finds the sudden absence of NT social expectations so disorienting that it results in a kind of "explosive decompression." Usually people who have this reaction are people who have been particularly strongly indoctrinated into passing for NT, to the extent that when the NT social pressures are gone, and they don't have to wear their "NT masks" anymore, they no longer know what to do or even who they are. They may feel panicked, or simply frozen into paralysis. The good news is that when this sort of strong disorientation occurs, it is temporary and is usually a prelude to a personal "blossoming" as the person reconnects with his or her suppressed self, and forms a strong attachment to autistic community.

- Sometimes as autistic people begin to understand autism as their natural way of being, they become angry about the things that have been done to them by people trying make them more "normal," or they experience grief reactions over the things they've lost through not being allowed to develop self-understanding and self-acceptance earlier.

- In rejecting intolerant NT prejudices that define NT characteristics as "good" and autistic characteristics as "bad," some autistic people react with anti-NT prejudice and start defining all autistic characteristics and autistic people as "good," and all NT characteristics and people as "bad." Fortunately, "NT bashing" on ANI-L or at Autreat is generally met with prompt rebuttals and calls for tolerance by other autistic people.

- Autistic immersion experiences, both at Autreat and in smaller gatherings of friends, are often followed by some degree of sadness, disorientation, and even depression upon returning to the NT world. One person reported suffering from significant post-Autreat depression every year for the first several years she attended Autreat. Eventually she said the depression stopped:

I think that the depression may be caused by the abrupt effect of saying goodbye, and having to go back to "The World" and thus abandon the AC part of the self. The realization that there would be more meetings helps to carry the AC essence inside, even when the other ACs are far away. (Sola Shelly, personal communication)

Some Autreat attendees have eased the separation by arranging to spend a day or two after Autreat with one or more autistic friend(s), sometimes sightseeing together and thereby re-entering the NT world in autistic company.

SUMMARY

In the last thirteen years, Autism Network International has grown from a small group of penpals meeting for the first time in a small apartment, to an international community of autistic people who meet online, in small informal meetings in private homes, and in our own communal space at Autreat. We have certain shared values in affirming the validity of our way of being. We have many common experiences both with the experience of autism itself, and with being autistic in a world of neurotypicals. We have a history of significant events experienced by our community. We have a dynamic, constantly-evolving set of customs and rules growing out of our shared experiences and our common needs. We have certain terms, expressions, and in-jokes that are distinct to our community. We have children whose parents are helping them grow up knowing that it's okay to be autistic, knowing other autistic children and autistic adults, knowing that they're part of this community. The children who attended the first Autreat are teenagers now; the children whose parents were among the early members of ANI-L are now young adults. It will be interesting to see what this first generation of ANI children will bring to our community, and to the world, as they come into their own.

REFERENCES

The American Heritage(r) Dictionary of the English Language, Fourth Edition(2000) Houghton Mifflin Company.

Christiansen, J. B., & Barnartt, S. N. (1995) *Deaf President Now!: The 1988 Revolution at Gallaudet University*. Washington, DC: Gallaudet University Press.

Cousins, S. (1993) Neural connections in Toronto. *Our Voice*, the newsletter of Autism Network International, 1 (3).

Douglass, F. (1855) *My Bondage and My Freedom*. In Library of America College Editions (1994) *Douglass Autobiographies*. New York: Penguin Books.

Dybwad, G. & Bersani, H. (1996) *New Voices: Self-Advocacy By Persons With Disabilities*. Cambridge, MA: Brookline Books.

French K. (1993) My personal holiday. *Our Voice*, the newsletter of Autism Network International, 1,(3).

Johnston, J. & Sinclair, J. (1996) Orientation to self-advocacy for parents and professionals. Presentation at Autreat, Canandaigua, New York.

Kennedy, M. J. (with Shoultz, B.). (1996, April). Thoughts about self-advocacy. *TASH Newsletter*, 22_(4), 27-28. Online at http://soeweb.syr.edu/thechp/thoughts.htm http://soeweb.syr.edu/thechp/thoughts.htm Kugelmass, J.A. (1951) *Louis Braille: Windows for the Blind*. New York: Julian Messner, Inc.

Lane, H. (1992) *The Mask of Benevolence: Disabling the Deaf Community*. New York: Alfred A. Knopf.

Putnam, P. (1979) *Love in the Lead: The Fifty-Year Miracle of the Seeing Eye Dog*. New York: E. P. Durron & Co.

Schwarz, P. (1999) The autism community as a neurological diaspora: Some cultural parallels and some practical responses. Presentation at Autreat, Canandaigua, New York.

Shapiro, J. (1993) *No Pity: People with Disabilities Forging a New Civil Rights Movement*. New York: Times Books

Shelly, S. (2003) Cousinhood: Who cares and other questions. Presentation at Autreat, Brantingham, New York.

Sinclair, J. (1988) Some thoughts about empathy.
www.jimsinclair.org/empathy.htm
http://web.syr.edu/~jisincla/empathy.htm
Sinclair, J. (1992) Social uses of fixations. *Our Voice*, the newsletter of Autism Network International, 1,(1).

Sinclair J. (1993) Don't mourn for us. *Our Voice*, the newsletter of Autism Network International, 1(3). Online at
www.jimsinclair.org/dontmourn.htm
http://web.syr.edu/~jisincla/dontmourn.htm
Sinclair, J. (1996) Parent-professional partnerships: Who's missing in this picture? Presentation at Autism Treatment Services of Canada, Victoria, British Columbia, Canada.

Van Cleve. J.V. & Crouch, B. A. (1989) *A Place of Their Own: Creating the Deaf Community in America*. Washington, DC: Gallaudet Univesity Press.

Williams, D. (1994) *Somebody Somewhere.* New York: Random House.

Williams, P. & Shoultz, B. (1982) *We Can Speak for Ourselves: Self-Advocacy by Mentally Handicapped People.* Bloomington, IN: Indiana University Press.

(A version of this essay appeared previously on autreat.com in January, 2005.)

Critic of the Dawn

By Cal Montgomery

I. It shouldn't have happened to you," people say. Slight emphasis on *you*. Institutionalization, they mean.

Sometimes they stop there; sometimes they finish the thought. "You're okay."

I remember the first people who taught me that I was okay and who stood naked in line with me, waiting for a paper cup of shampoo and a turn under the showerhead, on bath nights. Or, "You were misdiagnosed." And I remember the times I could not speak and had no keyboard, the times I slammed my head against a wall over and over until the staff looked for a helmet I couldn't remove, and I am sadly grateful that they haven't known a world in which communication and self-respect are possible only with blood and broken bones.

"But for some people. . . ." They're thinking of people who lived once in institutions, now in cardboard boxes, thinking those are the options. It's a false choice: the supports, not the people, have failed.

"That shouldn't have happened." Emphasis on *that*. They talk about regulations, oversight. I think of the glossy literature my parents read, the architecture they admired. They bragged about the place that "cared" for me. I think of the reality of that place, the powerlessness, the punishment. I cannot wish it on anyone.

My family will tell you it shouldn't have been so hard on them. They spent a lot of money, time, energy, getting me where they wanted me. Keeping me there.

I spent a lot of time and energy fighting guardianship. It was explained like this: if I voluntarily consented to what "my team" had already decided was going to be done to me -- the agitated stupor of drugs, the unrelenting pain of electroshock, the degradation of smiling "yes" while being told my every experience was *wrong* -- no one would file for guardianship. If I refused, they'd show a judge my labels -- I wasn't "high-functioning" enough to be taken to see him myself, they said -- and my parents would voluntarily consent for me the rest of my life.

Shotgun consent, sure, but they got it. When you choose between traps, you choose the one you might someday escape.

My sister got a job. My parents paid her college tuition, but there was no money for textbooks and incidentals. My sister has expressed her anger that I "got" so much while she worked.
I'd rather have a job than be tied down in an isolation room, but I suppose we have different goals.

ß

Martha Nussbaum published "Disabled Lives: Who Cares?" in the New York Review of Books, and people started talking about her portrayal of disability.

"She understands."

"Finally, our issues are getting coverage."

"It bothers me."

"How can she leave us out like that?"

And I began to struggle with my own response.

I struggle with her association of disability with "extreme dependency," with her quick assumption that caregivers -- or, as in Nussbaum's case, relatives -- speak for disabled people, with her assumption that disabled people are dependent on others for the development of their talents in a way that nondisabled people are not, with her assumption that "care" as we know it today is benevolent.

I struggle in the context of a focus on "the able disabled" who take certain cognitive abilities for granted, with the quick assumption that phys-dis leaders speak for people with cognitive impairments, with the assumption that all people, disabled and non-, develop as human beings unconnected to other people, with the assumption that the "care" families provide is always oppressive.

I struggle.

II. As I move through my life -- a disabled person -- two companions haunt me. They are imaginary, but in my dealings with other people, they are forceful. Sometimes other people cannot seem to sense me behind those phantoms. Sometimes I am forced into their masks, and falling out of character has consequences.

One I think of as an uncle. A descendant of Carrie Buck, of the Jukes and the Kallikaks, a cousin to the Rain Man and the wild children of the forests. You've seen him rocking in the corner, headbanging. He cannot speak and, people assume, has nothing to say. Sometimes he is a cute, incomprehensible child; sometimes a terrifying, incomprehensible adult. He is usually uncomprehending but sometimes manipulative; usually repellent but sometimes seductive. Violence swirls around him: sometimes he is a target, sometimes a perpetrator, sometimes both. He is an enigma, interpreted by others: he cannot define himself.

He embodies the stereotypes, the paradigms of cognitive impairment, of my own particular set of labels. He's no different from me -- but he is. Get me in the right situation, and we look exactly alike. Get me in the right situation, and you can see no resemblance. Bruce, I call him in intimate moments, after a caricature I once saw on television.

The other I think of as a sister. A shadow twin. The daughter my parents wanted in my place, pretended they had. The sister my flesh-and-blood sister wished for. Me, but with impairment denied, defused, removed. Me, but with grace, stamina, social skills. She speaks for herself -- then again, she doesn't have to. She's no different from me -- but she is. Get me in the right situation, and we look exactly alike. Get me in the right situation, and you can see no hint of resemblance. Mary, I call her, after the aunt whose other name I was given.

I am encouraged to disassociate myself from my uncle Bruce, just as women, as African-Americans, as physically impaired people have disassociated themselves from him. People suspect, believe, that segregation, exclusion, institutionalization, may be best for him, for others. Best for that nebulous *us*. Bruce, they believe, would never participate in disability politics. He'd never be able to. But he represents impairment. So often, when people talk about protection and care, they imagine loving my uncle in my place.

If I am pressured to disown my uncle Bruce, I am also pressured to pass for my sister Mary. She's more comfortable for other people. She, of course, would never waste time on disability politics. It would never occur to her. But she represents disability. So often, when people talk about barrier removal and leveling the playing field, they imagine freeing Mary to live my life.

I know I am not my uncle, because people tell me, in subtle and not-so-subtle ways. "You don't seem disabled," they say. In the tiny stress on *you*, I know my uncle, and I know we are being distinguished. People relax, ever so slightly, when they read the words on my communication board: they realize that even when I cannot speak, I still use language much like theirs. I know too well the agitated stillness when I cannot find words to make myself clear, cannot fathom others' meanings. In the sudden release of physical tension that betrays others' reassurance, I know my uncle.

I know I am not my sister, because people tell me, in subtle and not-so-subtle ways. They use words like *perseveration, echolalia, concreteness, self-stim, self-injury*. In these words, I know my sister, and I know we are being distinguished. People stiffen, ever so slightly, when they see stairs, when they realize they've touched me, when they spot throbbing fluorescents, when they realize the lecture isn't captioned and there is no text. In the sudden physical tension that betrays others' discomfort, I know my sister.

I also know that, had I been a part of my father's generation, Bruce, not Mary, would have been my twin. I am Bruce's heir in the way that today's disabled children are Mary's. I wonder, when they reflect on that heritage and how it has shaped them, what they will think. I wonder, too, how they will remember my uncle Bruce, and I recall my own fumbling for a heritage among half-formed stories of village fools and eccentric aunts, residents of Hartheim and Bedlam.

I choose not to emulate or to repudiate either of my phantom relatives. That decision reflects my understanding that there are those whose lives are dominated, with or without their consent, by phantoms much like Bruce or much like Mary. It reflects my conviction that the representations of disability that give Mary and Bruce detailed life are less than reality, are both more and less than truth, that I am being asked to choose between two stereotypes, not two realities. It reflects the heritage I claim as mine, the community, the communities, to which I believe I am responsible.

ß

"Disabled person," I call myself. Maybe it's time for a nod to terminology.

In Britain in the 1970s, disabled people began to criticize the link between physical difference and social death, began to draw a distinction between impairment -- which has to do with the ways we differ from one another -- and disability -- which has to do with the way impaired people are treated in a society that does not plan for impaired people.

Disability, on this understanding, is not *in*-ability but dis-*enablement*, and nondisabled people are not, in comparison to us, *innately able*. They are, rather, *enabled by a society* set up to accommodate their needs and not ours.

Disability is injustice, not tragedy; unequal treatment, not inherent inequality.

ß

I opened my textbook to the wrong page.

"We hold these truths to be self-evident," I read, "that all men are created equal." And I was hooked.

I was naïve: I was ten, and if I hadn't grasped the ways inequalities played out in the US, hadn't heard of disability rights, hadn't tuned in to criticisms of saying *men* and meaning *humanity*, I'd heard of slavery. But in that moment, I failed to make the connection.

We hold these truths to be self-evident, that all men are created equal . . . I thought it meant that every human being was valuable, none more than another. That everyone had a chance, none more than another. I thought it was simple; in my simplicity I thought it was true.

I was a child in love with a childish conception of equality. But I was in love.

The teacher spoke, and I turned to the correct page.

ß

The incantations that invoke Mary, call her up to stand between me and the world, are variations on a theme: I am the same. Bruce is banished. The incantations that invoke Bruce and banish Mary are variations on a different theme: I am different.

"Same as what?" you ask. "Different from what?" The reference point -- the imaginary person around whom society is planned -- is a pale and obscure figure, but those who have searched him out report that he is white, straight, nondisabled, educated, mature, moneyed, and male. Those whose sameness to this reference point, this mythical man, has been stressed -- whose struggle in his world has been blamed on choice, on moral lapse -- may quite reasonably insist on their difference. "Disabled and Proud," reads a tee-shirt. Those whose difference from him has been stressed -- whose exclusion from his world has been considered justified -- may quite reasonably assert their sameness. "I am not a puzzle. I am a person," reads a button.

As different people experience disability in different ways, have it attributed to different sources, adopt different tactics for different situations, there are shifts between the campaigns of sameness and the campaigns of difference -- and the disability community is shattered, broken into subcommunities with different traditions, different priorities, different dialects to explain different experiences.

ß

Let me talk for a moment about impairment. Impairment is about how we differ, one from the next.

I know that tactile defensiveness -- disliking touch -- is impairment, because I look around me and see other people seeking out exactly that kind of physical contact that is painful to me; because I notice that I come from a species that enjoys the mechanics of sexual reproduction; because I know the fiery pain of "friendly" touch. I know that prosopagnosia -- not recognizing faces -- is impairment, because I look around me and understand that not recognizing a face is almost always a moral failing or a moral judgment.

I know I am impaired by looking to others. I have looked to those who write psych, neuropsych, PT, OT, speech-language reports. To those who write books about people like me, who make careers working with people like me. I look to my interactions with nondisabled people, to the social and physical worlds they build for one another. They teach me about myself. They tell me what about me is strange to them, what makes them uncomfortable, what makes them laugh. They tell me *I am different*. They tell me how. And they tell me which parts of that difference are valuable, and which are emphatically not. They tell me about impairment.

I know I am impaired; I know that I have much in common with my uncle Bruce.

ß

Someday, they told me. Maybe . . . years from now. If I worked very hard. I might -- They couldn't guarantee it. They weren't promising. Just dreaming. Hoping. Imagining what I might achieve.

Someday I might go for a walk on grounds, unaccompanied by staff.

Perhaps it is enough to say that their dreams and mine did not coincide.

ß

But let me talk for a moment about disability. Disability is about a re-imaging of what it means to be treated differently.

If it is true that I know my impairment by looking to others, it is also true that I know my disability by looking to others. I look to those who attempt the same things I do, I look at the barriers they face, and I judge my set of barriers against theirs. If I cannot get into the meeting room, can they? If I cannot find meaning in my teachers' sounds, can they? If I cannot get people in power to pause while I make my points, can they? I look to others to tell me what about my life is limited, constrained, disabled. They tell me *my life is different*, and they tell me which parts of that difference should be accepted, and which should emphatically not. They tell me about disability.

I know I am disabled; I know that I have much in common with my sister Mary.

ß

You know, they told me, I don't look -- Nobody would have to . . . I could be just another crip.

And as if I were just another crip, they started with the jokes and comebacks.

"She asked me whether my toenails still grow; I asked her whether her hair still grows."

"They want cognitive disability representation? Why don't they just ask 'SuperChris': he's cognitively disabled."

"They may be able-bodied, but we're able-minded."

They didn't mean *me*, of course. I wasn't like *that*, wasn't like *them*. They meant no offense.
Perhaps it is enough to say that my vision of "the disability community" and theirs does not coincide.

ß

And, because disability is so identified with dependence, let me talk for a moment about that.

I am a dependent person. I eat food whose final preparation I handle myself, but which has come to me across roads laid and maintained by other people from stores staffed by other people -- and even those people didn't grow or raise or harvest or slaughter any of it. I wear clothes made by other people from cloth woven by still others. I am human: I depend on others. And this is called independence.

I am a dependent person. I need human contact, most of which I receive through an Internet built and maintained by many other people. I do not know my neighbors, but even face-to-face interaction requires someone's cooperation. I have learned from my time in isolation rooms that I can handle a while without human interaction, but that eventually it will become unbearable. I am human: I depend on others. And this is called independence.

I am a dependent person. The words I work with were taught to me by people who wrote and read them before I traced my first *A*. The language I work in is a living entity, shaped and grown over centuries by billions upon billions of speakers. The ideas I work on are part of a tradition nurtured by many thinkers. I am human: I depend on others. And this is called independence.

I am a dependent person. I do not -- have learned that I cannot safely -- live alone. I require the patterns of life to be modeled for me over and over again. I struggle to get, and to keep, jobs in workplaces designed for "plug-and-play" workers. I learn some things quickly and easily; I need to be explicitly taught many things that seem obvious to others. I am human: I depend on others. And *this* is called dependence.

Independent can mean *self-governing*. It can also mean *self-reliant*. It can deny others' influence on our decisions or others' support in carrying those decisions out.

Dependent can mean *controlled by others*. It can also mean *requiring the support of others*.

None of us, of course, is independent in either sense. We grow up in social contexts, supported and denied, enabled and disabled by those around us.

But some rely on supports which are so common as to go unnoticed, while others use support that is atypical and therefore apparent. Some supports are provided by the community as a whole and go unnoticed, while others are borne -- or not -- by a small number of people whose lives are profoundly affected.

So I know the ways in which I am dependent not by looking at how I depend on others, but by watching other people. I look to nondisabled people to tell me which kinds of dependence are recognized, which are devalued. I know the shame that comes with asking for "inappropriate" help.

Within the disability community, too, there are fault lines around which kinds of dependence we recognize, which kinds we devalue.

III. As I move through the public debates -- a disabled person -- I too often find one of my phantom relatives represented as a two-dimensional billboard figure, the balancing lessons of the other ignored.

There are those in the community whose rhetoric calls up my uncle Bruce in robust and noble detail, relegates my sister Mary to the status of supercrip or overcomer, or dismisses her as a wannabe.

There are those whose rhetoric evokes my sister Mary, strong and proud, and dismisses my uncle Bruce as too incompetent for disability culture, disability pride, disability rights.

There are people who call my uncle Bruce a threat to public order, people who call my sister Mary a whining opportunist, people who play "divide and rule" by attacking one or another representation of disability and encouraging defenses along -- but never across -- the traditional fault lines. And the fault lines that divide our community -- the distinctions between those whom we treat as blocked by barriers and those whom we treat as innately limited -- the very existence of the fault lines troubles me.

ß

In one sense I cannot bring myself to condemn people with sensory and mobility impairments who distance themselves from Bruce. No more can I bring myself to condemn women, people of color, and other groups for doing precisely the same thing. People make this move in exchange for better conditions, better opportunities, better lives.

But I recall that the price of distancing oneself from a stereotype is to reinforce that stereotype, and the related injustice, for those who cannot likewise distance themselves. It saddens me to watch. A disability movement -- disability rights or independent living -- which stresses "the able disabled" and overlooks "the unable" is less than it could be. Less than it should be.

In one sense I cannot bring myself to condemn people who can't imagine their loved ones benefiting from the ADA, who can't imagine their loved ones as full members of a society much like ours, who struggle against isolation in the name of integration, who work to create utopias where disabled people will be loved for what we are rather than scorned for what we are not, sheltered from hostility, free to live good lives.

But I recall how easily protective separatism becomes coercive segregation, and it saddens me to watch. A disability movement -- a protective movement or a normalizing movement -- which stresses "the most vulnerable" and overlooks "the capable" is less than it could be. Less than it should be.

Dismissing the struggle of those who make it to university and discover there that the lectures and texts are available only to others, dismissing the struggle of those who exert great effort to communicate pleasure and displeasure, diminishes the movement.

ß

In her provocatively titled article "Disabled Lives: Who Cares?" Martha Nussbaum begins with the stories of three disabled people. Jamie and Arthur are cognitively disabled children, and Sesha is a cognitively and physically disabled adult. The stories Nussbaum tells about them are only nominally *theirs* -- they are framed and controlled by the people who love them and care for them.

My uncle Bruce is splayed across these pages, posed by those who tell "his" story for him -- for he seems incompetent to tell it himself.

Nussbaum's view of disability is truncated by her unwillingness to consider the ways in which the physical and social environments limit our ability to develop human powers and to enjoy liberty and independence, the ways in which human dependence is highlighted or downplayed in a variety of ways. Her view is no more *the* view of disability than is one that says, "We may not *move* like you, but we *think* like you, and that's what's really important."

Her reliance on these three stories, on three books which explore -- in various ways -- the lives and loves and labors of family and paid caretakers, means that her view of disability, as expressed in these pages, is incomplete. She draws on an old and familiar series of clichés: disability as dependence, disability as innate limitation, disability as political voicelessness. She comes at disability through feminism and commits the traditional feminist errors about disability, rather than reaching for the vitality that a fully realized interaction between feminists and those concerned with disability can offer.

"Parents are the *real* experts," went the old parent-advocate slogan, challenging professional power over disabled lives. They demanded that their children be sheltered, nurtured, loved in the way that the best parents love their children. That was a wonderful advance: celebrate it. But more and more disabled people are now challenging parental power and the image of disabled people as children; and Nussbaum's article, which ignores those critiques, is much less than it could have been.

Nor does she accurately assess the present situation as compared to the past. She suggests that in previous generations, children like Jamie and Arthur, like the child Sesha was, would have died or been institutionalized. If she is thinking of reasonably well-off and recent Western families, she may be right. But there have been other families, other communities, in recent generations and earlier, that would have made a place for the Jamies and Arthurs and Seshas of the world.

Nussbaum's approach to "fair treatment" of disabled people draws on the popular images that give rise to Bruce, on the importance of all people "hav[ing] the chance to develop the full range of their human powers, at whatever level their condition allows, and to enjoy the liberty and independence their condition allows," on the supportive role that nondisabled people play. She assumes our limits are innate, our society benevolent. Those are not safe assumptions.

In discussing equality, she argues that many traits, like race and sex, should not play a role in determining social advantage. "[S]o, too, one would have thought, the facts that one person's body is more dependent than another's, or that one has a dependent aged parent, should not be sources of pervasive social disadvantage." But she seems oblivious to the extensive work that has been done on how -- not whether, *how* -- what we call impairment has been used to "justify" significant social disadvantage. The important critiques that have arisen from the paradigm that gives me Mary are ignored.

Following this well-trod path, Nussbaum urges that we learn to value those who cannot make the expected contributions to the larger community; she does not consider how the larger community limits who may contribute. She urges that we provide better support to those who are dependent, but she does not question how we decide who is dependent and who is not.

ß

Martha Nussbaum's error is not unique. My sister Mary lives in much of the writing in disability studies, work by scholars who have made a parallel but opposite decision to leave my uncle Bruce out.

"Nothing about us, without us," says the South African slogan; without a sufficiently broad definition of *us* and a sufficiently reflective approach from those thinking and speaking "about us," this slogan can be used to justify a change of regime, rather than a true revolution, for most disabled people.

ß

"Equal rights are not special rights," we shout -- but of course it is precisely the distinction between equal rights and special rights that we debate. It is precisely the question of when differences should be acknowledged and when they should be ignored that we cannot answer in unison.

Disability rights activists addressing dis-enablement have argued, as have other rights activists before us, that to build an environment -- social or physical -- that benefits some people and not others is discrimination.

Those who oppose these rights arguments say that the environment is fine, and that efforts to level an already flat playing field are just another form of discrimination.

Care activists, focusing on the in-ability of those for whom they care, argue that any playing field must provide "safe" areas in which to nurture those who cannot play, and protection for those who work to for that "safety."

Those who oppose these care arguments maintain that the rough-and-tumble competition on the field is natural, that those who can't handle it -- or choose not to -- should yield to those who can.

Rights activists present a picture of someone like my sister Mary and call it the face of disability. They argue that the Marys of the world can and should be accommodated -- but they also stress how easy such accommodation is. Care activists worry that those who cannot readily be accommodated -- some of whom, they suspect, cannot be accommodated at all -- will be left behind, left out, left unprotected.

Care activists offer a picture of someone like my uncle Bruce and call *that* the face of disability. They argue that those who are inherently alien to our society should be accepted, embraced in a different way. Rights activists worry that this acceptance of intrinsic inability will slow barrier removal.

There are two distinct debates here, two distinct understandings of disability.

ß

I read Martha Nussbaum's "Disabled Lives" and I chuckle at the play on words. Where she sees un-able lives, I see dis-enabled lives; where she sees dependence and inability, I see barriers.

And yet . . . the barriers are not so clear, not so easily addressed as some writers seem to believe, and it is not as clear as we might think how we should re-envision our society to welcome, to value, to enable all people to full membership.

I read Martha Nussbaum's piece and I struggle with it, and with the context in which I read it.

I read Martha Nussbaum's piece and I realize again that I wish I were reading "crossover" work that draws on the several traditions of disability, work that takes the best of each tradition and brings it together in something new.

I read Martha Nussbaum's piece with a sad sense of her limits, and of my own. "Disabled People: Who Cares?" is a piece about where we are, not where we can go.

("Critic Of The Dawn" appeared originally in the May, 2001 edition of The Disability Rag's Ragged Edge magazine.)

The Future (And The Past) Of Autism Advocacy, Or Why The ASA's Magazine, *The Advocate*, Wouldn't Publish This Piece1

by Ari Ne'eman

In recent years, a growing number of autistic people have begun to demand a more active role in the public policy, research, service-delivery and media discussions that impact our lives. As the national conversation about autism has increased in tone and fervor, we who are the targets of this discussion have not been consulted. To those who believe in the motto of the disability rights movement — "Nothing About Us, Without Us!" — this situation has to change. Sadly, the traditional autism community has been driven by a set of priorities different from our own. Led almost exclusively by those not on the autism spectrum, it has made harmful decisions without our input. In response, this new autistic community has behaved very differently, a fact that now manifest itself in many ways. From a growing number of self-advocate run autistic social and support groups popping up across the country to larger autistic-run and mostly autistic-attended conferences like Autreat and Autscape, self-advocacy is on the rise. In some respects, new online technologies have assisted the development of this community, as nonverbal communication and geographic distance become less relevant in the world of the Internet. In other respects, however, the rise of the autistic community has been the natural result of increased awareness and diagnosis, leading to more and more autistic adults who are ready to come together to ask, "Where do we go from here?"

Advocacy has always been a big part of the autism world, and the autistic community is no different. As the founder of a prominent autistic-run organization, the Autistic Self-Advocacy Network, I have had the pleasure of overseeing extensive efforts to increase the representation of autistic people in the policymaking, research, service-delivery and media about our lives. From working to promote the inclusion of autistic people on policymaking bodies and task forces to passing state-level legislation on issues such as community integration, bullying prevention, disability history, first responder training, adult supports and other issues, the Autistic Self Advocacy Network has played an active role in the rise in influence of the autistic community. Furthermore, through our partnership with the Academic Autistic Spectrum Partnership in Research and Education (AASPIRE),[2] we are laying the groundwork for a new kind of autism research paradigm, which includes autistic people as full partners in the creation and implementation of rigorous studies on issues relating to the quality of life of autistic people. Yet, at the same time as our community has increased in relevance and influence, we have also come into conflict with more traditional autism groups on how we should approach autism advocacy and public representation of the autism spectrum. It is our belief that the traditional priorities of autism advocacy, which focus on eliminating the autism spectrum rather than pursuing quality of life, communication, and inclusion for all autistic people, need to be reset. In this essay, I shall attempt to lay out a framework for where we need to go — and what has kept us from getting there to date.

The object of autism advocacy should not be a world without autistic people — it should be a world in which autistic people can enjoy the same rights, opportunities and quality of life as any of our neurotypical peers. These words, counterintuitive though they may be to many in the autism community, represent the future that we must guide ourselves toward. In the past decade, more and more of the autism discussion has been taken up by a focus on causation research, with little to no practical implications for the lives of autistic people, even as our population has been left behind by the progress that much of the rest of the disability community has enjoyed from a vigorous civil and human rights-oriented agenda. Existing service-provision systems are doing a poor job of serving the unique needs of autistic adults in crucial fields such as employment, community living supports, transportation, disability discrimination and rights protection. Our public school system is rampant with violence and abuse against students with disabilities, with students on the spectrum subject to a particularly high risk of injury and even death (National Disability Rights Network 2009). Crucial barometers of inclusion with respect to community living and access to the general education curriculum show that to be on the autism spectrum is to be left out of many of the most important innovations of the disability rights movement of the last 20 years.

As all this has occurred, what has the response of large portions of the autism community been? By and large, one of discredited theories about vaccines, pseudoscientific treatments, and the rhetoric of pity and despair. Even a cursory glance at the magazine of the Autism Society of America reveals many such examples, with advertisements for vaccine recovery and Applied Behavioral Analysis, whose initial aversive-heavy experiments claimed to bring half of all children subjected to its methods to "indistinguishability from peers." These programs lack the research foundation they claim. For example, Ivar Lovaas' promise of recovery through ABA was based on the theory and methods used with "feminine boys" at-risk for homosexuality (Rekers & Lovaas 1974). That fact alone should give anyone pause. Meanwhile, those who peddle these pseudo-scientific treatments collect hundreds of thousands of un-reimbursable dollars from families justifiably desperate for a way to secure opportunities for their children.

Curing Autism Vs. Improving Quality Of Life

What do we really want? Is it autism prevention? Given that research has shown that the autism spectrum is predominantly genetic in origin, the most likely form of prevention would be that of eugenic abortion, similar to what we have seen with the 92 percent rate of selective abortion in the Down syndrome community (Mansfield, et. Al. 1998). Surely, there are considerable ethical problems with this course of action. Do we want normalcy, the "indistinguishability from peers," that Lovaas-style ABA promises? Or is that just a proxy for the more tangible things people desire, like the ability to communicate or the chance to hold a job and live in the community? Most of us on the autism spectrum do not wake up in the morning and wish that we had never been born. Insofar as we desire normalcy, it tends to be as a mechanism for achieving the things we cannot access in our lives due to lack of support, inaccessible environments — social and otherwise — and education and medical systems that are not responsive to our needs. It is without a doubt true that autistic people across the lifespan face much more difficulty in many spheres of life. Yet, at the same time, the autism spectrum is inclusive of more than a series of impairments; many of the traits we possess can be, in the proper contexts, strengths or at least neutral attributes. For many of us, the prospect of cure and normalization denies essential aspects of our identity. The autism spectrum is defined as "pervasive" for a reason; while it does not represent the totality of what makes us who we are, it is indeed a significant part of us, and to pursue normalization instead of quality of life forces us into a struggle against ourselves. Recent research reveals what many of us are already aware of — that autistic people possess distinct strengths with respect to rational as opposed to intuitive decision-making and systematic, categorization-oriented thinking (De Martino, Harrison, Knafo, Bird & Dolan 2008). A focus on autism elimination instead of more targeted efforts to address specific obstacles to quality of life, be they social, medical or otherwise, ignores these strengths. To quote Simon Baron-Cohen, internationally renowned autism researcher, on the issue of prenatal testing and cure: "What if such a treatment reduced...[a] baby's future ability to attend to details, and to understand systematic information like math? Caution is needed before scientists embrace prenatal testing so that we do not inadvertently repeat the history of eugenics or inadvertently 'cure' not just autism but the associated talents that are not in need of treatment" (Baron-Cohen 2009). It should be stressed: none of this is meant to deny the very real fact that autism is a disability. It is only to point out that disability is as much a social as a medical phenomenon and that the "cure" approach is not the best way forward for securing people's quality of life.

The Concept Of Recovery

The oft-cited concept of "recovery" from autism is not only scientifically unsupported but also dangerous in that it removes the very supports that made progress possible for many people with autism. Moreover, by equating developmental progress with a change in the fundamental character of our brains, the recovery concept denies the natural growth and skill acquisition that occurs for all individuals, regardless of disability. It is unreasonable to assume that autistics will be the same at age 30 as at age 3. The claim that addressing the challenges and behavioral difficulties associated with the autism spectrum can result in a fundamental re-wiring of a person's brain, to the point that he or she is no longer autistic, is ridiculous. Proponents of a "recovery"-oriented philosophy ignore the myriad coping strategies and mitigating measures that many of us use in order to be successful. When a person is suddenly deemed "recovered," he or she may lose access to the very strategies and measures that allowed for progress in the first place. Families fighting school districts that attempt to justify the removal of crucial IEP services, based on a child's progress that these services made possible, are intimately familiar with this dilemma. The disability community at large struggled with this sort of perverse reasoning after numerous judicial decisions narrowed the definition of disability under the ADA, depriving those who have found ways to compensate and improve their ability to function through accommodations. Congress addressed this problem by passing the ADA Amendments Act at the behest of a broad array of disability advocacy groups (including the Autistic Self Advocacy Network). This legislation mandated that mitigating measures such as medications, assistive technology or "learned behavioral or adaptive neurological modifications" not be considered in determining whether a person has a disability under the ADA. This act recognizes the fallacy of the recovery model with respect to disability.

Addressing Our Challenges

That many of us need additional support in order to accomplish the same things as neurotypicals should not invalidate the legitimacy of our existences; no human being has been entirely independent since our hunter-gatherer days. The majority of us don't farm or hunt and kill our own food. Nor are most of us personally responsible for the construction of our own shelters and modes of transportation. The society around us provides additional support in a wide variety of ways, albeit geared mostly towards the needs of the typical majority. The additional difficulty, expense, and challenge associated with securing necessary support for those of us who diverge from that majority stems from the reality that we live in a world that is geared only to a particular kind of person. As with previous civil rights movements regarding race religion, gender, and sexual orientation, we need an autism and disability advocacy that aims to change our society's institutions — from our educational system and places of public accommodation to more specialized infrastructures such as those for long-term care. We need a world that is much more inclusive of a broader range of individuals.

Does this mean that we should not be engaged in trying to ameliorate the many challenges associated with being autistic? Of course not. What it does mean is that, first, we should target our efforts towards the real challenges we face, rather than towards a broader, nebulous concept of "curing" autism that is offensive to many of the people that it aims to benefit. Second, we should in every instance consider the fact that it is often social barriers rather than disability itself that pose the problems we face. When a person faces anxiety, let us look for a method to address that challenge — but while the answer may end up being a medication or other medical solution, for many facing this challenge, social rather than medical approaches may be more effective. If the anxiety stems from trouble interacting with peers, the solution may well be education that is responsive to the social as well as academic difficulties autistics face. Often the environments in which we educate our children tend to tease and bully someone for having a different kind of mind, which is as wrong as oppressing someone having a different color skin. The same goes for problematic behavior, which for many nonspeaking autistic people is one of the only forms of communication available. By providing people with the education, assistive technology or other tools necessary to empower communication, these difficulties may be largely alleviated. Beyond that, when addressing other autistic traits such as categorization and sequencing behavior, lack of eye contact and a departure from social norms, we should give serious thought as to whether the problem lies with the behavior itself or the social stigma that surrounds it. If it is the latter, the path of previous civil rights struggles to broaden the scope of acceptable attributes may represent a more ethical solution.

In many instances, the answers are not yet apparent for us, particularly in realms like communication, which poses one of the most pressing and important areas of challenge for our community. However, our existing autism advocacy and research agendas have not placed finding solutions to these issues high on their agendas, preferring to focus on environmental or genetic research aimed at providing for "cure" or "recovery," If we make the effort, we are likely to find ourselves surprised by what a true civil rights struggle will yield for us. Only a few short decades ago, it was assumed that three out of every four autistic people had a co-existing intellectual disability (mental retardation was the term at that time) and that autism was caused by "refrigerator mothers." Today, we know that neither is the case, in part because of those individuals and groups whose priorities have been responsive to the true needs of autistic individuals. At one point, it was assumed that the inevitable future for the vast majority of people with developmental disabilities was institutionalization. Today, we have new legal and social services infrastructures that are creating a new reality oriented around community living supports. If we set as our goal the full realizations of rights, opportunities, and quality of life for all autistic people regardless of age, ability or place in life, and if we then follow up with vigorous advocacy and research, we will no doubt face future pleasant surprises as well. It is only by undertaking this as our priority that we can succeed in creating a world that accepts and supports neurological diversity just as it has come to accept and support a wide array of other diversities across our society.

Autism Heroes

Finally, we need to recognize that there has been a problem with our old guides. The heroes that have been put forward to the autism community have not measured up to their billing. Better ones are available. Should we admire Bernie Rimland, who mocked community integration as a pipedream and peddled a steady diet of quack cures to desperate parents forced to shell out thousands? Should we admire Jenny McCarthy, who has tried to revitalize a sagging career by plunging the autism community further into a discredited obsession with vaccines? Should we continue to support Autism Speaks, which uses corporate and celebrity influence to milk dry the autism community while returning only a tiny fraction of the money it raises for services in the communities from which it was raised?

Better exemplars exist, such as Justin Dart, who laid out and fought for a dream of inclusion for people with disabilities that led to the Americans with Disabilities Act. Let us instead turn to people like Judy Heumann, who fought discrimination against those who would sideline her because of her disability, and eventually rose to become Assistant Secretary for Special Education in the Clinton Administration, or Ed Roberts, who fought discrimination to get equal access to a college education, and then created a network of over 400 Centers for Independent Living (CILs) across the nation. It is a stark and clear choice — between pity, quackery and financial exploitation and civil rights advocacy, hope, and the prospect that disability and quality of life don't have to be mutually exclusive propositions.

The Cure agenda has failed us, as a goal and as a guiding philosophy. We can do better — we owe it to ourselves and to those for whom we long to build a better future, predicated on the idea that there is more than one way to get what we want and that we don't have to focus on making everyone the same for us all to have a chance to be happy.

Works Cited

- Baron-Cohen, Simon. "Autism Test 'Could Hit Maths Skills'." BBC News. 7 Jan. 2009. 25 May 2009 < http://news.bbc.co.uk/2/hi/health/7736196.stm>
- De Martino, Benedetto, Neil A. Harrison, Steven Knafo, Geoff Bird, and Raymond J. Dolan. "Explaining Enhanced Logical Consistency During Decision Making in Autism." *Journal of Neuroscience* 28.42 (2008): 10746-10750.
- Mansfield, Caroline, Suellen Hopfer, and Theresa M. Marteau. "Termination Rates After Prenatal Diagnosis of Down Syndrome, Spina bifida, Anencephaly, and Turner and Klinefelter Syndromes: A Systematic Literature Review." *Prenatal Diagnosis* 19.9 (1999): 808-812.
- Reikers, George A., and O. Ivar Lovaas. "Behavioral Treatments of Deviant Sex- Role Behaviors in a Male Child." *Journal of Applied Behavioral Analysis* 7.2 (1974): 173-190.
- *School is not Supposed to Hurt: An Investigative Report on Restraint and Seclusion in Schools.* Washington, DC: National Disability Rights Network, 2009. Print.

Endnotes

- This piece was solicited by *The Advocate*, which then declined to publish it.
- http://www.aaspireproject.org
- http://www.aaspireproject.org/
- http://www.aaspireproject.org/

(A version of this essay appeared previously in volume 30 of Disability Studies Quarterly in 2010.)

Retrospective At The National Press Club (transcript)

by Ari Ne'eman

Events like tonight call on us to do more than just give thanks. They call on us to reflect a little bit, and ask some important questions. So, let's start with one of the most important question to scholars, philosophers, and folks lying awake at night: why are we here?

What are we doing here? What is this all about? And I don't just mean why are we here at the National Press Club tonight, but why is the self-advocacy movement important? Why is it important that people with disabilities talk for ourselves, and that we fight against that which is about us without us? Why does self-advocacy matter?

When Scott and I co-founded ASAN five years ago, the national conversation on autism was frankly very different from what it was today. Most people's ideas of autism were shaped by <u>Rain Man</u>, various public service announcements promoting pity and fear, and television shows that contracted what I like to call Very Special Episode syndrome. Some of you may be familiar with Very Special Episode syndrome. It's a very, very concerning public health epidemic upon which a television show contracts a disabled character for an episode or two. Fortunately they're usually able to kick the habit pretty quickly, sending us back to the institution, or the school where we belong. Usually the non-disabled characters learn a very important lesson along the way. It's a great frustration of mine.

But when folks talked about autistic people then (and often now, but we're making progress), they often assumed that they're only talking about children. Because of that, a lot of people told us when we were getting started that the time wasn't right for an advocacy organization run by and for autistic people. They said the public and the autism community were not ready. You should wait a while. You should give them more time. They'll include you when they're feeling a little bit more comfortable. When they get around to it. You know, when they're sure.

And the past was very daunting. It seems like nobody had ever done this before, although we later learned that was not the case. The odds were against us. Under other circumstances, we might have taken that advice but we didn't, and I want to tell you why.

Before we started ASAN, I remember reading an email from a young autistic woman who was writing to an online support group she belonged to after having a singularly horrific day. In the morning, she went to an autism fundraiser where the organizers spent their time talking about how people should give in order to help these poor, unfortunate souls. People like her who they said could never hold a job, never live independently, never have any friends, and never be included in their communities. In the afternoon, she decided she'd had enough of these folks and looked up new autism organizations. She discovered that one of the leading autism groups in her country Canada had recently testified to the Canadian parliament saying that autism is worse than cancer because the person with autism has a normal life span.

Finally, to try to unwind in the evening, she decided to watch some television. Of course, she promptly discovered in a commercial break a public service announcement comparing the odds of having an autistic child—a child like her--with the odds of being in a fatal car accident.

After describing the various elements of this rather unfortunate day, she wrote in her email, "Why do they hate us so much? What did we ever do to these people?"

I understand what she meant perfectly. As a matter of fact, I'm sure I've said the exact same thing many, many times growing up, and probably even still today. And I say that knowing perfectly well that it isn't about hate. I know that even those that we disagree with have the best of intentions. I know that even the most vile and fear-mongering advertisement or fundraising effort is, in some perverse way, motivated by love. But what became immediately evident at that point, and what drove us to found ASAN, was that good intentions and love were quite frankly just not enough. Even love, in the absence of empathy, can be harmful. When people that you talk about, or set policy on, or conduct research regarding, are not in the room, even good people feel licensed to say horrible things. You cannot help people through pity and fear.

So we decided that an organization was needed. A unified voice of autistic people speaking for ourselves was needed. ASAN grew, supported by autistic people and our allies in the parent and professional community. People saw our mission and values as their own.

But we needed other partners. We needed to find other people who would support us. We were - and we are - a new community. We needed to figure out: where are we going to get friends when the situation looks hostile politically and practically for us, and, more importantly, how are we going to define ourselves? Not just by what we didn't like about how others approached us, but also by speaking to an autistic experience in this country and this world in positive terms. It's very interesting, we found the answer to both of those things in the same place: the broader disability rights movement.

We soon discovered we were not the first group of people with disabilities who were not happy with the dominant narrative about both disability in general and our particular disability. I remember the first time I spoke to the folks over at AAPD and ADAPT, and so on and they were dealing with the same issues that we were. It took us a bit of time to realize it, but soon it was clear that—I think everyone's always surprised when they learned this about themselves—we weren't as special as we thought we were.

And we were thrilled to learn that there was this whole movement, and other organizations: this broader community of people that we could draw on for strength. We came to see our work through the eyes of past disability rights struggles. We knew we weren't alone because names like Ed Roberts, Justin Dart, Judy Cuman, Marka Bristo, Jacobis Pengrove, Judy Chamberlain, and countless others spoke about a history of leadership by and for disabled people that went further back than we had ever dreamed of. Disabled people who have brought power and hope to those of us who are too often written off by society. And in the process of doing so, perhaps more importantly, built a sense of kinship and community that went beyond any particular advocacy campaign or initiative.

I'm not a wheelchair user but when I see pictures of those who are crawling up the Capitol steps to fight for the passage of the ADA I know that they were fighting for my rights as much as they were fighting for anyone else's. I'm not deaf, but when I hear and when I read about the Deaf President Now protests at Gallaudet I see something that speaks to me as a disabled person in a very personal way. There is a broader disabled experience in America, and we as autistic people are part of it.

Now, the prejudices and ignorance that I spoke of earlier haven't gone away. But we're fighting it, and we're making progress. More importantly, we're offering an alternative. We're finding ways to make real progress in the practical challenges that face us, such as healthcare access.

ASAN is partnering with several major research universities to utilize community based participatory research methodology. It's a great technique in which we're involved not just as test subjects but as partners in the research going on about us to come up with new tools for physicians on improving healthcare access experiences. We're creating resources written by and for us, like our new navigating college handbook. But more importantly, we are building a sense of community just like any other minority group. We have the same legitimacy, and we should have the same rights. Any minority group looks to a sense of community to make it through tough times.

I want to close by sharing a quote from Ed Roberts, the father of the independent living movement, talking in a speech he gave upon the victory of the 504 sitters. I bring it up not just because Ed Roberts was a fantastic orator, and not just because Ed Roberts and the others who participated in the 504 sit-in, quite frankly, gave to our generation a gift that I fear that we may work the rest of our lives without ever being able to repay, but because, speaking beyond being the president of ASAN or presidential appointee or anything else I've had the honor to be in the last five years, when I was a child in the special education system and I was looking for a source of hope, and when times were darkest for me, I discovered these words. They made all the difference in giving me the strength to speak on my own behalf, but more importantly to work for the rights of others to do the same.

> We have begun to ensure a future for ourselves, and a future for the millions of young people with disabilities who I think will find a new world as they begin to grow up. Who may not have to suffer the kinds of discrimination that we have suffered in our own lives but that if they do suffer it, they will be strong, and they will fight back. And that's the greatest example that we, who are considered the weakest, the most helpless people in our society, are the strongest, and will not tolerate segregation, will not tolerate a society which sees us as less than whole people. But that we will together, with our friends,

reshape the image that this society has of us. We are no longer asking for charity. We are demanding our rights.

(The text of this speech was delivered at the Autistic Self Advocacy Network's fifth anniversary fundraiser by ASAN President and founder, Ari Ne'eman.)

The Beginnings of Autistic Speaking Day

by Corina Becker

It started sometime mid-October last year. I was browsing the internet, following links off of Twitter to new places I hadn't been, when something caught my eye. A new autism awareness campaign, it advertised itself as a way to raise money for charities around the world and for people to understand autism better. Curious, and ignoring the growing dread in the pit of my stomach, I clicked the link and took a look.

What I found was Communication Shutdown, an event started by a group in Australia that prompted people to refrain from going on social networking sites such as Facebook and Twitter for one day, November 1st. It said that it would help people to understand the communication difficulties that people with autism struggle with, and this will help people to know autism better. Also, for a $5 donation, people would get a charitable app to send out tweets and status updates throughout the day on why people were being silent for the day, and the money would go to certain autism charities in people's own countries.

Let me just tell you, as an Autistic person who uses Twitter extensively for pretty much everything, I was not impressed. As I wrote in my post on October 15th, Real Communication Shutdown, there are many issues with the campaign, beginning with the sensory-overload design of the website, and going on to the basic assumptions made by the organizers. To quote myself:

> "... it relies on the assumption that everyone participating uses Twitter and Facebook to communicate. While I realize that these sites make communication easier, it is not the only way in which NTs can communicate online, and thus subverts the entire exercise of the campaign.

> "I was recently asked by a person on Twitter to participate, and I responded that there wasn't much of a point, since I am Autistic, and do not require to learn about difficulties that I myself face in communicating. I pointed out to this person that Twitter and Facebook are two of the sites that actually allow Autistics to communicate and connect with others in the community, so I will not be disappearing from the Internet, as it is my lifeline. I also remarked that this is a flawed simulation, since a non-Autistic person still have the capability to text on their phones, and speak verbally, and so would not be totally comprehending the true reality of Autistic disability."

I went on to suggest that a better way for Communication Shutdown participants to simulate the full extent of the possible communication difficulties Autistic people face: a complete and utter communication disconnection. No internet, no phones, no texting, no note writing, no speaking. Nothing.

Do not communicate at all, and maybe they'll understand the frustration that causes Autistics to lash out, to hit, bite, scream, and all the other "bad" behaviours that just get blamed on autism. That's what I thought, but then I realized the simulation was flawed. Even if people were to resist the temptations to cheat, it would be too easy for people in an uncontrolled environment to come to the wrong conclusions. Without someone controlling conditions in the simulation, and then providing a structure for feedback and to guide responses towards the purpose of the simulation, it would fail. A simulation, in all honestly, isn't to convey the reality of others perfectly; it's impossible to do so due to the wide spectrum of unique people on the spectrum specifically and in humanity in general. A simulation is to present a piece of a reality in a way that another person who does not normally experience that reality can in part understand the reality of others.

Therefore, as a large-scale simulation, Communication Shutdown will be a failure. Never mind that in this tech-savvy, media-driven generation, there will be an enormous pressure to at least sign in and message to people privately. In fact, given how addicted youth seem to be to their electronic devices, it was basically guaranteed that there would be participants who still signed in during Communication Shutdown.

Knowing this, I impulsively proposed that non-Autistic people be silent and that Autistic people be as loud as possible on social networking sites. I called for "Real Autism Awareness," for Autistic people to:

use this day to flood every social networking site we know with our accounts, our experiences, what it feels like to be Autistic. Every sensory pain, every communication frustration, every account of being bullied, every wondrous moment, every peaceful calm, every instant of understanding and joy. Let them hear our voices and take back the autism community.

In my next post, I realized other Autistic people felt the same way as me, and I took it one step further from a proposed alternative, to an actual alternative. Whimsically calling it Autistic Speaking Day, I expanded on the purpose of what would come to be known as ASDay: to acknowledge our difficulties while sharing our strengths, passions, and interests, with the intent of raising autism awareness and battling negative stereotypes about autism.

I published the post on October 18, 2012, and then started to tweet links to it at a fairly consistent rate. To be honest, I did not expect that much would come from it. I was prepared to write a short post on my blog, linking to my past post and not saying much else other than I was sitting on Twitter, sending out tweets about my life as an Autistic. I really did not expect the responses I got.

I got some responses from someone running Communication Shutdown, but her comments did not satisfy me to call off my counter-event. In fact, it made me angry and I began to be more aggressive with my promotion of ASDay. I got some criticisms from other people as well, which I addressed later in a blog post, especially after I noticed ASDay gaining a lot of attention. It seemed that some people were unable to comprehend that 1) ASDay wasn't just about countering Communication Shutdown, but had the purpose of promoting Autism Awareness in our own way; 2) that we weren't asking people to donate money to anything; 3) that even people with the right intentions can make mistakes and those intentions do not excuse them from criticism and protest from the Autistic community; and 4) that all Autistics of all ages and "ability" levels can participate..

But what amazed me was the flood of support, agreement and pledges to contribute.

Apparently, I wasn't the only one who felt there should be an opposite of Communication Shutdown. Browsing other blogs, I became aware of other similar events. I decided that it didn't matter what each of us were calling it, but that we were all doing the same thing, with the same goals in mind. So I thought we might as well work together, and agreed to dedicate a few hours here and there with the other campaigns online. I still thought that ASDay would just be me and maybe a few others, tweeting obsessively throughout the day.

Until Kathryn Bjornstad commented on my blog with the Facebook link, I had no idea how big my idea had gotten. After clicking on the link, I think I just sat there for at least half an hour, stunned at how many people had already joined up to participate. I don't think I can accurately describe the feelings of jubilance I felt, and success. In a way, just by having so many people say, "Yes, I will not be quiet, I will speak up," made ASDay a smashing success before it even began.

It was then I started to realize what I had started. I felt electrified with energy and a rush of excitement. I remember a point where I thought "It's just not me, so now I can't slack off." And so with my next entry, I started to get to work, making logos to spread around and getting involved with the Facebook group. Someone made a twibbon of it, and another person suggested the hashtag #ASDay when I realized that my original tag #AutisticsSpeakingDay was really too long. I also addressed the criticisms, which I mentioned above.

As November 1st got closer and closer, I became more and more busy. Both Kathryn and I were contacted by news networks, including ABC News (Australia), 4ZzZFM News, Examiner.com, and the Washington Times for interviews through email or just to have permission to quote what we've already wrote. I was also asked by Steve Silberman, investigative reporter for Wired magazine, to write a guest post for ASDay on his personal blog. Between this and moderating the ASDay pages, I ended up not having time to write a detailed post for ASDay and simply picked out what I thought were some of my best blog posts.

I spent the day on Twitter, something like twenty hours straight, talking to people through tweetchat on the CoffeeKlatch, or on my own. People would contact me with a blog post they had done, and I'd share it on Facebook for the large list Kathryn compiled. I tried to read them all. The sheer amount of people openly talking and sharing information, and the responses throughout the day still amaze me. The goal of ASDay was to get people to learn about autism directly from Autistic people, and it was working.

From what we could track, we had over 500 participants from all over the world from as far as Indonesia and Turkey, over 80 blog posts, and we were messaging blog posts to over 2000 people who were invited to the event on Facebook alone. We have no clue how far the event reached just by "word of mouth" over the Internet.

As ASDay started to come to an end, we started getting an incredible about of feedback. I was very pleased by the responses from parents, family and professions about what they had learned from the day. As Jeanne Holverstott put it in a lovely post,

> "#ASDay became more than just another day. It was a large-scale dialogue about daily struggles, successes, and challenges that we didn't know about, couldn't guess about, and, perhaps, never dreamed of. Lifetimes of day-to-day experiences congealed to document what it's like to be a person with an autism spectrum disorder. #ASDay was a living, breathing, and talking personal and community history book with pages filled by unsung heroes with powerful stories."

We also started getting responses from Autistic people. The thanks and success for putting ASDay together I defer; the success of Autistics Speaking Day is not mine alone. It is the combined efforts of everyone involved, even in the smallest of tasks. It is a beautiful expression of community.

However, that is not why we immediately decided to run ASDay again. There was another result of ASDay that we hadn't quite anticipated, but was definitely welcome: empowerment.

Throughout the blog posts and feedback responses, we realized how much ASDay was an inspiration for a lot of Autistic people. There have been people who have started blogging, and continued blogging, from this event alone. Other Autistics who already blog felt encouraged to be open about their diagnosis and blog regularly about their lives as Autistic people. On several accounts, Autistic youths have felt empowered to start getting involved with their local autism organizations and become active in the autism/Autistic communities.

When I read these responses, I cried. I still cry when I think about them. I'm awestruck at how ASDay impacted people with such a resounding effect. Through these responses, I've realized the value that ASDay had to other people. For me, it was just another awareness campaign, one of the many I've participated in since becoming an active member of the Autistic community. For others, this was the starting point for their own journeys and inauguration into the community as Autistic members.

Even though we started as an awareness campaign, ASDay has become so much more. It is a chance for involvement and support for many Autistic members, it is a source of empowerment, to be able to speak and express oneself and know for sure that there are people listening. It is a chance for communication within our communities, to share information, our experiences and our lives.

With this in mind, Kathryn and I decided to continue running ASDay each year, for as long as there are Autistic people who want it to keep going. This year we decided to plan a little more ahead than the impulsive rush we did last year. We're using social media and word of mouth again as our primary means of organization and advertisement. We opened up a blog so that we can compile all contributing blogs into one place, as well as a new Facebook page and a Twitter account.

We may not be a counter-event to Communication Shutdown anymore, but the rest of our goals for ASDay have remain the same: To raise not only autism awareness, but also acceptance, and to battle negative stereotypes about autism by advocating for the inclusion of Autistic people in the community, and offer a forum to broadcast the messages of Autistic people and non-Autistic allies to as many people as possible. We welcome Autistics of all ages and "functioning" to participate in sharing their stories and messages, in whatever form is the most comfortable to express. We also welcome our non-Autistic allies to share in this day of respectful community and communication.

We hope that all of you will join us on November 1st!

(A version of this essay previously appeared on thinkingautismguide.blogspot.com in 2011.)

Current Realities

Loud Hands & Loud Voices

By Penni Winter

The State of Autism Today

Autism as a diagnosis - as opposed to the actual condition - has been around since the 1940s and Asperger's since the early 1990s. Yet what have we gained? What real understanding is out there? As we look around in 2012, misconceptions, misunderstandings, maltreatment and downright dangerous fallacies about autism are rife.

The Normalisation of Autistics

One of the biggest and most insidious maltreatments involves the concept and practise of what I call 'normalisation,' which springs out of the belief that Autism is an inferior or 'wrong' state. Thus 'becoming normal' is seen by many parents and therapists as the ultimate goal, the only one worth pursuing, because being autistic is such a Terrible Thing, and the aim of all therapy is to make us 'indistinguishable' from our 'normal' peers. Autism thus becomes something to be got rid of, no matter what sacrifices must be made. Some would even rather see their child dead than autistic.

This normalisation can involve many different therapies and practises. Let me make it clear – it's not *what's* done, but *why* it's done. Some of the same therapies, such as social skills and life skills training, I know are used by those who don't subscribe to the Big Bad Autism viewpoint. They are seeking instead to simply grow their child's capabilities *as an autistic person*, an approach I have started calling 'Maximisation', and a goal I wholeheartedly support₁. With normalisation, on the other hand, the ultimate goal is simply to rid the individual of any outward sign of their Autism.

The normalisation approach is likely to be marked by any or all of the following: an insistence on 'quiet hands', the suppression of stims such as walking on toes or rocking, the quashing of sensory overload reactions, the labelling of our special interests as 'obsessions' and consequent restriction or denial of them, an insistence on eye contact, a refusal to allow the child private time alone, direct criticism of autistic behaviour or personality traits, and no doubt others I haven't yet discovered. If they succeed in their goal, or even approximate it, the NTs around the autistic person congratulate themselves--and sometimes the autistic person--for this 'achievement.'

What they don't see, however, is the real cost of this normalisation, which can be very high indeed. The people taking this approach I'm sure are mostly motivated by concern. However, they are subscribing to one huge fallacy – the one which says that the Autism is somehow separate from, and 'burying', the 'real' (i.e.: normal) person underneath. Not so. *Autism runs all the way through.* It's a deep neurological difference. It can no more be stripped away or 'cured' than our gender or race can be 'cured' or taken away. It's that central to our being.

An autistic child who grows up knowing that something which is that intrinsic to their very selves is so hated and loathed by those around them, who has those same adults demand that they suppress, deny and 'get rid of' all evidence of it, is not going to grow up feeling good about themselves. They will likely grow to hate their Autism, and themselves with it. Even if they don't have a formal diagnosis, it's still possible they will hate their 'weirdness' or 'difference' anyway, and will likely feel almost as much pressure to be 'normal'. As young adults, they may come to refuse to identify as autistic, and thus deny themselves support and community with other autistics. The chances are they will suffer from depression, anxiety disorders, deep anger and resentment, low self-esteem, or similar problems. Many will struggle to maintain their 'passing' façade and have chronic anxiety around being 'found out.' They may have problems with drink or drugs, drop out of school or jobs, or even attempt suicide. Some succeed.

This is not theoretical. I have spent decades of my own life straining to make myself over into that elusive 'normal,' and hating myself for not succeeding. I saw myself as 'less than' others, furiously lashing myself for my--as I saw it--weakness and stupidity. I lived with chronic depression, overwhelming anxiety levels, and rock-bottom self-esteem. The more normal I tried to be, the less normal I secretly felt – and the more of a failure. Even when I was able to 'pass', I lived with what I now call 'imposter anxiety,' the fear of being exposed and rejected – "*You're* not normal!" Years of involvement in the feminist movement, the New Age movement, counselling and self-improvement of various kinds, could not budge any of this. It wasn't till I discovered my Asperger's, and found others who also had it, that I began to shift my viewpoint.

This pressure of course came from within, but I wouldn't have begun it if hadn't first felt pressure from others. Nor am I the only one. While experiences of course vary from one person to another, the general rule seems to be the more pressure is put on an autistic to be 'normal', wherever it's from, the worse the person feels about themselves as a consequence, and the harder their life becomes. Read, for instance, what it *really* meant for Julia Bascom to be forced to have 'quiet hands[2],' or read Rachel Cohen-Rottenburg's description of what she calls 'over-compensation[3],' or of the young autistics she has met who struggle with hating their autism[4]. Or read Amanda Forest Vivian's response to a newspaper article on the suppression of stims: "People with ASD have real problems. That some of us walk on our toes is not one of them[5]." Dip into any autistic-run forum or some of the open Facebook groups for those on the spectrum. Read what adults on the spectrum have to say, about their lives and their experiences. Read, and weep. Weep for all the lost years, the lost people, the lost opportunities, the potentials never realised.

Autistics as 'Not Properly Human'

And this goes deeper than simply having our Autism suppressed. In many respects, we are not even seen as fully human. There's a common fallacy, for instance, that we are limited in or even totally devoid of any capacity for love or caring, or indeed just about any kind of emotions--almost robotic-like soulless automatons. An example is an article last year in a New Zealand magazine on an autistic child. It was sub-titled, *When Love Is a One-Way Street*--even though the mother and a subsequent TV program on the same child, revealed he *is* capable of affection[6]. He just prefers to spend lots of time alone, as do many on the spectrum--which really says only that they need solitude, not that they are incapable of love and affection.

A similar and related fallacy is the one that we are incapable of empathy or compassion. Professor Simon Baron-Cohen has done us no favours in his claims that empathy is, "what makes humans human", and then says we have none[6]. To be fair, he explains that it's 'cognitive empathy' we don't have (i.e.: the ability to recognise emotional states in others, by way of non-verbal signals), but that we do have 'affective empathy' (i.e.: if we realise someone is upset, for example, we do have an emotional response). Unfortunately, this distinction is lost on most people, and the common belief, fed by media alarmism, seems to be that we lack *any* capacity for empathy.

Most of the myths and stereotypes about Autism feed into this 'not quite human' viewpoint. For instance, that the typical Asperger's person is a young, male computer nerd, with no social life, has poor personal hygiene, who is more interested in ASCII than actual people. Or that we have no sense of humour, aren't able to joke, do sarcasm or irony, etc. Or the idea that we have 'empty lives,' devoid of the usual things that others focus their lives around, while our actual interests are ignored or judged a 'waste of time,' or as further evidence of our 'wrongness.'

This dehumanisation can and often does have a devastating flow-on effect. If we are not seen as fully human, then we can be treated however others wish. If we don't have feelings like normal people do, then we can be freely bullied and abused, rejected and excluded. If we have no sense of humour, then it doesn't matter if others jeer, ridicule or poke fun at us, and so on. If our lives are 'empty,' then they are seen as 'worthless.' In common with other disabled people, it's presumed we lack 'quality of life.' We become sidelined, marginalised, invisible, our rights as human beings ignored. In extreme cases we've even been murdered by close family or caregivers – and when that happens, it's seen as an 'act of mercy', and the sympathy is usually for the *murderer*, not the victim, who becomes almost forgotten[8]. This is true in very few other types of murder.

Autism as Tragedy

Our Autism is called a 'tragedy' or even, by some parent groups, 'the enemy' to be fought at all costs, and the [apparent] increase in our numbers is referred to as an 'epidemic,' as if Autism were some dread disease. We're said to 'ruin' our parents' lives and break up marriages[9], and we get discussed in terms of the 'burden' we are on our families, the 'difficulty' we cause others. What we might feel or think or want is hardly ever even asked – because, oh yeah, that's right, we don't *have* feelings or needs. It's the parents and families who are focused on, because they are deemed to be the ones that 'matter', not the individuals with Autism.

Even as adults, we're presumed to have nothing worth contributing to the discussion 'about' us. Our experience and our concerns are dismissed[10], our attempts to present our viewpoints ignored, and we are all too often excluded from participation in groups and on issues that concern us, or at best given token roles. And then, to add insult to injury, we're even told that if we can speak at all, then we're not 'really' autistic, and therefore can't speak on behalf of other autistics (though how, if *we* can't speak for them, those who definitely *aren't* autistic can either, is left unquestioned). These critics often make erroneous assumptions about our levels of independence, or ability to communicate verbally, and thus we are dismissed as being unable to understand those who are 'lower-functioning.'

I fear I have painted a very bleak picture here. To be fair, there *are* parents of autistic children who do not subscribe to the 'normalisation' approach, who are not scared of or negative about their children's Autism --and who *are* willing and prepared to listen to us, in order to help their children become all they can be--and incidentally to help us, if they can. Some even write their own blogs. Unfortunately, they tend to be individual voices, scattered and drowned out by the doom-and-gloom trumpetings of the big Autism organisations, via a co-operative and complicit media.

On Autistic Community and Culture

There's still so much that is horrible about the way we are treated; it is breathtaking. How can we turn this around and change a world that is so unaccepting of us? My belief is that becoming part of the autistic community has to be the first step. Without it, we are isolated and alone, and it's almost impossible to break free of the pressure to be 'normal,' and the consequent self-hatred. The community of autistics, while not perfect (but then who is), is crucial to developing strong self-esteem, and to a realisation of our essential humanity and self-worth.

For instance, when I first began to think I 'might' be autistic/Asperger's, if I had read only books by the 'experts' on autism, dropped solely into parent-led forums, and/or digested only the 'scholarly' or 'scientific' websites and mainstream news media articles, I would have come away with my negative view of autism reinforced. My stereotypes further entrenched and my self-esteem (never high) consequently even more rock-bottom. I would either have rejected altogether the idea of being autistic, or seen myself as something terrible, inferior, my 'autistic' qualities as things that needed to be 'changed' or ripped out of me. Either way, I would have continued to see myself as 'wrong' in some inherent manner.

But thankfully, I was fortunate enough to stumble across several Aspie-led forums, autobiographies such as *Pretending To Be Normal*[11], *Congratulations! It's Asperger's Syndrome*[12], *Born On A Blue Day*[13], and the online writings of people such as Ari Ne'eman, Dave Spicer, Jane Meyerding and Jim Sullivan, the author of the seminal piece *"Don't Mourn For Us*[14]." These were pivotal both in my coming to identify as Asperger's/autistic, and also in coming to see that being so was not a tragedy or an inferior state.

In the forums, for instance, so often it would happen that someone would share an experience, a reaction or a thought pattern they'd had, and others, including me, would respond "Really? You do that/have that too? I thought I was the only one!!" When this happens often enough, the individuals get to feeling "gee, maybe I'm not so terrible after all, so deficient, so weird, so… worthless…" And then there's the simple acceptance we granted each other, for all our 'quirks,' which came as a relief after so many years spent in an unaccepting world, where criticism and put-downs and jeers were more (and still often are) our usual fare. Within the Autism community, we are forging friendships, establishing networks, and valuing and validating each other.

These and many more such experiences led me – and so many of my new acquaintances and friends – to see that we were and are not how others have sought to define us, that our 'funny little ways' do have merit, that we were and are human beings, with the right to be ourselves in all our eccentric glory, and to be treated with respect. That respect, sadly, is all too often still not forthcoming from the world at large.

We are Equal

Autistic rights are disability rights, which are human rights. We are all poorer for the lack in any one group of these basic rights. Yet, a while back when I wrote a piece called, *Five Things We'd Like People To Know About Adults on the Spectrum*, I listed the first of these as, "That we are human beings, first and foremost." When this was reposted on another website[15], one person commented, rather indignantly, that 'of course' we are human, it shouldn't need to be said. Yet it does. It does.

Because stereotypes are just that – stereotypes. I could write an entire book just on debunking all those tired old myths. Suffice to say that we are capable of a great deal that we're not supposed to be, even if we do it in a different way. The supposed 'lack of empathy,' for instance, is in direct contrast to the experience of many autistics, that in fact many of us suffer from *too much* empathy, and often either don't know how to express it, or find it too overwhelming and have to withdraw from situations[16]. There is now even an entire Autism and Empathy website dedicated to disproving this myth[17]. Rachel Cohen-Rottenburg, who runs the website, has also done a fine four-part analysis of Professor Baron-Cohen's Empathy Quotient Test on her blog, questioning many of the assumptions behind the questions[18].

And then there's humour – most of us *do* have a sense of humour, though we tend to find different things funny. If we don't laugh at others' jokes, it's probably because either we don't find them funny (e.g. racist, sexist, or cruel jokes), we're having trouble working out whether the person is actually joking, or we maybe didn't hear the joke properly because of auditory processing issues. Many of us can even do sarcasm and irony, though we can have trouble handling other people's sarcasm, as often we can't tell whether it *is* sarcasm or not.

Nor are our lives 'empty' and meaningless. Many are married or have partners and even have children--some of whom are on the spectrum themselves, and some who are not. And while the unemployment rate is high amongst autistic adults, nonetheless, we do work or have worked at all sorts of jobs and professions, including many we're not 'supposed' to be able to do. A recent query in a Facebook Asperger's group revealed a long list of jobs we've done, or still do – video editor, chef, postman, special needs teacher, music teacher, carpenter, lawyer, welder, university lecturer, electrician, janitor, librarian, waiter, retail worker, X-ray technician, self-employed craft worker, volunteer firefighter, and many, many more. We are artists and writers, graphic designers and videographers, musicians and photographers, actors and performers. Some suffer a good deal of work-related stress, and many of us feel forced to hide our autism in order to keep those jobs. But that doesn't detract from our being able to do them--simply that we fear others will *perceive* us as being unable to because of it.

We also have many and often absorbing interests (NOT obsessions), which give us great pleasure. These range widely, and include such things as Japanese anime, other cultures, music, cats, genealogy, martial arts, science, theology, map-reading, history, sports, art, astrology, singing, cars, astronomy, research, languages, photography, Autism itself, and yes, even computers! This is but a sampling of the things we are interested in. Many autistics belong to churches and/or community organisations, do volunteer work, participate in sports and cultural activities, and just about all the other things 'normal' people do. We just like to participate in them in our own way.

Even those who are deemed 'lower functioning' have many things that interest and absorb them – hubcaps, spinning wheels, lamp-posts, twirling ribbons, flashing lights, washing machines, running water, etc. Who has the right to say their lives are 'meaningless', simply because these aren't 'normal' interests that others their age have? And it's now being discovered that those deemed 'lower functioning,' usually because they are unable to communicate verbally, are not as 'empty' within as others have assumed[19]. The dividing line between 'higher' and 'lower' functioning is proving more and more of a myth.

Our lives are definitely, definitely not empty, and *we* are not empty, not soulless, not unfeeling, not devoid of all the things that make a person 'human.' We live, we laugh, we love, we give, we care, we bleed--oh how we bleed.

The core of Autism is not an emptiness, but a unique way of being, of thinking and feeling, of relating and reacting to the world. *In itself,* this way of being has as much value, as much of a right to exist and to reach its full potential, and as much to contribute, as being neurotypical has. It is simply *different.*

We are human beings. While I do believe that yes, we have the responsibility to act as responsibly and as politely as we can towards our fellow humans[20], we also have the right to simply be our true selves, in all our eccentric glory. We shouldn't have to 'prove' that we are human. We want and need to be accepted as we truly are, not as substandard or 'fake' NTs. If the world could just stop ranting about 'tragedies' and really *look* at us and *listen* to us, get to know us, they would come to see we are as human as they are.

On Being Autistic Advocates

Of course nothing will change for us without our making it happen. However, advocacy, or being an 'activist,' as my generation would have called it, could potentially mean a wide variety of things for each individual. It might mean simply resisting that vile and often damaging pressure to be 'normal.' Or just no longer trying so hard to please and placate. It could mean letting our stims show, or ceasing to suppress our symptoms of sensory overload, or our 'weird' way of walking or talking or moving. It could mean 'coming out' to friends, work colleagues, teachers, or even family, if we come to a realisation of our Autism as adults. Or perhaps we might dare to speak up when we come across ignorance about Autism or abuse of an autistic child.

Or it could mean we sign petitions, write, or do public speaking or presentations. We might also join in the agitation for certain law or government policy changes or against loss of services. We could participate in Autism organisations, trying to change them to be more 'autistic-friendly,' or build our own organisations. Being an advocate could also mean asking the hard questions--the uncomfortable ones-- or pointing out awkward facts to both NTs and those on the spectrum. It could also include attempting to answer them.

Building a strong 'autistic rights' movement in effect includes a wide range of things: developing community amongst ourselves and creating a new and more positive identity, developing new analyses of the ways we are oppressed and marginalised, getting across to the rest of the world a new perception of what it means to be autistic, and of course, campaigning for our human rights. There is room for all of us to play our part. And whatever we do, however we do it, we can do it with 'loud hands' and 'loud voices,' and loud whatever else we need, in whatever way that works for us individually or collectively. Let us be our real autistic selves, loud and proud, and show the world what we truly are.

Yes, I know that many autists are busy to the point of stress simply surviving their own lives, and don't have much energy left over for any kind of advocacy, however gentle, or their lives are such that they are constrained from it. I know how daunting it can seem, and how tired you feel. Oh, how I know! But we are all part of this, simply by existing. And if we all did something, however insignificant it might seem, all those little things would in time add up to a Big Something. "Rome wasn't built in a day," nor will we change our plight overnight. There's a lot of work still to be done. I don't want this to sound like an autistic version of, "Workers, you have nothing to lose but your chains!" a-la Karl Marx, or too happy-clappy or idealistic. But it *is* time for change - because the current situation is untenable, unbearable, and downright unjust. There is and has been simply too much pain. It cannot and must not continue.

1. See my blog post on this, on 14 November, 2011, at http://strangeringodzone.blogspot.com/2011/11/behavioural -therapy-normalisation-vs.html

2. Julia Bascom, 'Quiet Hands', October 5, 2011, at juststimming.wordpress.com/2011/10/05/quiet-hands/

3. Rachel Cohen-Rottenburg, 'On Passing, Over-Compensation, and Disability', February 19, 2012, at http://www.journeyswithautism.com/2012/02/12/on-passing-overcompensating-and-disability/

4. Rachel, 'Autism Parents: It's Time to Stand Up with Us', January 8, 2011, at http://www.journeyswithautism.com/2011/01/08/autism-parents-its-time-to-stand-up/

5. Amanda Forest Vivian, 'Autistics Speaking Day post', November 1, 2010, at http://adeepercountry.blogspot.com/2010/11/autisticsspeakingdaypost.html

6. Donna Chisholm, 'Autism: A Mother's Story', *North and South*, Auckland, New Zealand, April 2011

7. Simon Baron-Cohen, various writings, most recently in *The Science of Evil: On Empathy and the Origins of Cruelty*, New York: Basic Books, 2011.

8. See for instance commentary by Zoe Gross on the murder of George Hodgins, Mar 17, 2012, at http://illusionofcompetence.blogspot.com/2012/03/remembering-george-hodgins.html; or Rachel's commentary on that and other recent murders of   autistics, 'This is What You Get', April 4, 2012, at http://www.journeyswithautism.com/2012/04/04/this-is-what-you-get/

9. Kennedy Krieger Institute, May 19, 2010, '80 Percent Autism Divorce Rate Debunked in First-Of-Its-Kind Scientific Study', at http://kennedykrieger.org/overview/news/80-percent-autism-divorce-rate-debunked-first-its-kind-scientific-study/

10. Rachel, 'Saving a Theory, Dismissing its Subjects', January 1, 2012, at http://www.journeyswithautism.com/2012/01/01/saving-a-theory-ignoring-its-subjects/

11. Lianne Holliday Willey, *Pretending to Be Normal*, London, Philadelphia: Jessica Kingsley, 1999.

12. Jennifer Birch, *Congratulations! It's Asperger's Syndrome*, Philadelphia: Jessica Kingsley, 2002.

13. Daniel Tammet, *Born on a Blue Day*, London: Hodder & Stoughton, 2006.

14. Jim Sullivan, 'Don't Mourn For Us', http://www.autreat.com/dont_mourn.html, retrieved 13 March, 2009.

15. 'Five things we'd like people to know about adults on the spectrum', reposted by Hilary Stace on Aug 19, 2011, at http://humans.org/2011/08/19/five-things-wed-like-people-to-know-about-adults-on-the-spectrum/

16. Maia Szalavitz, 'Asperger's Theory Does About-Face', May 14, 2009, at http://www.healthzone.ca/health/mindmood/article/633688--asperger-s-theory-does-about-face/

17. http://autismandempathy.com

18. Rachel, 'A Critique of the Empathy Quotient   (EQ) Test', Parts 1-3 & Conclusion, Aug 6 – 15, 2011, at http://journeyswithautism.com/category/empathy/

19. John McKenzie, 'Autism Breakthrough: Girl's Writings Explain Her Behavior and Feelings', ABC News, February 19, 2008, at http://abcnews/go.com/Health/story?id=43112238&page=1 #T4AKEHpqw8o

20. See my posts on this, Jan 10 – 25, 2012, at strangeringodzone.blogspot.com/search/label/aspie lack of manners

Dear Younger Self

by E

Dear Younger Self,

It's not just you.

You really are different. And there's nothing wrong with that.

Yes, it is hard. No, it doesn't get better.

You get stronger.

You will always have to be stronger. You will always have to try harder. You will still be considered weaker and lazy by many people who watch you struggle, hamper your efforts, and put you down. Even the ones who don't see you as broken will often assign you full-human-being status only in principle, rather than being able to understand fully. This partial acceptance must be nurtured because it is all many people can achieve and it makes things better for you and others. However, you must be willing to understand that in many situations it is more harmful and humiliating than no acceptance at all, and in those situations, force yourself to endure without it.

People really are as scared of you as you think. Yes, their fear is perplexing and terrifying in ways they will never have to know, but much more importantly, it can be made useful. Scared and ignorant people often talk about us as useless and try to change our very nature without admitting this is what they are doing. A fearless and knowledgeable person will be able to encounter others as they exist in the world and use fear and ignorance in transcendent ways.

They really are scared of new ideas and/or change. You will work hard for accommodation, etc. and not get it, only to find out it's already being enjoyed in a more forward-thinking community. The media coverage will not tell you what it took, the family arguments behind closed doors, the role self-advocates played and what they did for how long. It will say only that parents/teachers/government "gave" this right to disabled people because they, the normal people, "felt" like it, because it was "right" for "their" community, or because they reasoned that this particular group of disabled people "could still end up being valuable members" of that community. This will make you feel incredibly disheartened, frustrated, and alone. It will also strengthen your resolve if you remember to believe in yourself, even when not a single other human being does.

Of course, this is difficult because people don't like a lot of the things you do or are.

For instance, people don't like it when you identify with someone who is apparently "more" disabled than you are. Since you happen to be "verbal," they really don't like it if you identify with someone who can't produce meaningful speech. When you naturally identify with someone who has trouble producing meaningful speech because you are often forced to speak when/where/how others demand, and have that speech put in the context of the other's choice (usually related to the broader culture), while the ways you supplement your speech with other types of communication are ignored. It seems odd that people would so adamant that the verbal and nonverbal must be at odds with each other. But that is how the majority thinks, and as far as thinking goes, you are firmly in the minority. It should not be lost on you in this example that in order to stop fearing the natural affinity of the verbal and nonverbal who communicate in alternative ways, people would have to be comfortable letting you speak when/how/where you want.

Of course, it doesn't matter if they "allow" you to do anything or not, you must do it anyhow, if it is right. So what do you care what anyone tells you about who you should and should not identify with or when and when not to speak? Yes, they will hate/ridicule/try to silence you. Don't mind them and keep signing/hopping/babbling.

They really do kill us. They really do want to, though they say it's disagreeable. They really do hurt us because they are hurting too, or because they can or because their worldview depends on it. One thing people don't talk about is that sometimes "they" are actually "us" in one way or another. We forget that fact when "they" refuse to include "us" and maybe that's what "they" want, to keep being "them."

The rules for being a "them" are:

"They" want you to be ashamed, and they call this "help."

"They" would like to remind you of your failures, often induced by them in the first place, as a rationalization for the amount of control they would like to take over you.

Sometimes, one of "us" becomes or thinks s/he is one of "them," and the same unfortunate rules apply.

Younger self, your older self would like to make you safe, but it doesn't work like that. Your older self would like to have all the answers for how to deal with people who want you complacent, different, or dead. Frankly, their motives are just as puzzling now as they ever were. The best thing your older self has ever been able to posit is that they see themselves in you and would no longer like to see that part of themselves. They want to smash the mirror that is you. They are much more fragile and needy than you realize, because they seem strong when they take advantage of your weaknesses, and they feel strong, too. Often, the spell is broken the moment you show them you won't cooperate. There are many, many people who will voluntarily feel broken, useless, selfish, inferior, and guilty for someone else.

There are plenty of people who will forsake their judgment. If you are not an easy target, and if they haven't picked you for personal reasons, a victimizer will be happy to go elsewhere.

The guilt one feels for not being who one is "supposed" to be can go away. The guilt one feels for not being perfect in a world where perfection will only get them up to normal standards can even go away sometimes. It can go away when you meet others like you, because there are others like you and you will meet them. Right now you feel left out of meaningful relationships with others. Remember that feeling, and all the loneliness and confusion it brings, because when you grow up and meet others like you, they will ask you how the hell you survived, and you have to remember and tell them. And it is not only for this purpose that you remember. You remember because there will be moments when someone who went through the exact same experience says something about it that is incredibly wise; something you yourself may have half-formulated and forgotten about, and in just in that moment all the abject feelings of shame, loneliness, and anger fall away from both of you. There are people who live their whole lives without understanding what a connection like this is, to someone who may be from an entirely different walk of life and defined in a completely different way by society, is or can be. They don't know because they coincide so well with others like them that they never quite develop relationships that go beyond coincidence. If someone has difficulty relating to you because you are different, consider that you may be the first person they have encountered that helps them go beyond this type of relationship. It may be frustrating for both of you, but if you persevere you can give them a gift. You have things to offer. You do not have to feel guilty for your differences.

Sometimes, that fleeting feeling of connection will not feel like enough. You'll want allies, you'll want understanding from your own family, help such as proper accommodations, what everyone deserves. You'll wish for the authorities in control of how you live, support yourself, and learn to understand you enough to give you the things you deserve. You'll feel incredibly naive for having bought into what people have told you about yourself, as if you have betrayed yourself. At the same time someone you thought might just possibly know where you're coming from says something so ignorant and cruel that it breaks your heart. You will want long-term friendships, both with people who are "like you" and people who are not. You will have to be very forgiving--more than most, it seems--in order to accomplish this. You will have a natural affinity not only for loners and outsiders, and people whose value is not readily seen by most others, but also for people whose own personal or group history has involved them in struggle somehow. This is an especially good thing because these groups of people have often learned to be much more accommodating and understanding of others. They have a lot to give you.

And sometimes you will even offend your allies. People don't always like to talk about this, but you need to know it happens. Sometimes you'll see that look in their eyes that you instantly recognize. You're behaving like a "them." You didn't know better, but maybe you should have. It's hard to admit, because you know how you feel when someone does it to you. You would like to think you don't do that sort of thing. It sounds trite, but the truth is everyone makes mistakes. You and everyone else have been picking up signals about what is fully human and what is not from the time you were unable to think for yourself. When these things come up, it's good to examine them and get rid of them. Don't put up barriers to your own improvement by making excuses for your own ignorance.

You're already used to doing way more than your share when it comes to bridging gaps. Use this super ability to transform yourself and your world.

As you start to relate to people as an individual and as part of your found culture, you will start celebrating other people's victories-- victories that some may not even be able to understand--victories of people like you, that allowed them to realize themselves in ways you would like to realize yourself. The alienation from yourself that is so often enforced by well-meaning people who have told you you are wrong and defective is cracked every time this happens, and a bit of light shines through. If this keeps happening, someday you'll have a clear, unimpeded view of your own value as a person and of many other things that are mistakenly measured in terms of being either "whole" or "lacking."

If you continue to persevere in your search for connection both with yourself and the outside world, you will realize something strange and almost scary in a transformative way. It will become evident that you are not just you at all. In fact, people who tell you that you are broken, different from others (or sometimes they even call you "unique" and "special"), are only trying to make you feel small, discourage you into coinciding with them rather than trying to relate with you, and that's not how respect works. You need to show people how to respect you, and you must know your own language before you even attempt to teach it to the broader culture. It's people like you who will teach you your own language: about what was done to you, about your victories which you may not even realize were victories, what you've lost, what you've won, and what you still hope to gain. You will need to figure this out so you can tell it to those who come after and they can use it to make their lives a little better, do the same to make someone else's life a little better, and the cycle can continue.

And this is the most you can ever hope for: For all of us to keep trying to be recognized for who we really are, as individuals, just like everyone else. To celebrate our joys and victories.

And it is enough. Because we are enough.

Loud Hands

by April Herren

I have loud hands! I need help finding my place in a room. I can't tell where my body is in relation to things. I need to continually feel my surroundings to know how I fit in my kind little place. I might look pretty weird to the general public, but it is how I can keep myself connected in the world. I really might not want to have loud hands. It is a part of who I am. I could not stop if I tried.

I might just get my nice high not holding a beer or glass of wine, but by holding my objects really, really close to my face and concentrating on them. My objects might look like normal everyday items, but to me they help me to function in a world that is not prepared to deal with me.

I might have Autism, but I am incredibly bright. I live independently in my own apartment. I have help with my everyday living tasks. My mom lives close and is helpful. Life is good. The world just isn't prepared to deal with me.

I might like to maybe try not to listen to the world, but I have to live in it.

I might like to educate the world by writing. I love to write. I might need more little MEs to kindly tell the story of what it is like living in a world with Autism. I need little kind people to be open to my movement differences. It is how I make it in a world where I don't fit in. I need people to accept me for who I might be, not for my movements. I might look very different, but inside I might like to be accepted for who I am. I might need more help than most people, but I might not need criticism from people I don't know.

I might not like people to judge me. I am very independent; my life is my own and I might not look independent. But I am the one making the choices. Opinions of others matter, if they might listen to my opinion as well.

Now I might not need my mom to help me justify my independence, but I still need the support from her. My mom is a big part of my life. She helps me manage my life. Some things are harder for me because my body doesn't work correctly.

I can't sit still. I can't do normal everyday tasks. I need little kind helpers to help with these things. I might not be very successful without them. I have wonderful support. To the average person it might seem weird, but I can't function without it.

My Autism is my friend. It is my friend who helps through life's crazy times. I can't imagine feeling feelings without my Autism. In a crazy sort of way I feel that my Autism is a person all its own. I just feel that I might not like who I might be without my inside self. I might hope to be like this because it is who I am. I really might try to control my compulsions, but they are so much a part of me that I don't know who I would be if they went away.

My inside self is a side of myself that I don't share with many people. I need my life to have meaning. My life might have a deeper meaning that my Autism knows. I think I have a definite place in this world.

I have my newfound helper to help me with my writing. I now have ways to express myself. I get to write three days a week. It is wonderful to be able to express myself. I might like more time to type more. It is such a great release. I love the sense of freedom I get when I am writing. My writing might not be published yet, but I am working very hard at it. I might someday be published, but for now I might need more kind help to get my writing finished.

Just having the time to write is my biggest challenge. My mind is always ready but my body rarely listens. I like more time to write but I never know if my body might listen. Listening might look more like my body is following its own rules, but my body does follow its rules. Really my body listens to itself. Really don't have much control over my body much of the time. Really don't have much control over many things most of the time. I might feel out of control with my life in the hands of others most of the time.

You don't need someone with you all the time--I do. I need someone just to be safe! You might make your own meals; going forward, I have to have all of mine made for me. You just feel like having something to eat and you help yourself. I need someone to help me get anything. You don't even have to ask for something to eat. I have to ask if someone will listen!

There might be some tough things I have to deal with, but not being able to talk is by far the most difficult thing I deal with. I use facilitated communication to communicate. People need to be trained extensively to be able to help me. I can't speak and I need others to intentionally help me type letters on a letter board to type words.

There is no rhyme or reason to the way everyday things might create my helpers' tough challenges. I just might do fewer things for myself. Does it really matter? To you I look uneducated and instead I am very smart; I just can't control my impulses. You think I am rude but my body really does not listen to my mind. To be stuck in my body is not easy. Time forces you to deal with things that you might not want to deal with. It takes a village for me to master even the smallest tasks.

Helping me is a very big task; just trying to listen is hard for me. It is hopefully just my highest ever teaching task that I might accomplish. I need to feel every accomplishment. I need very free servants to help me. Help needs to be friendly but firm. I need strong helpers to help me be safe!

Getting good helpers is a must for me to be safe and successful. Very strong helpers don't keep me from being myself; they help me to control my compulsions so I can function more perfectly. Because of my Autism, rarely am I without anyone. They are a continual part of my life. I need them just to get by. They can make my life great or horrible. Little helpers really need to help me get through the day.

Helping me with my life choices is important. They get me ready for the day. You get ready on your own. I need everyone getting me ready to be successful. You button your own pants; I need help to button mine. You get your own breakfast; I need help getting mine. You just love to do whatever it is you want, whenever you want. I can't do things whenever I want. You can play music whenever you want; I need help turning it on. I need help just being me.

My youthful understanding openly listens to my heart but I can't always hear it. My heart might like love, but the reality might not happen. Just knowing that my life might help open little kind places that others can learn from is enough love for me. I need new love in my life, but a nice life is just going to have to do. A nice life is my destiny. I might just like kind love, but I need beautiful love to listen to me. I might like open love to have my life kindly opening my mind.

My life is my own to live like I want. I want my life to be mine. I might not want to live my life in a sheltered little place without people looking at me. I openly might like living my life picking up little pieces of litter, that my inside self loves so I can help others. Litter is ugly, not kind. Kind people don't litter. Litter is only hurting the people who litter.

My life is like the world covered in litter. It might look like a just hurting mess, but in reality I might look like my life needs cleaning up. Others might not look like me, but underneath the mess, my mind is just like yours. Like my nice high I might get from my objects; I get the same feeling picking up litter. I like the newness of it. People might like the kindness I have. I might just have more kindness than most people.

My highest goal is to listen. I need help listening. I kind of hear things in slow motion. My little ears can't hear like little ears are supposed to. My ears don't hear like your ears. I hear just what the real thing really sounds like. You hear the sound that you like, but I hear just jumbled sounds. You hear in different loudness, I hear just one loudness. You hear sounds with real tones, I hear things very flat. You can differentiate between different sounds, I hear one loud sound.

My hearing is just kind of like my mind; a jumbled up mess of sound, kind of like when you hear the telephone ring. Other people kind of ignore the sound, but I can't. It bounces back and forth in my head all day. My mind gets full of noise. It is just miserable. Kind of like others might feel if they heard the phone, the juice maker, the washing machine, and the doorbell bouncing around in their head all at the same time. You might just go crazy. That is just a feeling of hell!

Maybe little helpers might not have help to know that I hurt when there is too much noise. I might not listen in real time, but I do hear like you do. You hear words that might not mean much; I hear little jumbles of sound. You hear high sounds, I hear only low sounds. You hear pitch, I hear only one tone. You can't imagine just how horrible it is to hear like I hear. My hearing might not be like yours, but it is kind of like popular music is playing in the background.

I need more help to listen to people. You might listen hearing little bits of jumbles, but I hear just little jumbles of noises. You hear little flicks of sounds, but I hear little bursts of sounds. My ears just don't hear like they should. My hearing is different than yours. My hearing might not have the level yours has. I just hear things differently than you do. I just have little hearing differences. I kind of might not hear people when they whisper. I kind of hear in little true lumps. I listen in groups of sound.

I kind of often feel like my life is people helping me remember. It is kind of just one big jumble of hearing trouble. I like my unfortunate life! It just isn't like yours; my life is really kind of like yours. I just need more help like getting ready. Going out helps feel more normal, but I just might never be like others.

Autistic Community and Culture: Silent Hands No More

By Elizabeth J. Grace

Four Vignettes from Four Decades, To Start

1980-something

In the early eighties before I got kicked out of high school [in the days when manifestation determination laws didn't cover Autism yet], a friend of mine said she didn't want to be friends anymore because I was just way too "intense." I knew what she meant, of course, but I had no idea what to do about it, other than to get my other (accepting but mischievous) friend (whom I had nicknamed "Kick-Butt") to help me write yet another jangly folk-punk anthem commemorating the unfairness of life. The first-mentioned anti-intensity friend never got to hear the song, which may partially explain why she recently found me on Facebook and wanted to be back in touch. I said yes to that because she works with transportation, which has two reasons for being a good explanation: (1) transportation is awesome, and (2) she deals with passengers—so by now her daily life is probably a giant bundle of intensity. Also, she contacted me, which was a nice overture, I thought. And most of all, being older, I've come to believe that being a teenager is pretty much automatically jangly folk-punk anthem-worthy for just about everyone.

1990-something

In the early '90s I met a man who said everything through lines from famous movies, television shows and commercials. He had grown up in an institution, and autism was considered rare back then, so the people at work (a sheltered workshop) assumed he was just spouting quotations for no apparent reason or to stim. And maybe sometimes he was stimming--why not--but most of the time he was clearly saying things, and I heard him and translated. Finally, I was able to convince some people to listen and learn. "Miraculous!" they said; I was a genius, putting two and two together like that, a code-breaker. But I was not a code-breaker. I could secretly hear him because what he was saying made complete and logical sense, and it was worth the risk of saying so even though I was 'staff' because he deserved to be heard by others and I knew they would be able to listen if only they found out how to do it. But I thought of it as a dangerous risk, you must know that I did. I was 'staff'; I got to drive the forklift. I had made it.

2000-something

In the early years of the new millennium I was in graduate school with some people who wanted to be school psychologists. I wanted to be an education researcher. We all had to take a required class together from this famous Autism Expert. One day, some of the psych majors came into class chattering excitedly because they had discovered (I think it was) Grandin's *Thinking in Pictures*. "Look, Dr. Famous Person", they said, "we found a book where we can get insider knowledge of what it is like to be a person with autism from the horse's mouth!! She even writes about what it was like for her as a child!!!" I listened, silently, first happy but then biting on my teeth and sitting on my hands as the professor answered. "That's fun and interesting", he said, "but it won't tell you anything. You remember what we learned about Theory of Mind, don't you? By definition, a person with autism does not know what it means 'for life to be like something for someone,' so she cannot possibly get the concept of what it is like to be herself. In order for you to learn about things you need to read research. Do you understand?"

I could not tell if they understood, but they nodded and looked hurt. They did not look as hurt as I felt, because my hurt was mixed with anger and dread fear. I stopped going to that class, despite the mandatory nature of it, because it felt unsafe. It did not seem like a good idea to hang around with professors who might believe me to be incapable of research by definition of who or even what I am, if they had known. I was going to make it. I was going to be Dr. Grace, and he wasn't going to stop me, so for now: steer clear.

2010-something

Now I am that education researcher and professor, Dr. Grace, though I don't really run around calling myself that as much as I thought I was going to and sometimes when people do call me that, I space it because it's not the name I've been used to for so many years. I'm not tenured yet; then I really will have made it. But I'm getting there, knock on wood. But here's a funny other thing that recently happened that reminded me how deep this thing is. Online and at home, I'm fine with myself, and I'm so happy to have found community. I can talk about my culture, and I do, and I will in a minute here, after one more vignette. So first, this one more wee story about how the silencing goes so deep that it even becomes self-silencing.

Last year, we were asked in a faculty meeting to write down a list of our areas of expertise and pass it on, so that we could have a master list of faculty expertise in the department. Susan Gabel, sitting next to me, is a critical theorist, in Disability Studies in Education. She glanced at my list and said, "Hey! Where is Autism??" And I said, without missing a beat, "Oh, I am not an Autism expert." She looked at me aghast, and laughed, and said, "Now, I know you don't love those folks, but you NEED to be what an Autism expert IS!!" "Ahhh! I said", getting it and starting to laugh too. "Okay, hand me back that list." Because I was thinking a cross between two things: one bad and one understandable. The bad one was the internalization of the false value that I never finished that class and didn't have the Autism Expert™ imprimatur. Which, feh, I'm a little embarrassed to admit that was inside my head. The understandable one was why would I want to be in their club? But the new one that Susan helped give me was this: I would want to be in their club so as to take it back. Occupy Autism Expertise. Once I can figure out that pesky issue of what it is like to be me, that is.

Autistic Community: Oxymoron?

Now a word to the people who have squinted or such like at me when I talk about Autistic community: Cut it out. A doctoral student was having trouble finding people to do his study, so I offered to ask around in the community. But no, he wanted people with *autism*, you understand, not the kind of people who hang around in communities. I said, "Student's Name, can you imagine why what you just said might have had a tendency to piss me off a little?" "Not really", he said, "isn't the autistic community really parents?" Well now that is something I could see where he would have reason to believe--but he really had to go right now, he didn't have time to get schooled by me, no not at all, nohow. He told his dissertation director I couldn't help him.

Once I was in the room when a visiting Autism expert told the preservice teachers that kids with Autism didn't care if they had friends--didn't want them. I had planned not to interrupt, but I had to bounce up here. "'Scuse me, just curious, how do you know that info? Well, they don't act the way I would act if I wanted friends, you know? Cool, that's possible. Okay, so class, what's the real moral of the story here?" And the pre-service teachers were all over it. You can't tell by looking at how a kid acts what they are thinking, it's not that simple; kids are not you. Yay! What can you do? You can assess by interview, journaling, etc... but people express things differently....That Autism Expert is my Facebook Friend now because she didn't freak out. She guessed why I felt the urge to make sure that didn't stand. She is a good egg. And furthermore, she follows the community news as an ally and no longer says that type of thing. Now, when she visits classes, she points them to people's blogs!

The Word 'Autism' Itself Started It

So people think we are in our own little worlds because of the word made up to describe us. But we can be in the world together.

Autistic Culture

Many things about Autistic culture are small, linguistically noticeable things that delight my students when they find out about them. For example, because it is not obvious to many Autistics when someone is being sarcastic. Due to the fact that many of us can be literal in the way we take in information, we have a written convention used by many of us in which we announce sarcasm as if it were an html tag, as in, "I love it when people say I don't even know what it is like to be my own self, and can't have a community because I am too into my own self, which by the way I don't even know what that is!" /sarcasm

Another thing I find is that the locus of Autistic culture being online because we are so spread out geographically has been also very useful for other cultural reasons. Many Autistics feel shy and socially awkward. Others are more comfortable using typing as a primary mode of conversation while being able to speak with difficulty in their everyday life. Even if an Autistic does not use oral language at all, there is no differentiation with that in terms of typing, in the way it looks online. This puts all of the Autistics together on the same page.

Encouragement

It is part of the culture to be very encouraging and to take a great deal of time explaining things, even many times. I have noticed that in Autistic culture, re-explaining is considered polite and thoughtful. If I do not understand something and you explain it to me many times in slightly different ways until I get it, this is seen by me and likely to be seen by other Autistics as an act of kindness and patience. Whereas in culture clashes of mixed community with adult Autistics having frame clash issues of trying to explain things to parents of Autistic children, it seems from the evidence that the non-Autistic parents of Autistic children may interpret this as a form of aggression.

From inside my head I can tell you that when you do not agree with me, I often believe I have not explained properly. This is borne out in informal discourse analysis of texts created in online iterations in the Autism community. Within the Autism community alone, multiple explanations seem to apply not to disagreements but to literal not-understandings and learning curves.

Because of this culture of explanation, it is also safe in Autistic cultural circles to openly proclaim that you do not understand a thing, or get a joke, or know what something is. This is not only safe but common practice. "What is that?", may be a response to a pictorial post or "I don't understand the politics", or "Is this real?" The person posting this in an Autistic environment does not need to worry about getting flamed for being a n00b, but rather will need to worry about the number of explanations that may appear in the inbox if Facebook or whatever the social network is being used is set to receive individually.

On the flip side, it is safe to say that you know what something is, and that you understand it, or care about it, you are allowed to explain it without being viewed as a know-it-all dork, or so it seems.

A paralinguistic feature online is the use of smileys or emoticons, which are very useful, or else the names of facial expressions within brackets as in <smile>. Or giving people a hug by writing actions that you are doing that, or putting their name in parentheses. People show a great deal of caring online.

Speaking of a great deal of caring, I met my wife online. She is not Autistic but she thinks I rock (bad pun but I love it—and my rocking, by the way, is something our twin sons seem to find great comfort and delight in) and she also loves it when I do what she calls "echo-lail."

Most of all, she tells me she loves my hands; the way they move, the way they express. She touches them a lot with her magic hands, lovingly, as if to say, "I want to know you more." (Long live the Internet for showing me where to find this angelic woman in addition to Autistic culture, and, while I am at it, Search Engines. What a magnificent invention those are.)

Finding the online Autistic community and its attendant culture has been so life-affirming and (the opposite of silencing) to me that it has enabled me to come out of my shell socially in the dominant culture as I have practiced having friendlier social skills online and then taking them into Real Life.

Also, I have been able to discuss Autistic Culture and News with pre-service teachers as well as Disability Studies doctoral candidates and other doctoral students. I think one of the key features of the robustness of Autistic community culture helping me get braver and what it means to me in my life is that I am planning to start an Autistic Self Advocacy Network (ASAN) Chicago Chapter next month, so we can march in the Disability Pride Parade.

This is despite the pesky fact that I cannot start the chapter nor do that march online-only. But that is okay today: the culture and the community put the power behind me.

Perfectly Autistic, Perfectly Me

by Karla Fisher

"I think you have an Autism Spectrum Disorder."

The doctor looked at me and waited for my reply. I was furious with him and considered for a moment how I might hurt him and get away with it.

"Doctor," I spoke quietly, suppressing my real anger with amazing control, "I am a productive member of this world, very highly functioning and this has absolutely nothing to do with grief, which is why I hired you. Or did you forget?"

I was in grief therapy at the insistence of my boss. Since my father's death just a few months earlier, I had been having this problem with seeing the world in details. Sitting in our one to one weekly meeting, I told her that I could not build up the details of the places I was in, so that I could not tell where I was, nor could I put thoughts together or do my job. I just assumed she would know exactly what I meant. I assumed everyone built up rooms from pieces. Instead she sent me here. She made me come see this "head doctor."

I hated doctors and especially had no respect for the field of psychology. I had had the displeasure of seeing them in action two times in my past and neither time impressed me at all. The first time was after the birth of my first child. I was told that I had 24 hours' time to recover from this major ordeal and I was so shocked from the experience that I knew I would need it. When the nurses asked me if I wanted to see my baby within the first few hours of my recovery, I told them that I would rather rest for the 24 hours as I assumed that my baby was well cared for at their facilities. Next thing there was this very young and profoundly stupid shrink standing next to me, asking me about why I did not wish to see my daughter. I was exceedingly angry with him and told him off after explaining the logic. I could not believe how I was treated, as if I might be a bad person. It completely boggled my mind that this logic was so beyond these idiots.

The next time I saw a shrink was when I wanted to return back to my job as a Russian Linguist at the National Security Agency. I had previously been in the military and served as a Russian Linguist but got out to have my child. Once she was a bit older and could handle daycare, I desired to return to this work, only now as a civilian. So I went through the process of the applications and tests, lie detector tests, and interviews. All went well but I did not receive an offer to return. I was informed of the decision to not hire me by a friend. He told me that I did not pass the psychological evaluation. He said that they told him there was something not quite right but could not articulate exactly what. I rolled my eyes at the stupidity but had no choice but to go back to rebuilding my career from another angle at that time. I did this by kicking, clawing and scratching. I did another tour in the military, had a few failed jobs and eventually found my way into high tech (a place that finally accepted me).

Now, having been employed for more than 20 years in the booming high tech industry, I was finally settled and respected as a senior engineer in a job that I loved. But now this... again?! All I wanted was go back to work and instead of helping me, he pinned me with this? I left that session scared, angry and determined to prove him wrong.

Alas, all the research I did and all the tests that I took only proved him right, and so began the process of actually accepting this new truth. Anger followed. Autism is a disability. It has hurt me in many, many ways throughout my life. I worked so hard to do things that other just seemed able to do. I suffered physical exhaustion, high blood pressure, anxiety, panic attacks, and ulcers. Doctors thought I was too stupid to care for myself when I did not know that I had infections due to my hyposensitivity. They did not understand me. All my relationships with partners dissolved due to a lack of appropriate emotional reciprocation. They did not understand me... Jobs were lost as I was inexplicably fired. There were ridicule and misunderstandings too numerous to recount or count. They did not understand me... And this all due to this thing that was in me. I wanted it out. Every morning I woke up with a pit in my gut as I realized this was not a dream. It was my new reality. I wanted a cure. I wanted to be fixed. But that was not an option, so every day I pushed out of bed and made it through the day. And every day I learned more. And every day this autism thing became less and less a thing of anger as I realized that I was still the same person and I learned to advocate as an autistic. Eventually I started to come back to a place where I could work again, and through self-advocacy with my peers and my boss, for the first time in my life, I was being really understood.

A year later, in the hallways at my place of employment a voice calls out,

"Hey guys, get in here! Karla is drawing again!"

"Awesome! I love when Karla draws."

I pause at the whiteboard to wait for the others and to reflect on the significance of the statements. In that moment, thousands of images appear in my mind. In all of them, I am drawing on whiteboards or chalkboards or paper or creating PowerPoint documents with pictures. I am teaching by pictures. It is how I communicate and how I have always communicated. But only recently did I learn that others do not do this. People have often told me how much they admired the pictures and the unique insights, but still I never saw it as anything special until that moment.

Learning happens for me by absorbing data, either from other pictures or spoken words or text, and that data input produces thousands of points in space in front of me at very specific locations. They look like dim stars. With each data point comes many more images, colors, and senses loosely tied to it but not tangible enough for reason. For weeks or months (sometimes years), I work to categorize and sort these images until there is enough clarity that the thoughts can become words. It is completely insane to me that I see so many data points connect but others do not see these. It frustrates me endlessly that I cannot help them to see it all because of my inability to explain... to language... Why is it so hard? Uuuugh...

But then one day, it is there. I see the picture that is actually cohesive enough to put words to and share with others. Words that I hope will give my audience insight to the connections that I am making. Insight to the different perspective that I have... the one the others missed. And out it flows. Sometimes it is halting and sometimes it takes several sessions, but with persistence and lots of help, I manage to squeak just a tiny portion of what I know and what I see out to the world. And the world receives it and they reward me with a salary, employment, patents, trophies and trinkets. But that does not matter to me. I do not seek their rewards. I seek instead to see that the work that I do and love is valued. And I think it is.

It all feels surreal in this moment to be me as the room fills up with my peers awaiting the next picture and subsequent insight to our current program. There I stand, eccentric and strange to these other beings but yet admired. And there I stand, recognized and rewarded for this thing. It all comes together in that moment that this is exactly what people love about me and that this thing... this "Karla is drawing again!" thing... is really all about autism. For whatever bad autism is in me, it is also this good. But more importantly, it is integral to everything about me. And in that moment I finally accept that autism is me. It is me just as my eyes and hair and skin are also me. There is no parsing the autism from me without losing me... and that is not only okay, it is perfect. Perfectly me...

The room is now full and everyone quiet so it is time to continue with my drawing. I turn back to my whiteboard and reiterate my work to the point where I was before being interrupted. Then I continue. When it is done, the board is filled with scribbles and forms seemingly in random places with lines of connection and words splattered here and there. There is an occasional algorithm thrown in for good measure. Some of the attendees have questions. Some adjustments are made real-time as I work out the answers on the board. Finally, I am spent. The board is a mess and the engineers in the room are all seemingly excited. I watch them take notes or take pictures of the board with their cell phone cameras. They praise me for having this insight. We all go back to our lab to work on this new direction...

A few hours later it is 5:00 PM and the energy in the lab shifts towards quitting time. Some of them leave in groups to go out to get a drink. Many of them have families and I hear them make calls to tell their other family members that they will be home shortly. One by one, they take off until it is quiet and I am alone in the lab. The low humming from the computers relaxes me and I see my dim stars of data. They are teasing me with insights that have no words as they light up like shooting stars and show connections. Images appear. Now my work really begins. I am filled with wonderment and joy and my mind goes quickly to work, parsing how to categorize the images and make these insights actualize into words.

Becoming Autistic, Becoming Disabled

By Anonymous

I was born autistic; I was born disabled. I was never supposed to know. I was supposedly born normal, smarter than most, a bit different, but normal. The specialists I saw—speech, social, LD—these were not for an autistic, disabled child. I had a speech impediment, a difficult time coping, and ADD (with dysgraphia); but I was, on the whole, a normal child. The fact that I bit my tongue when angry was a personal failing, and the scorn I received was well deserved. My repetitive movements were just me being immature. My complaints when something was too loud, or if I heard a troubling sound, or my clothes were irritating, were just me acting out and calling attention to myself. After all, it wasn't like I was disabled. I would have to learn to quiet my hands and body; to ignore the strange sensations. I would have to struggle to make myself indistinguishable.

I learned autism from the media. Autism was Rain Man, a human computer without normal emotions. This was autism. This was not me. Autism was not me. Autism was people who could not speak, who could not make decisions, who do not appear to be thinking at all. I could think, and speak, and make decisions.

Autism was a country I did not know. Autism was an alien landscape that I did not comprehend. I had never been there, or so I was certain. I was autism's orphan.

Disability was something I did know. Disability was my mother's wheelchair, the chairs and braces I saw in school. Disability was Geordi LaForge, Helen Keller (the book and movie character, not the real person), and Stephen Hawking. Disability was physical impairments: blindness, deafness, 'lameness,' perhaps a missing limb, lost through trauma or missing from birth. I was able-bodied, so disability was not me.

"Autistic-like tendencies," my mother said to the neurologist while I was being poked in the face with the annoyance stick: it was my first label, one I'd had for years. I had autistic-like tendencies, but I was not autistic.

"Autistic," my sister said, after making it clear that she wasn't supposed to tell me, a secret I was never meant to hear. I protested that I was too smart to be autistic. Autism, you see, could not be smart. Autism had no thoughts, could not speak, did not make choices, had no future. Autism could not be me.

When I was sent to special ed for "fighting," I railed against the labeling. Special ed was where they put the lesser people who didn't belong in society. The short bus, complete with the wheelchair figure on the back, was where I did not belong. I was a normal person, a worthy person; I did not belong there. A horrible mistake had happened. Two years later, beginning special-ed high school, my special-ed principal tried to talk me out of taking mainstream Spanish. He said it was too "difficult" for a special-ed student, and I didn't need a language. I only needed the lesser diploma that doesn't get you into college.

Sin embargo de cuantos años pasan, yo todavía no sé, y creo también que nunca sabré, si eso es perdonable. Pero, yo sé que si yo hubiera escuchado a él, yo nunca podría escribir esto. [Regardless of how many years pass, I still don't know, and I also think I never will know, if that is forgivable. However, I do know that if I had listened to him, I would never be able to write this.]

The newspaper told me that disability activists were protesting a new statue of Franklin Roosevelt, for showing him "sans wheelchair." That was just silly. Disability was not an identity, was not a culture, was not a country. They didn't have a history, so there was nothing to erase. Disability was nothing more than an impairment. Autism Awareness Month came and I had a laugh, "autistics aren't aware," always making sure not to remember my label, to cling to my normalcy. The TV commercials announced, "1 in 166: the numbers say, it's time to listen," and I nodded my approval. Something had to be done, a cure had to be found, so these lesser people could be made whole and valid, like me.

In college (where I went having earned the full diploma), I was a bright student with a few quirks. The fact that I didn't take notes, and hadn't since high school, was just an odd quirk. My strong attraction to African history and politics was another odd quirk--nothing more. My occasional difficulties with other students, or the fact that I didn't manage to date normally, was a moral failing on my part. I had not been working hard enough to understand people, as I was certain everyone had to do. I graduated, studied abroad twice, and got my Master's degree. These were all things that proved my normalcy, my worthiness.

Years went by and the weight of passing without knowing took a greater toll on me. I suppressed thoughts and memories constantly. I chose not to remember those words I had heard, the definitions I had read. In a moment of epiphany, I would realize perfect links between the traits of autism and the life I had lived, then I would work hard to forget those links. Doublethink is the art of holding two separate, irreconcilable thoughts at the same time, and I was certainly doing plenty of that. But what I was really doing was turning willful ignorance into an art form of its own.

Then the dam broke. After 24 years of denial--of conscious denial at that--I stared truth in the face. It didn't happen all at once, of course.

There were still days and nights of ever-more-conscious denial, of futile resistance to reality. Finally I turned around, not to face the truth, but to succumb and surrender to it: I had an Autism Spectrum Disorder. When I accepted the truth, I went to sleep feeling relieved of so much. Of course I wasn't really autistic, not like one of 'them,' I simply had Asperger's, and was therefore still a mostly-okay person; even superior, but lacking in some areas.

I read *Pretending to be Normal*, my first foray into autistic literature and history, but not really, because the title said "Asperger Syndrome." That was still a comfortable label to wear, more so than autistic. "On the autism spectrum, but just barely," "semi-autistic," "sort of like autism," "similar to autism" and, of course, "aspie". These were the descriptors I chose. They set me apart. I didn't need a cure, but those others certainly did. I joined the WrongPlanet forums, spoke to the people, became a good Aspergian--self-diagnosed, of course. Slowly I accepted the label of autism, autistic, but "high-functioning," always "high-functioning."

I read more and I read the right things. Through some contacts on the forums I found Kassiane Sibley's blog, and later, autistics.org. I read things from people considered high-functioning, people considered low-functioning, and people who seemed to defy functioning labels altogether. These were people sharing their thoughts which, though each unique, all had something deep in common. They described their autism as not simply a minor characteristic, but the defining characteristic; without which the person they were would be dead. They took pride in their autism.

I felt the need to contact Ms. Sibley myself, and with a little searching I found her through AIM. She spent most of the night answering questions, discussing concepts, and dispelling the myths I had been holding, and for that I will always be grateful. She also became my friend, and eventually a close one, and for that I will always be even more grateful. That night I became Autistic and proud.

I was 25 before I finally went for my first official Autism diagnosis, as far as I know. I was already autistic, but not yet autistic. When asked why I was pursuing my diagnosis, I said it was for the Schedule-A federal employment program for the disabled, but that wasn't the whole truth. The truth is that I wanted that diagnosis--I needed it--as my certificate of naturalization to the country of my birth, and the community I now called home, no matter how freely I was waved in by the border guards. With the diagnosis, I was officially autistic. When my papers were reviewed by the Virginia Department of Rehabilitative Services, I was officially disabled.

"You don't really see yourself as disabled, do you?" my father asked. I declined to answer, and shrugged my shoulders. I didn't want to have the conversation. I still had no place in disability culture; if the notion of me being disabled seemed strange to others, it was downright bizarre to me.

A few years later at my government job, I made my first official request for an accommodation. It was a rather simple matter: I couldn't be stuck in a room with only fluorescent light for hours on end, and my coworkers could not blast their music at whatever volume they saw fit. Most employers have a rule on music volume anyway, and I even offered to bring my own incandescent lamp. Even then, it was anything but easy to do. I had been trying hard not to ask for it; not to ask for anything special. I had suffered in silence for a long time because that was what I expected of myself, what I had been trained to believe was expected of me.

I was not ready to make a specific reference to autism, only using the words "disabled employee" in my email, and noting that my disability was not visible but was documented. After sending it, I felt nervous, like I had crossed a terrible line. There I was, again asking for things others didn't need, again calling attention to myself, asking others to work around me. Even though intellectually I knew I had done nothing wrong and everything right, and had a right to reasonable accommodations, I still felt in the pit of my stomach that requests of this nature would not be tolerated. I felt a degree of certainty that I would be criticized, even berated and maybe fired, for daring to suggest that I had needs. A few minutes later an email came back saying that my requests were approved.

March 30, 2012, a few days before my 30th birthday, I held my candle on Union Square. A young man was dead, murdered. Like me, he was Autistic; like me, he was disabled. He was murdered because he was Autistic, like me; he was murdered because he was disabled, like me; he was far from the only one. I read names of those who were disabled, like me, who had been murdered for being disabled, who had been murdered for being like me. I was surrounded by people who were disabled, like me. They listened to the names as I read them. They knew me as one of them, disabled, like them, like us. We were the disabled community, and we were mourning our own. I was joining with the other cripples to participate in disabled culture and in disabled history.

That night, I became disabled--and proud.

Non-Speaking, "Low Functioning"

by Amy Sequenzia

I am autistic, non-speaking. I am also labeled "low-functioning." This label is a pre-judgment based on what I cannot do. It makes people look at me with pity instead of trying to get to know me, to listen to my ideas.

I am a self-advocate and I can type my thoughts. But at the moment I show up with my communication device and an aide, my credibility, in the eyes of most neurotypical people, is diminished.

This is a constant battle for non-speaking autistics. Even the ones among us who have demonstrated, many times, their capabilities, and who have succeeded despite all the hurdles a disability imposes, these successful cases don't seem to be enough to end the myths: that a non-speaking autistic cannot self-advocate; that the so-called "low-functioning" cannot think by themselves and cannot have ideas or opinions.

We can, and we do. We keep moving forward despite the many labels we are given because it is assumed we need others to speak for us, to decide for us. Labels like: "low-functioning", "severe", "mentally retarded", "needy", "incompetent". They all show how the neurotypical world sees someone like me. Someone who looks "more different", acts "more different", needs more help with things pre-determined, by the neurotypical, as simple tasks.

Looking very disabled or needing more physical help does not make us unable to think, being critical, being able to analyze.

There are too many neurotypical "experts" claiming to know more about us than ourselves. They say they can make us "better", as if we are "not-right" or "wrong". Most of them never thought about asking us what could make our lives more productive, less anxious; or trying to understand a non-speaking autistic who has not yet found a way to communicate. All the conversation has been about "fixing" us, with the expectation that we finally look and act "more normal."

Autism is a big spectrum. Some of us have better cognitive function; some of us might have intellectual disabilities; some take medication; most, if not all, have sensory issues. The ones labeled "low-functioning" need aides for everyday tasks.

For example: What does it mean if I don't pick the right shape when asked? For the "experts", it probably means that I am, in their words, "mentally retarded". It is, in reality, more complex than that. It could be that my mind is obsessing over something else; it could be that I had a seizure or that the anti-seizure medication is making me extra drowsy; it could be that I believe I deserve a better treatment, since I am an adult and I am past childish tests. Even if I am indeed intellectually disabled, the fact that my opinion is being ignored remains.

Non-speaking autistics that fail to make eye contact, and that can't say, or are never asked, why they can't, also receive the "low functioning" label.

Forcing someone to make eye contact or insisting on assessments more appropriate for a child – with the inevitable "good job!" – are nothing more than a training program, a useless one. It causes more anxiety and does nothing to improve our self-esteem.

All the labels given to us only help to make myths seem like the reality. By classifying a non-speaking autistic as low-functioning, one is lowering expectations for the autistic individual. He or she is not given a chance to express him/herself and maybe show hidden abilities.

We, autistic, have tried hard and accepted the neurotypical way of doing things to make it easier for non-autistic people to understand us, interact with us. Despite some progress there is still very little reciprocity. This is even more evident when the autistic person is one of the so-called "low functioning." There is little patience in listening to us. When one of us succeeds, he or she is considered an extraordinary exception.

Look around. There are many of us trying to be heard. We did not put the "low" in "low-functioning" and we are speaking out. It is also up to the non-autistic to reciprocate in this communication exercise.

(A version of this essay appeared on shiftjournal.com on January 11th, 2012.)

And Straight On Till Morning

by Meg Evans

The stories that we tell our children from their earliest days determine the course of their lives. So it has always been with humankind; ever since bright-eyed children gathered in the firelight to hear the hunters' tales of the grand sagas painted on the cave walls, dreaming of greater adventures yet to come.

I grew up with parents who believed strongly in the power of stories to shape impressionable little minds. They had only one TV, which they kept in their bedroom, and they usually left it turned off so that I wouldn't see disturbing images such as crime reports or Vietnam War body counts. They were careful about what they said in front of me. I developed a worldview based largely on the children's classics. The stories of Peter Pan and Heidi were my particular favorites around the time I started kindergarten.

That had its drawbacks, however, as my parents and teachers discovered. Wholesome as those stories might have been, they didn't say much about going to school. Heidi spent her days running around with the goats in her little Alpine village, raised by a grandfather who didn't see the use of education. The March sisters of *Little Women* didn't go to school, except for the youngest sister Amy, who quit going after the teacher whacked her hand for hiding limes in her desk. And of course, Peter Pan lived in Neverland—second star to the right, and straight on till morning—where he spent all his days adventuring and never had to grow up.

So there was a considerable gap in my defining set of cultural narratives, which the adults in my life couldn't quite fathom how to remedy. I told my kindergarten teacher that I was Peter Pan and she must call me Peter, or I wouldn't answer. When the class drew pictures, mine were full of crocodiles and fairies, even if they were supposed to be about something else. If the end-of-recess bell rang when I hadn't yet finished some imagined epic quest, I saw no reason why it should matter if I stayed outside rather than going back into the classroom. I climbed trees to get out of the teachers' reach if I didn't feel like doing what they said.

At some point I was taken to be evaluated by child psychiatrists. This was handled in such a matter-of-fact way that I didn't think any more of it than other kinds of doctors' appointments. The word "autism" was never mentioned in front of me; it wasn't until many years later that I came across it by chance in an old document, while looking for something else. All I knew at the time of the evaluation was that my brain waves had been measured and, in part, found to be consistent with dreaming while I was awake. I liked the sound of that, although I didn't know why anyone would consider it significant. From my point of view, it was perfectly natural that the world should be made of dreams.

In those days, an autism diagnosis wasn't any help in getting school services because the schools didn't yet have a mandate to provide special education. They could, and often did, expel young children for autistic behavior or anything else out of the ordinary. The school where I went to kindergarten made it clear to my parents that I wouldn't be welcome to return the following year. As with everything else, I wasn't told about it at the time.

My parents enrolled me in another elementary school within walking distance. That turned out to be less convenient than they expected, however, because it was all too easy for me to walk home when I got bored. Of course, I was told many times that I had to stay for the entire school day. But I didn't pay much attention to that demand, which struck me as unreasonable when compared to the adventurous days of the children in the stories. After that, my parents tried another school far enough away so that walking home was out of the question. Unfortunately, its courtyard had a large and very inviting tree, which the students were strictly forbidden to climb. I didn't last long there either.

During that year I had a live-in babysitter, Marilyn, whose main task was to prevent me from wandering off and playing in traffic. Sometimes she told me creepy ghost stories when my mother wasn't around to disapprove. Marilyn lived in a small apartment on top of our detached garage, which I thought was proper because in so many books, the governess lived in the garret. I believed that we were poor, just as in Louisa May Alcott's description of the March family, because we had only one servant. Also, I wore a cousin's hand-me-down dresses. I didn't worry about it because, as the stories earnestly admonished, one mustn't fret about not having new modish frocks when others less fortunate are begging for their dinner.

My mother, surely at wit's end about what to do with a child who had acquired the sensibilities of a nineteenth-century aristocrat, at last hit on the idea of bringing me into modern times by way of Nancy Drew. Those books didn't do much to improve my school behavior, though, besides keeping me quiet when I read them at my desk instead of paying attention to the teacher. The pre-feminist Nancy was not in college and had no future plans beyond a vague notion of marrying her boyfriend when he got his degree. She spent all her time solving mysteries with her equally footloose 'chums'. After a while, my mother managed to find a more accommodating school where she could "park me", as she later described it. But ultimately, not much was done beyond waiting until I met the inevitable fate of Wendy Darling and other heroines of children's literature tragically cast out of fairyland—in other words, I grew up.

Today we live in a society that has become more understanding and accepting toward children with developmental disabilities. Most of the institutions have been or soon will be closed, bringing a deplorable chapter of history nearer to its end. Schools are now required to provide services and teachers have learned more about how to accommodate children's individual needs. Federal and state laws prohibit disability discrimination, both in education and in the workplace. Self-advocates, parents, and professionals are working together to improve community supports and services. Autism is no longer thought of as a horrible shameful word, never to be mentioned above a whisper. And yet, we are not where we need to be.

Had I been born 40 years later, it's likely that my parents would have been advised to get me ready for school by way of social stories telling me what to expect and behavioral exercises showing me what to do. No doubt I would have been more obedient as a result. I wonder, though, how much of my confidence and happiness today comes from those early years when I imagined myself joyously dancing barefoot in the wildflowers like Heidi and flying through the night sky sprinkled with fairy dust like Peter Pan. I wonder how much smaller and more constrained my world might feel now if the stories of my childhood had been about conforming to other people's expectations.

Having raised a son and a daughter, both of whom are now in college, I know that a large part of a parent's job consists of setting boundaries. Children need to learn how to live in society; they can't be left to run wild. They must be taught that there are rules about behavior in the classroom and elsewhere. But it's also part of our job to encourage them to explore their world and pursue their interests, within reasonable limits of course, so that they can learn how to set their own priorities and to make decisions wisely. They must be given enough freedom to develop the self-confidence and optimism they will need to navigate today's complex society. First and foremost, they need a solid foundation of acceptance.

Acceptance begins with the stories, the dreams, from which both our personal and our collective social worlds are made. When our cultural beliefs include assumptions about what certain kinds of people can and can't do, barriers arise from such beliefs just as surely as if actual concrete walls blocked our progress. These barriers go beyond basic civil rights issues such as being denied access to schools and employment. They also exist in our minds, in how we are taught to think of ourselves and what we can do. For something to be accomplished, it must first be imagined. If a child grows up hearing others speak of him in terms of tragedy, burden, and deficit, he will likely internalize these views, and all of his dreams for his future will disappear.

As we work to create more opportunities in society for ourselves and our children, we are storytellers above all else. When we focus on developing inclusive education programs, ending employment discrimination, making community services more widely available, and many other worthwhile causes, we are crafting social narratives centered on acceptance and inclusion. Such stories form a backdrop for the scenes of a strong, confident, successful life.

(A version of this essay appeared previously on autisticadvocacy.org on April 24th, 2012.)

The Incapable Man

by Bev Harp

I

Incapable of returning love. In the Philippines, in Mandaluyong City, a party is held to celebrate the telling of the story. He is forty-four. The book was his mother's idea and she conveyed the story to its authors. A party is held in lieu of a wedding.This man will never be married, incapable as he is of returning love. The article telling the story of the party for the biography of the man who will never marry, who is incapable of returning love, is filled with references to unconditional acceptance. Unconditional love. The value of autistic people is mentioned. Someone is trying.

I read the story. I read it again. I think about it for days, I can't let it go. Incapable of returning love. People have said things about me; more often, I have seen things. In their eyes, like a mix of confusion and anger, compassion and pity. There may be a word for this mix, but I don't know it. These looks happen far less often than they used to. After all, I have had 50 years to learn how to make myself understood.

II

"Andrei paints, reads, plays a portable organ and xylophone. He has the comprehension of a second grader, but paints like a pro."

The story says so. What is music, what are painting and poetry made of? Not only talent, not just skill, but emotion and comprehension are components.

Growing up, the arts saved my life, over and over. This is not hyperbole. While half of the bookshelves in my room filled with volumes on death and suicide, no one seemed to notice. Placing objects in a room is not considered standard communication. The other shelves contained books of modern and contemporary poetry and art. For years, these were my closest friends, quietly agreeing that nonstandard ways of communication held value. "So much depends /upon/ a red wheel/barrow/ glazed with rain/water/ beside the white/chickens." This poem was much like the way I talked, the way I thought, and this poem was important. Evocation of the Apparition of Lenin was important. Rothko's paintings meant something to me. Pollock's did. Not something translatable. I was not alone.

III

I turned 50 last month. A party was held. I invited some of the people I care about, as many as I could afford to entertain, as many as would fit into the room. I designed invitations, shopped, prepared food, arranged activities and music. Other people helped too, assisting with the last minute food preparations, and designing an elaborate menu of mocktails to go along with the mid century theme I had chosen. Still others helped by keeping the party social, remembering the things I tend to forget, the introductions, the place to hang up the coats.

Placement of objects in the room was intended to communicate. To explain in words what the styles of the late 1950's through early 1970's mean to me, I would risk being tedious and dull. Do you really want to hear why I think that Noguchi table represents the malleability of hope in the face of mortality? Or that the starburst clock, encompassing at once the tragedy of Hiroshima and the promise of space travel, makes an eloquent statement on humanity's relationship to technology? The party offered an opportunity to paint the picture wordlessly. To show it. To share something about myself with the people I care about, to have them enter a place in my imaginary world. By which I mean real.

IV

"The book talks about the ways in which an autistic child is accepted and nurtured with unconditional love despite the dam of a mental handicap separating him from others."

The separating/dam. What does it mean for a person who does not like being in large groups, who prefers even solitude, to host a party? This is not a rhetorical question. Because I worry that it might mean self-indulgence. In the dominant language. To invite people to try enjoying the things I enjoy, maybe this is not called "sharing" but "demanding" something of people. I worry that it is wrong to celebrate my survival. I worry that it is seen as wrong to communicate in my own language. In the past, I have seen things. I worry. Anything I say or do might be evidence.

More goes on in the minds of others than can be demonstrated or seen. My mind. Andrei's mind. Your mind. There is a genetic agreement that smile means happy, that tears mean sad. When you don't see these signs, you may assume that emotions are also lacking. When an answer is not given to a question, you may assume the one questioned does not have the information. Or has the comprehension of a second grader. Or does not wish to communicate with you. The assumption is automatic, yet comes packaged with the opportunity to question. I might have assumed that my family, not reading my signals, wished I would kill myself. That would have been incorrect, though I had communicated and they had failed to respond in kind. We never did speak the same language. And love? I have had to accept over and over that it will not come in the ways I expect, but in the native language of the ones bestowing it. Like Andrei's parents, like anyone's parents, I must constantly adjust my expectations. This is not my hardship or your handicap, not a cause for self-congratulation. This is just the hard work love is made of.

Just Me

by Amy Sequenzia

I wrote about being labeled "low-functioning" and how this causes damage to my self-esteem.

But it is not only this label that can cause the same type of damage. Labels, in general, put us in a box and "living" in such boxes causes too much anxiety.

When people read what I write, and when they like what they read, they sometimes seem to think I am some "super spectacular" autistic with a very different label from the usual "low-functioning".

On the other hand, when some people meet me for the first time, they don't believe I am capable of intelligent thoughts.

Functioning boxes are not definitions of who we are. They are simply a very narrow view of our complexities.

I am a person who needs a lot of help--and I mean a lot--with everything. I can think independently, but I need someone to ask me if I want to type my thoughts. I need someone to read small prints to me. I need someone to hold my communication device for me. I need someone to direct me to a better place or to help me position myself better before I type.

But the words are mine and it feels good to be able to express myself. I can show that I am intelligent.

Once I meet people or when I know I will meet people who know me only through my writings, my anxiety level is so high, I can act in very strange ways. I can look very childish and silly and I am very self-conscious about this. I can also seem uninterested, but this is only a self-preservation mask. I find it hard to communicate even if I have a lot of things I want to say. Then I need time--quiet time--to process all that might be happening. And I need to focus, which requires a lot of energy.

This is only an example of how deceiving and not helpful labels can be: I could be thought to be "high" or "low" functioning by the same person at different times, if only one aspect of my life was considered.

I am writing this because I know some of my friends, autistic friends who are labeled "high-functioning", have the same kind of anxiety when, for example, they meet other people or when they are expected to show to a live audience how amazing they are. Some of them, despite not needing a full-time support person like I do, rely on very elaborate charts to be able to go through daily routines.

They could also ask for more support, but they are seen as too "high-functioning" to need accommodations or even understanding.

Functioning labels create more anxiety because the boxes we are put in deny us the right to be a little complicated and different. And yes, I think I have this right.

Someone like me should have the right to look and be very disabled and not have our sometimes hidden abilities questioned, especially if the doubts about our abilities are based on how we look and on how much help we need. This increases our anxiety and makes the neurotypical world so much more difficult to navigate.

The autistics somewhere else on the spectrum, like some of my friends, should be allowed to deal with their hidden disabilities without being called "not autistic enough" and told they "have it easy".

The box they are put in is a trap: they are disabled but they don't look disabled enough to be allowed to have support for their disabilities. This increases anxiety.

I am not a genius trapped in an uncooperative body; I reject the "low-functioning label". I believe my friends who are more independent than me have some of the same issues I have. I believe some of them also reject the "high-functioning" label.

These labels bring a need, external to us, to be, look or act in certain predetermined ways, or forces us to prove our ability to have intelligent thoughts.

These needs are determined by the neurotypical world and enhances the anxiety already so present in our autistic lives.

I can't speak for my friends, but labels hinder my life. I reject labels. I am just me.

(A version of this essay previously appeared on ollibean.com on July 12, 2012.)

What They Do To Us

Quiet Hands

by Julia Bascom

Quiet Hands

1.

When I was a little girl, they held my hands down in tacky glue while I cried.

2.

I'm a lot bigger than them now. Walking down a hall to a meeting, my hand flies out to feel the texture on the wall as I pass by.

"Quiet hands," I whisper.

My hand falls to my side.

3.

When I was six years old, people who were much bigger than me with loud echoing voices held my hands down in textures that hurt worse than my broken wrist while I cried and begged and pleaded and screamed.

4.

In a classroom of language-impaired kids, the most common phrase is a metaphor.

"Quiet hands!"

A student pushes at a piece of paper, flaps their hands, stacks their fingers against their palm, pokes at a pencil, rubs their palms through their hair. It's silent, until:

"Quiet hands!"

I've yet to meet a student who didn't instinctively know to pull back and put their hands in their lap at this order. Thanks to applied behavioral analysis, each student learned this phrase in preschool at the latest, hands slapped down and held to a table or at their sides for a count of three until they learned to restrain themselves at the words.

The literal meaning of the words is irrelevant when you're being abused.

5.

When I was a little girl, I was autistic. And when you're autistic, it's not abuse. It's therapy.

6.

Hands are by definition quiet, they can't talk, and neither can half of these students...

(Behavior is communication.)

(Not being able to talk is not the same as not having anything to say.)

Things, slowly, start to make a lot more sense.

7.

Roger needs a modified chair to help him sit. It came to the classroom fully equipped with straps to tie his hands down.

We threw the straps away. His old school district used them.

He was seven.

8.

Terra can read my flapping better than my face. "You've got one for everything," she says, and I wish everyone could look at my hands and see *I need you to slow down* or *this is the best thing ever* or *can I please touch* or *I am so hungry I think my brain is trying to eat itself.*

But if they see my hands, I'm not safe.

"They watch your hands," my sister says, "and you might as well be flipping them off when all you're saying is *this menu feels nice.*"

9.

When we were in high school, my occasional, accidental flap gave my other autistic friend panic attacks.

10.

I've been told I have a manual fixation. My hands are one of the few places on my body that I usually recognize as my own, can feel, and can occasionally control. I am fascinated by them. I could study them for hours. They're beautiful in a way that makes me understand what beautiful means.

My hands know things the rest of me doesn't. They type words, sentences, stories, worlds that I didn't know I thought. They remember passwords and sequences I don't even remember needing. They tell me what I think, what I know, what I remember. They don't even always need a keyboard for that.

My hands are an automatic feedback loop, touching and feeling simultaneously. I think I understand the whole world when I rub my fingertips together.

When I'm brought to a new place, my fingers tap out the walls and tables and chairs and counters. They skim over the paper and make me laugh, they press against each other and remind me that I am real, they drum and produce sound to remind me of cause-and-effect. My fingers map out a world and then they make it real.

My hands are more me than I am.

11.

But I'm to have quiet hands.

12.

I know. I know.

Someone who doesn't talk doesn't need to be listened to.

I know.

Behavior isn't communication. It's something to be controlled.

I know.

Flapping your hands doesn't do anything for you, so it does nothing for me.

I know.

I can control it.

I know.

If I could just suppress it, you wouldn't have to do this.

I know.

They actually teach, in applied behavioral analysis, in special education teacher training, that the most important, the most basic, the most foundational thing is behavioral control. A kid's education can't begin until they're "table ready."

I know.

I need to silence my most reliable way of gathering, processing, and expressing information, I need to put more effort into controlling and deadening and reducing and removing myself second-by-second than you could ever even conceive, I need to have quiet hands, because until I move 97% of the way in your direction you can't even see that's there's a 3% for you to move towards me.

I know.

I need to have quiet hands.

I know. I know.

13.

There's a boy in the supermarket, rocking back on his heels and flapping excitedly at a display. His mom hisses "quiet hands!" and looks around, embarrassed.

I catch his eye, and I can't do it for myself, but my hands flutter at my sides when he's looking.

(Flapping is the new terrorist-fist-bump.)

14.

Let me be extremely fucking clear: if you grab my hands, if you grab the hands of a developmentally disabled person, if you teach quiet hands, if you work on eliminating "autistic symptoms" and "self-stimulatory behaviors," if you take away our voice, if you...

if you...

if you...

15.

Then I...
I...

.

They Hate You. Yes, You.

by Amanda Forest Vivian

I always think about Danny, who was not really named Danny. It's too bad I can't use his real name because it's one of my favorite names. I'm sure he's forgotten me but I can remember his name, his face, his favorite subway train, and the words he made up.

He was a kid I met this summer at the school where I interned. I have written about him several times, sometimes at length. And although he was my favorite kid at the school, that isn't why Danny is always surfacing in my mind, tiny in his big t-shirts, flinging himself around and reciting things.

It's through Danny that I found out for sure, this stuff is about me.

Because the first thing people use on us is always, "It's not about you." When I was a kid, when I first started reading about autism rights, it was so *instinctive*: of course it's wrong to say "cure autism now." Of course it's wrong to say autism is a tragedy, a disease, it's wrong to give kids electric shocks, it's wrong to say you thought about killing your kid in a video about eliminating autistic people from the gene pool. Like Sinclair says it's wrong to mourn for a living person. All this stuff was plain and clear and bright, and I was autistic, and I was being attacked.

Right?

Well, not to anyone else.

Because, of course, if I told anyone I was autistic, they said I was lying, or I had a different kind of autism that made me smart and talented, so I wasn't like Those Kids, the kids who needed to be cured. And that I should think about their parents, about the money and time to care for a person like that, about the dreams that are shattered when your kid is really autistic, not smart autistic, the real kind. So in my late teens when I put myself through my paces, when I figured out my deficiencies and set myself to systematically eradicating them, one of the deficiencies I eradicated was my use of the word autistic. Because you shouldn't use words people don't understand. And you shouldn't use words that will make someone feel bad, someone who has a kid who's Really Bad, Really Disabled. Because you're not that.

And I met some autistic kids and they were not much like me, and I didn't know to apply what I knew about myself to them, because I couldn't see what they were feeling inside. But I liked them. Then I met some people with intellectual disabilities and I liked them too; after a brief nervousness because some of them looked so different from me, and made noises I didn't understand, it was easy to like them. They were people who liked drawing, holding hands, looking at pictures, having a boyfriend, eating, music, animals, and the rain. I could see that these people weren't on the surface very similar to me, but I liked being around them almost more because of that, because it made me feel happy and chastened to misjudge them again and again. To be proven wrong when I thought I could quantify them just because I knew more words.

So by this point, I was pretty much sold, even if I wasn't Really Autistic, on the idea that people with developmental disabilities matter. Because I was around them all the time and it was obvious they mattered. But still, I felt my position was that of an outsider, an ally. I had opinions but I didn't necessarily feel that I had much right to talk about them; I didn't feel I had as much right as the parents or teachers of people with developmental disabilities.

And then I interned at this school.

And I started out thinking: wow, ABA is so cool. I've heard negative things about it from other Not Really Autistic people, but who am I to talk about what these Really Autistic kids need? They can't even *talk*. They might bite themselves or something. What the hell do I know about that?

And then I met Danny and the other kids in his class. High-functioning kids. Verbal kids.

Tony, who had been nonverbal a few years before, was incredibly hardworking and sweet. When he went into the school director's office and turned out the lights as a joke, I laughed, but she said, "Tony. Look at my face. How do you think that made me feel?" She stood there looking grim until he apologized.

James was stressed out and upset; one of his teachers leaned towards him, staring fiercely into his eyes, talking with cold, strained-sounding words, the kind of voice I called "static" when I was a kid. James looked scaredly back at her, wriggling his hands around in his lap. "*James*," she said. "I know you're upset. But what you're doing with your hands looks silly." This boy, all the tension in him being channeled into something harmless, something she had to look under the table to see. His tension was silly. His discomfort was an inconvenience. He was eight or nine years old.

And Danny with his words. "Danny's an interesting kid," the school director told me. "He likes to be in charge." Danny and I were walking, holding hands, and when I responded with concern when he told me he was tired, another teacher told me, "He's playing you." It's true that Danny was a bossy little boy; when we played restaurant, he replied, "No, we're out of that" again and again until I ordered the food he wanted to pretend to make. And his love of subway trains spilled out everywhere. He was supposed to write a story about a sad princess, and he did, but half the story was about the princess's friends taking her on the subway to cheer her up. He was supposed to write a crossword puzzle and the clues were things like, "Transfer is available to ____ North." The school was full of subway maps, since many field trips involved subways, and Danny would sometimes just lean over a desk, pressing his face into the shapes and colors, whispering his favorite schedules to himself.

Danny just liked words. When he was using his special words, the weird words he scrounged for or made up himself, he would find himself jerkily hopping across the room, speaking in a squeaky voice, his small face tense with excitement. "Presentation" was a weird word for movie, "document" was a way to talk about the letter he had typed on the computer for his parents. "I went to the barber," he said when I commented on his newly short hair, and then, with a rush of joy, "*but I like to call it the hair shop!*"

I like words too. It was hard to watch Danny's teachers nudge him, sit down with him, say, "Danny, the word 'presentation' is a little weird; you need to say 'movie.'" It was hard to watch the way they looked at him, pointedly, until he stilled his hopping and lowered his voice to a more standard pitch. When Danny found out my middle name is Wood, he completely tripped out on it, hammering pretend nails into my stomach and giggling, "I'm gonna build something out of you!" "*Danny*," a teacher said, "don't be weird. You and Amanda were talking about names."

It was the word weird. Nothing foreign my whole life. Tracing words and shapes in the air, crossing myself, my mom asking me a lot of questions, "Have you been feeling the urge to do that lately? Why do you do that?" with so much static it was clear I'd better keep my hands as still as possible when she was around. Running jerkily up the stairs at school, I couldn't help myself until I was fifteen or sixteen, despite the older boys laughing to each other--"is she trying to race you?"

Movement just consumed me that way. And being a thirteen-year-old who said "suppose" and "quite" when no other kids did. Just loving words too much, finding it hard to stay away from the strange ones. And getting too excited. Being weird is not that alien for me.

So my divisions broke down a little, because I was watching a kid just like me, and I was learning, in very specific, qualitative terms, what they thought of people like me. I was so nervous about keeping myself still and using the right words because I thought they wouldn't let me intern there if they knew I was actually like Danny, that I didn't think he was weird at all. All of Danny's teachers had been taught to grimace and say how annoying it was when he talked about trains. They watched *The Office*, but they never ever laughed when Danny told flat, self-referential jokes on purpose, twisting the ones he had been trained to say. I thought Danny was funny. Every time I talked to him I felt nervous about doing something that his teachers would think was wrong, and I also felt bad about perpetuating the attitude he was being taught, that none of the things he loved mattered.

So from specific to general, from Danny to James and Tony, to Max and John. John's teacher made him walk, in stiff, clean steps, and if he started doing anything that looked like skipping or jumping, she grabbed his arm, said "*No*," forced him again and again. Max liked to move his arm in circles while he was watching TV, so he was hauled off into an office, pushed down into a chair, had mouthwash forced into his mouth while he cried. They told me they were narrowing it down, he was moving less and less. Max and John didn't talk. James and Tony didn't talk as well as I do. But I move too much, and I move wrong, especially when I was a kid, and in that school I saw what they do to kids who move wrong.

I realized that, actually, a lot of it was about moving wrong. Or talking wrong, if you could talk. Or just taking too much initiative--wanting to make up songs, like Danny did, or playing a practical joke, like Tony did. That these kids looked and acted different and the school wanted to control them and make them as still and docile as they could possibly be. Watching them treat hopping, rocking, and neologisms like you'd treat a bomb on an airplane--it was like being at summer camp with a kid from the south, sitting in a car uncomfortably while he said he'd kill a gay person if they ever came near him. Wanting to say, no, it's not anything important; *I'm* like that, see? But I didn't talk in the car and I didn't talk in the school.

This is too long. It's hard to even explain it. I just have to say, for the millionth time, that this whole functioning level thing--yes, it matters in certain ways. I can buy and cook food for myself, while a severely autistic person probably can't. I can hide the way I move and talk better than other people can. But this doesn't really have much to do with politics, because when people claim that "cure autism now" and the disease and the Judge Rotenberg Center are not about me, well I beg to differ. The only reason they're not about me is that I'm old and verbal enough to not be vulnerable to that kind of abuse. They would be all too happy to practice it on me if they could. Autistic people do not get abused because they are low-functioning, they get abused because they do weird things.

So, the old-school ABA trials? With Lovaas?

This is a kid getting an electric shock:

This is why:

If you were in the wrong place at the wrong time, the wrong age, the wrong functioning level, this could be your life. This what people like them think about people like us.

(A version of this essay previously appeared on adeepercountry.blogspot.com on November 21st, 2009.)

I Hid

by Alyssa Zisk

I knew.
I knew what I was, what I still am.
I say what because so many of you see, well, that, as a what, not a who.
So I hid.

I hid because I knew.
I knew what would happen if anyone found out.
I knew that if anyone who could diagnose me, who could label me, ever
got near me,
       the game would be up in a moment.
I knew what they did with kids like me. With the Autistic kids.
We didn't take hard classes. We didn't even take normal classes.
What we could do was ignored to make the time to get us the abuses
we needed.
But it wasn't called abuse. If you're autistic, it's "therapy."
So I hid.

I passed.
Not for "normal," of course. I could never have done that.
But I could pass for merely weird as long as I avoided the people who
thought they were helping.
If you're just weird, you can take whatever classes you want.
If you're just weird, no one bats an eye when you have two pairs of
pliers in your bag.

If you're just weird, you can spend a month in another country.
All that's OK, as long as you're just weird, not Autistic.
So I hid.

I had "quiet hands," and no one even had to hold them down.
If no one knows you move like an Autistic, you don't, right?
I looked at people's foreheads.
No one notices you're not looking them in the eye if you look at their foreheads.
I made sure my teachers knew I was smart.
The top of the class can't be Autistic, right?
I was hiding.

But someone noticed anyways.
By then, I was in high school.
In high school, it's harder to make you do anything, unless you're already not quite human.
They have to convince your parents to force the issue if you don't want to be evaluated.
Who's going to convince parents who went through life with the picture of autism most of us still have?
The kid in the corner who doesn't talk or look you in the eye, who bangs his head on the wall?
He's autistic.
The girl who's been doing her best to pass for merely weird, who flaps her hands when excited?
Not autistic.
Hiding was working. Not going was working.
I kept hiding.

Because I knew.
I knew that even in high school, that label would give them too much power.
I knew that the Autistic needed to be made normal in ways the merely weird could escape.
I knew that we were somehow broken and needed fixing.

I didn't want to be fixed.
I kept hiding.

The problem is, hiding yourself is hard.
Maybe some people can do it forever.
I can't.
All the problems are still there, and I'm terrified.
I'm terrified because I still know.
I know I'll be an object of pity.
I know that some people will still see me as less human.
I know those same people will see me as broken.
I know they'll try to break the person I am in order to fix the person I never was.
I know they'll think I'm trapped in the shell of Autism, not the shell of normalcy they want to force me into.
I know I'll be "too Autistic to understand," except when I'm "not Autistic enough."
I know I'll be ignored.
But I also know that nothing will change unless we make it change, and those same people won't.
So I know that I have to do it.
I guess I can't hide anymore.

Speech, Without A Title

by Julia Bascom

Hi. My name is Julia Bascom and I've had it easy.

I had it easy. What this means is that in fifth grade I was the smartest kid in the class. I also did a lot of hiding under my desk, and I talked funny and moved stiffly, so the other kids formed a club. It had only one rule, the golden rule: you couldn't talk to Julia.

I changed schools at the end of the year. I kept breathing, but then, I had to: I had it easy.

No one beat me up. They didn't have to—I did a good enough job of that on my own.

I have a friend. We'll call him Martin. Martin is autistic, like I am, although he doesn't identify that way. In fact, nothing would make him happier than being just like everyone else. See, Martin and I are different. We both know that being different, being autistic, being disabled, is dangerous. We've both been bullied. We've both *had it easy*. We've both seen what our alternatives are—be just like everyone else, or don't be anything at all.

The difference between Martin and I is that I know without a shadow of a doubt that *this is wrong*. Martin doesn't.

Martin and I became friends because we were both worried about each other. Martin was worried because apparently no one had ever taught me how to pass for normal. I was worried about Martin and the way he was quietly twisting himself away. I only got more worried when he tried to teach me how to blend in, how to pass, when he yelled at me senior year for looking *like that*, because *don't you know you'll get hurt, don't you know you'll die, looking like that?*

I have another friend. We'll call her Maria. Maria has also had it easy. She's autistic like me, but she is more visibly disabled than I am. What this means is that when we went to get ice cream two weeks ago no one would sit near us. What this means is that people think that because I help her count out the money to pay for her order I should be ordering for her. What this means is that Maria is not permitted to just neutrally exist in public. Getting ice cream becomes an act of war.

I work with middle school students with significant disabilities in a mostly self-contained classroom. Some of them have had it easy—no one will talk to them, the other kids run away when they see us coming, the teachers don't want them in their classes, but no one gets beat up. Some of them have permanent brain injuries from abuse. Like Charlie. Charlie goes into murderous rages and has almost killed people–he's the sweetest kid, but someone decided to beat him enough that he doesn't feel the world is safe for him. He's right.

Kaley hasn't been to school in two months. The social workers are sent away from the house and the state is content to leave it at that. I don't even know if she's still alive, and no one seems interested in finding out. Roger, who can't feel or control his tongue, was kicked out of his foster home and into an institutional placement three days before Christmas because he eats too messily. His ex-foster mother now visits him regularly and expects him to call her "mom" and say that he loves her.

She says she loves him too.

The hell of it is, the world agrees with her.

Here's the thing about being disabled: it sucks. It's horrible in a million different ways, and not a single one of those ways is *because I can't do this* or *because I have this impairment.* That would be too easy. Instead, every single reason translates roughly to *because people are awful.* Sometimes, for a minute, for a day, for a week, I think I can forget that. I delude myself into thinking that the reason I can buy ice cream without five different hostile stares, can be allowed to work in a school, can be invited to the occasional party, is because people really are okay, and not just because I have learned how to fake being *normal*, being *human* well enough to avoid some sort of weird ability-based xenophobia.

I'm wrong, of course.

I just spent seven hours at a conference about bullying. Here's the genius behind really good, really effective bullying: it turns the victim into their own worst bully. I told you I never got beat up for being autistic. I want you to take a good look at me. See my glasses? Those are because I damaged my eyes banging my head in tenth grade. See the spots on my arms? Those are from where I tried to gouge out my skin all through high school. See the scars on my face? Those are a little more recent—same idea though: self destruct. There are a million more I can't show you—even the insides of my cheeks are scarred. I can't tell you how many pairs of sheets I've had to throw away because I woke up covered in blood—I'd tried to pick myself apart while I was sleeping.

I didn't do this because I was depressed, or scared, or because I hated myself. I didn't *want* to hurt. But I knew I had to. When I hurt, I was in my place. And smacking my head against a wall for an hour a day was ultimately less painful than trying to convince myself, let alone everyone else, that I was maybe, possibly, worth something just the way I was.

The thing about bullies is that, although they never go away—I went to a different school with different kids after fifth grade, but there were always plenty of bullies to keep me remembering—they cannot be with you every second of every hour of every day. They can do hundreds of subtle and nasty things to you, and they will, but eventually they will need to pee or go home or at least sleep. So what they do is program you so that you can continue to bully yourself in their absence. I still hear the chanted *retards* in my head whenever I play with a strand of beads. I still believe, in my stomach and pulse, the way you know to *run from a lion* or *don't jump in the campfire*, that *I shouldn't be here.*

I don't need someone yelling at me to sit down, shut up, stop flapping—I do these things automatically now. No one needs to tell me that I'm worthless—I get that. Message received, message believed, message drilled into my bones. No one has to threaten and force me into some version of myself that is less visibly disabled, less obviously autistic, less real and I guess less threatening—I've carved off all those edges of myself into a smooth facsimile of what I need to be.

(That's the only reason I've ever "had it easy". Because I *could do that.* Because I have, or had, the rare ability to pull myself apart and twist myself into some new shape when ordered. I'm lucky, in other words, that I don't have any glue holding me together. Lucky to be broken, because then there is nothing left for someone else to break.)

What I've just described is "having it easy", and it's actually not easy at all. It's complete and utter psychological and emotional warfare, and there is no winning for us—they, the bullies, set the rules and the terms and they always win. Millions of us live like this every day—we have it easy, we can't complain, this isn't something that can be solved with curb cuts or an act of legislation, and so we die the death of a thousand cuts.

I told you about Martin, earlier. Martin always beat me on quizzes in class, but there is one thing I know that he doesn't. I know that *this is bullshit.*

Here's the secret. There is, in fact, one way to beat the bullies. See, what they want is to work themselves out of a job, to have you doing their dirty work for them. They want *you* to beat yourself up. So the way you win is by stepping out of the game entirely. The way you win is by knowing, being absolutely and irrevocably and 100% positive, that *they are wrong.*

It's the tiniest thing.

It's almost impossibly hard. How do you discover the world's best-kept secret: that despite what you've been hearing since you were two and your parents started dragging you to doctor after doctor and the other kids stopped playing with you that you are actually *perfectly **fine**, just **fine**?*

When you are disabled, you are *sick* in every sense of the word. Disgusting, scary, dangerous, broken, wrong. Lesser. I knew this, had it memorized and lived my life accordingly. But one day I met someone else who was sick. "You're sick!" I protested when they insisted on acting like a human being.

"Yeah, I am." they agreed. "So are you."

And then one morning I woke up. I was still sick. And I was also *fine*.

I was fine.

There is no equivalent to a GSA for disabled kids. We have to pass it on like a secret. *You're okay. We're okay. Everyone else is wrong. We have a right to be here too. We're not just sick. We're not in doctors' offices all the time. We're okay.*

We need that support, need some sort of physical community. Passing it on like a rumor isn't enough. The moment we realize that the hateful people who fill and control our lives are *wrong* is the moment when everything can finally start to change. That moment shouldn't even have to happen—it should be something that we just always know.

Things won't get better until then.

Good-bye. My name is Julia Bascom, and I am, always have been, and always will be, *fine*.

Thank you.

This Is Why

by Julia Bascom

So you need to know about Kimba.

I met Kimba three years ago. I walked into the lifeskills classroom at the middle school, and he was moaning and flapping in the corner. I kind of wanted to do the same thing but I didn't, which meant that the teachers mistook me for a neurotypical like them, which meant that the first thing I got to learn about Kimba was that "he just tried to throw a chair at me."

I learned a lot of other things about Kimba in the next few days. I couldn't sit within four feet of him, because he would attack me—he didn't like anyone except his aide, and he went after her pretty regularly too. He had successfully convinced the teachers for an entire semester that he couldn't read at all, only to be foiled when they gave him a puzzle of animal names and he completed it perfectly. The only words he said were "NO!", "BUH-BYE!", and "ONE-TWO-THREE-FOUR-FIVE!" screamed like something was breaking. About a month after I first met him, I learned two more things: he was a foster child, and the previous night he had attempted to beat his foster mother to death and had almost succeeded.

Here's what I learned about Kimba over the next three years: he is incredibly intellectually gifted. He taught himself to read. He has a system in which he classifies every person he encounters as a different animal based on personality, appearance, relationship and attitude towards him, and the pleasantness of their encounter. He may be autistic, he may have various brain injuries, he might be selectively mute, he definitely had lead poisoning. He uses language obliquely, employing rich and innovative metaphors. He analyzes the symbolism in Disney movies, but his favorite television series is *Kimba The White Lion*. He taught himself how to use Google. He speed-reads. He spent the first nine years of his life in one of the most horrifically abusive environments my state has on record.

Kimba and I, now, spend most of our time in lifeskills together. We are virtually inseparable. I was the one who proved that he could read far above the level he was assigned. I am the only person he willingly lets touch his speech-generating device when he's having trouble finding the words. He's held my hand when I randomly dissociated, and he's grabbed my phone and texted KIMBA when he thought I was spending too long talking to the White House. When he wants to bang his head, now, he grabs my hands and I squeeze at his ears until he can breathe again. He puts his hands on my head and does the same for me.

For three years, Kimba and I have stood (often literally) hand-in-hand, united, in our very different pain and very different ways, against a world designed to shut us out. I curled around him when he was having flashbacks and he copied my bitch-face and employed it against incompetent substitutes. I foiled his plans and told his general-ed teachers that he could, in fact, read very well, and he tried to teach me how to wink. When I left lifeskills for a while to attempt college I said good-bye and he held on and wouldn't let go. I came back, defeated. We saw each other again and smiled with mouths that had forgotten how.

I wonder if he got so mad at me for going to Washington because he had overheard what was going to happen next.

While I was sitting in a humid room and watching as people stared at me and explained that the world would be better for everyone if we inconvenient autistics just didn't exist, plans were being made to put Kimba away. While I was getting job offers for my distilled fury and ability to wax eloquent about how my life sucks, it was being decided that the considerable, unbelievable, overwhelming progress Kimba has made in every respect over the last three years isn't good enough. While I was staring in disbelief as Geraldine Dawson pontificated about the suffering of "autism families", people were sitting at tables, sipping stale coffees, and deciding that, since Kimba hasn't recovered *quickly* enough from his trauma, he needs to be institutionalized.

It was announced today, and finances should be finalized by next week. On Wednesday, June 22nd, Kimba will complete the seventh grade at the middle school. He will eat an end-of-the-year cupcake that we will make, as he will not be invited to participate with his general-ed class. We will carefully gather up the last of his projects and load them into the same battered backpack he's had for three years, a backpack that will be thrown away with his projects that night because he won't need it—any of it—any more. We will pack up his device, the notes we'll have scribbled to his new staff saying *he can read very well, actually, and here is a Kimba-to-English dictionary, you'll need it if he ever decides to talk to you* and the notes we'll have labored over for him: *love you, miss you, you've grown up so much, it's going to be okay.* We'll smile, we'll lie, we'll tell him that he will love his new school and that we'll be allowed to visit.

On Wednesday, June 22nd, we'll say good-bye and try to memorize what his smile looked like.

On Thursday, June 23rd, he'll disappear into a residential program.

They said they know he loves animals. He can work on their farm.

I now count three kids I know and have worked with who, since December, have been institutionalized. This is three out of ten. Five out of fifteen, if I push the timeline back a year. We incarcerate people because they kill other people, because they rape or because they steal or because they make our world unsafe—and now, apparently, because they are just a little too inconvenient. Funny. You don't even get a trial when your crime is drooling or not talking, when your sin is PTSD or autism, when the thing you did wrong was being born and then not quite meeting expectations.

You just get put away.

I wanted to tell you about Kimba. I wanted to ask you what I am supposed to do tomorrow morning. I wanted to say that it doesn't matter that things this wrong aren't ever supposed to actually happen; they do anyways. I wanted to see if maybe, now, you understood—I don't write to touch, to *inspire*, to move people, I write because this happens every day, I write because *how are we supposed to keep on*, I write because a thirteen year old boy is being taken away.
I wanted to tell you about Kimba, because you have to understand that he underlines everything I say and write. I wanted you to meet him before he's thrown away like human garbage. I wanted someone to give a damn. I wanted to tell you about Kimba because, because, *because*...

....because I can't save this one, because I can't save him, because we have sixty-two days, because oh god, oh god, I can't save this one, because I forgot that even this tiny little somewhere-only-we-know only exists because nowhere is safe and nothing is allowed us, because oh, oh, oh. Because they are taking Kimba away.

Because thirteen is too young to die.

Grabbers

by Julia Bascom

It's a grabbers vs. flappers warzone.

On the one side are the flappers. We wave and twist our hands in front of our faces or slap them against our chests. Our heads punctuate our moods and the music against the wall. Our knees don't bend as we walk on our toes, our fingers pick at cuticles or scratch patterns against our forearms and cheeks, and we'd rather watch spinning pinwheels than drown in another person's eyes.

(Our joy is our own, and we communicate it differently, perhaps holding privately onto it, or pouring it out into another person. But soon we learn from the grabbers that our joy should be our shame, our movements not our own, and so we withdraw.)

What else is there to do when you are surrounded by grabbing hands but shrink in on yourself?
The grabbers don't believe that we can be happy or find meaning unless we are *exactly like them*—and that's really the goal, being *just like everyone else*, and so there is not even a second of hesitation in their eyes when they slap our hands down onto the table with a shriek of *"quiet hands."*

The hands are everywhere.

They're at our chins. *"Look at me,"* with a face pressed in so close to yours that you count the pores until they force your gazes to meet. They grab our hands, *"don't do that, people will think you're retarded."* They smack away picking fingers, because our foreheads must be pristine and easy-to-look-at for them. You turn away, pull away, try to put some distance in so you can breath, and they grab your hands, your hips, your shoulders and twist you back. You bounce your leg— surely you are allowed this?—and they press a hand to your knee, stilling you. Everyone taps their pencil, but when you start their hand closes over yours and won't let go.

"Please let me go!"

But protesting just means you need to be grabbed more often, with harder and more insistent hands, until you realize that the way you move is fundamentally *wrong*, as wrong and deficient and disturbing and *dangerous* as you are, and if you want to be counted as a "you" at all you must let them grab you until you can stop your self. The most basic human thing is just *existing in space*, and you quickly realize that you do even *this* wrong. Is it that you take up too much space, or just that you do it too differently, moving in an entirely alien way and triggering some sort of dormant xenophobia?

In the end it just comes down to *you are wrong, and for that you must be punished*. It simplifies to *your body is not your own, but it is mine*. And you learn that a relationship, if you can call it that, always has two roles, a flapper and a grabber, and *you will always be grabbed, and never be permitted to grab back.*

Inhumane Beyond All Reason
The Torture of Autistics and Other People with Disabilities at the Judge Rotenberg Center
by Shain Neumeier, J.D.

They call what the Judge Rotenberg Center does to people with disabilities treatment. That's why it still happens.

For over forty years, JRC has used painful methods of controlling the behavior of Autistic people, people with intellectual disabilities, and people with mental illnesses. This includes long-term mechanical restraint to a four-point board, food and sensory deprivation, social isolation, and, most infamously, electric shock. Labeling these methods as aversive behavioral modification, and even aversive therapy, JRC has not only been allowed to use them on their students – both children and adults – but has in fact received the approval of parents, state agencies and courts in doing so.

JRC follows what its own administration has called a "radical Skinnerian" behavioral approach, relying on the principles of operant behavioral conditioning – namely, arranging an individual's environment to provide rewards for appropriate or desired behavior and punishment for unacceptable or unwanted behavior. JRC's founder, Matthew Israel, became fascinated with these principles after taking a class with B.F. Skinner, a pioneer in the field of operant conditioning, and reading his book, a novel called *Walden Two*, portraying a utopian society that was based on the ideas of behavioral psychology while he was a student at Harvard University. He in fact decided that it was his life's mission to create such a utopian community, and, to this end, worked under B.F. Skinner during the course of his studies.

Despite the fact that Skinner's actual research was performed on rats, pigeons and other animals, Israel, after graduating from Harvard, went on to try to apply these concepts to people following his graduation in 1960. Specifically, in the next decade, he started two communes in the Boston area that attempted to replicate the society that Skinner had written about in *Walden Two*, as well as an organization called the Association for Social Design, which had the aim of creating communes like this in cities across the world. In the following years, however, these efforts fell apart. While Israel attributed this to personal conflicts among the people living in the commune, others who lived in the communes and who were part of the organization reportedly became disillusioned with his vision, which required them to live their lives correcting one another's behaviors.

That being said, Israel's time in the communes gave him an experience that contributed significantly to his decision to start a behavioral modification program for children. Specifically, at the Arlington commune, he lived next to a housemate whose three year old daughter, Andrea, engaged in rude and sometimes violent behavior such as intruding into his room and whacking people over the head with a broom, as well as more typical childhood behavior such as screaming and crying. With his housemate's consent, he started to use operant conditioning in order to address these behaviors, rewarding her by giving her treats and going on walks with her when she behaved, but flicking her on the cheek when she acted out or cried at being punished. After a number of weeks of this, he only had to look at her and shake his head for her to stop doing something, and in this way became what he would later call a "charming individual."

Despite the fact that Skinner himself did not support, and in fact actively opposed, the use of punishment as a means of behavioral modification, Israel drew upon the methods he had used in correcting Andrea's behavior in forming and running the Behavioral Research Institute, which would later become JRC, in 1971. Originally a day school located in Providence, Rhode Island, BRI began with only two students, one of whom was Autistic and one of whom was diagnosed with schizophrenia. Over the next several years, it opened up residential homes for its students in other parts of Rhode Island, and, eventually, in Massachusetts. It also opened up a second facility under the same name in California in 1977.

As it has since, the program relied on rewards and punishments for specific target behaviors to the exclusion of psychotropic medication. BRI rewarded students for good behavior with verbal reinforcements, food and toys. On the other hand, at the time, its repertoire of punishments, or aversives, included things like spanking students with spatulas, giving them hard pinches or muscle squeezes, spraying them in the face with water and breaking ammonia pellets directly under their noses. The program also involved the use of physical and mechanical restraint on students, both in emergency situations and for punitive purposes. Even at the outset, these punishments were used not only for aggressive and self-injurious behaviors, but in response harmless ones such as crying and failing to follow directions, which it classified as "noncompliant," "disruptive," and sometimes bizarrely "health dangerous" behaviors. The idea behind this general use of punishment – which JRC uses even now to defend it – is that successful operant conditioning requires that a person's entire environment be altered in order to provide rewards and consequences for behavior, including minor or seemingly harmless ones. In particular, it emphasized, and continues to emphasize, the need to address so-called "antecedent" behaviors, or harmless behaviors that it said could lead to or were an alternate form of target behaviors.

Even before BRI began to use electric shock, many opposed its use of aversives. Disability rights advocates argued that its use of aversives constituted abuse in any amount and that there were other, more humane and community-based alternatives available, even at the time.

Additionally, in 1979, investigators from two New York agencies visited BRI as part of their oversight duties on behalf of New York students attending the program, and reported it to be the "singular most depressing experience that team members have had." In particular, it noted that students exhibited red skin and scrapes from BRI's use of corporal punishment, and that they were "controlled by the threat of punishment."

Despite these criticisms, professional organizations like the American Psychological Association openly supported BRI's use of aversives, saying that treatment providers should have the option of using them to address aggressive and self-injurious behaviors. B.F. Skinner himself, despite his well-known objection to punishment, came out in support of his protégé's work, claiming as late as 1987 that some people with severe developmental disabilities who exhibited dangerous behaviors could not be reached by any other method. According to Israel, Skinner's views on the subject were much stronger than that, in that apparently, when he had shown Skinner video footage of his working with BRI students and the type of behavior they engaged in, Skinner had responded by saying, "I didn't know. These aren't people; they are animals."

BRI's strongest support, however, came from parents of students attending the program. This is how it managed to defeat an attempt by the Massachusetts Office for Children to close it or otherwise stop its use of aversives. After the OFC, which had licensing authority over the program, banned further placements of students at the program in the aftermath of a student's death there, BRI and a number of parents whose students attended it brought a series of lawsuits, which eventually ended up before Chief Justice Ernest Rotenberg of the Bristol County Probate Court in Massachusetts. In response to BRI's bringing a self-injurious Autistic girl before him, Judge Rotenberg ruled in what is called a substituted judgment hearing that the child, who was legally considered unable to make decisions for herself as both a minor and a person with a severe disability, would choose to continue to undergo the aversive program at BRI if she was in the position to do so.

While the litigation continued even after this decision, the parties eventually settled in 1987. The outcome of this was a consent decree, under which the OFC bound itself, and any other state agency that would have licensing authority over BRI's treatment practices, to not interfere with BRI's operations as long as the program had a court-approved treatment plan for every child on which they wanted to use aversives. Court approval, according to the consent decree, would depend on parental consent, a treatment plan developed by BRI's clinicians, the opinion of two oversight committees, and the same substituted judgment hearing process that Judge Rotenberg had used in deciding to order the continued use of aversives on that first autistic child who came before him.

This attempt at oversight was, and continues to be, insufficient to protect children and adults from the misuse of aversives at the program. JRC's certification reports in recent years have revealed that the mandatory oversight committees haven't even been meeting regularly, let alone carrying out proper individualized reviews of treatment plans. Furthermore, both judges hearing the cases and attorneys appointed to represent the interests of JRC students independent from their parents or doctors regularly accept JRC's proposed treatment plans by default, even in instances where there has been testimony by experts showing that this treatment would be completely unnecessary and inappropriate. The result of this is courts approving treatment plans that include the use of aversives and that can be changed to include entirely different behaviors without further approval.

In spite and on top of all of this, the mere existence of the consent decree has given JRC and its use of aversives legitimacy, and worse, enforceability. Not only has JRC been able to market and defend its practices to the public as court-approved by individualized review, but it has also been able to use it to stop the state of Massachusetts from interfering with their use. In particular, in the nineties, it sued the state Department of Mental Retardation for making another attempt to ban it from using aversives and to ultimately close it down. The case went all the way to the highest court in Massachusetts, the Supreme Judicial Court, which also sided with JRC, forcing DMR to pay huge amounts of attorney fees and to temporarily lose authority to regulate the program in punishment for what it found to be contempt of court. Since then, state agencies have been wary to even enforce regulations that JRC has actively violated, let alone take any more aggressive stand to protect the rights of JRC students. For instance, when a former JRC staff member attempted to report abuse and neglect of students to a state agency specifically charged with investigating such incidents, he was told that they could do nothing, since the use of aversives that he was reporting were legal.

Both legal and parental support for the program has continued even after a slew of preventable deaths at BRI throughout the 1980's, starting with that of twenty-five year old Robert Cooper in 1980, who died from a bowel obstruction after BRI failed to provide him with medical treatment before his condition became fatal. The state neither found nor held BRI responsible for his death. Five years after that, the situation repeated itself when Vincent Millitich, a student with a seizure disorder, asphyxiated after having a seizure while being restrained for "making inappropriate sounds," with his head in a helmet and forced between the knees of a staffer and plastic cuffs on his hands and feet keeping him in his chair. While his death led to OFC's attempt to close BRI and a later negligence lawsuit resulted in a judgment against BRI and some of its doctors, the program was officially cleared of responsibility for Millitich's death.

The relevant authorities made the same call when it came to the death of Linda Cornielson, a 19 year old nonspeaking woman with a developmental disability, in 1990. Cornielson, whose mother later said she had had no prior stomach problems, had been clutching her stomach in pain and refusing to eat while at BRI. The treatment staff thought that she was acting out, and proceeded to treat her symptoms as a behavior problem. Over the course of the two days leading up to her death from a perforated stomach ulcer, staff repeatedly used aversives – namely, muscle squeezes, spatula spankings, pinches and ammonia pellets - on her, including 57 such applications in just the four hours before she died. In an investigative report after the incident, the Department of Mental Retardation concluded that what they had done to Cornielson at BRI had been "inhumane beyond all reason" and had violated "universal standards of human decency." Even with this damning language, and with a verdict for Cornielson's family in a negligence lawsuit, the state did not, in the end, hold BRI responsible for her death. In all, six students have died at the program, and, in five of these cases, the most that it has had to face in terms of consequences has been civil lawsuits for money damages.

The one exception to this impunity came in the form of the state of California's response to the death of 14-year old Danny Aswad, a student with intellectual disabilities, while he was mechanically restrained to his bed facedown for over an hour at BRI's west coast facility. Even though the coroner had listed Aswad's death as somehow being the direct result of his intellectual disabilities and congenital malformations of the brain, the state Department of Social Services pursued an investigation into it, and into BRI's program as a whole. Among other things, the investigation revealed that BRI had used aversives excessively and unnecessarily, such as on a deaf child for failing to obey verbal commands; had deliberately concealed a student's bruises caused by the use of aversives from doctors and state agencies; had prompted students to act aggressively for the purpose of punishing them or demonstrating that they were aggressive as part of what it called behavioral rehearsal lessons; and had retaliated against students whose family members questioned the treatment program or threatened to make complaints. BRI of California, such as it was, did not survive the resulting lawsuit, and entered into a settlement agreement with the state in 1982 under which it agreed to stop using aversives and to ban Matthew Israel from involvement in its operations. However, the program continues to operate in California under the name of Tobinworld and is run by Israel's wife, Judy Weber.

Meanwhile, BRI's east coast facility continued to use the same methods it had used since it had opened, in fact the same ones that the California branch had been banned from using, despite the aforementioned two attempts by the state of Massachusetts to shut it down. Following its first victory, it not only changed its name to the Judge Rotenberg Center – both in commemoration of the Chief Justice of the Probate Court after his death and as a warning to anyone who would try to close or interfere with the program – and moved all of its facilities to Massachusetts, but it also introduced the use of electric shock as an aversive. For a couple of years, it used a relatively weak device, called the Self-Injurious Behavior Inhibition System, with a shock lasting a tenth of a second that reportedly felt like snapping a rubber band against one's skin. However, because of the extent to which the program used it on students – including one instance in which an autistic student named Brandon Sanchez was shocked 5,000 times in a single day – it began to lose its effect as students became inured to it over a period of months and years. When its representatives approached the developers of SIBIS to request that they make a stronger device, though, the developers refused.

As a result, the program designed and began to manufacture its own device, which it called the Graduated Electronic Decelerator (GED). The GED's shock was designed to be, and is, far more powerful than that of SIBIS – three times as powerful, in fact, with shocks lasting for a full two seconds. The device consists of a battery pack and five electrodes – two attached to students' arms, two attached to their legs, and one to their stomachs, and is activated by student specific remote controls carried by JRC staff. JRC has described the level of pain inflicted by the GED as being no worse than a bee sting. Students, former staff members and visitors to the program who tried the GED on themselves have disagreed strongly with this assessment. One JRC survivor compared the feeling to that of being attacked by a horde of wasps, and investigators and former staff members report that the GED regularly caused burns, which were bad enough that it became medically necessary to stop shocking students for a number of weeks.

Still, students became inured to the pain caused by the GED through repeated use in the same way they had to SIBIS' shocks. Thus, only a couple of years later, JRC designed and began to use a still more powerful device, the GED-4, which was three times as powerful as the original GED. Additionally, they eventually designed and began to use other shock devices, such as a "GED cushion" that would shock a student who got out – or fell out – of their chair without staff permission. By means of these devices, electric shock became the primary aversive used at JRC, replacing the use of techniques such as spatula spanks, pinches, muscle squeezes and ammonia pellets that Matthew Israel thought too risky for staff and, supposedly, students.

Even with the introduction and widespread use of the GED, JRC's opponents in the Massachusetts legislature and the disability advocacy community were and have been consistently unable to get any legislation passed that would ban it and other aversives. Like in the lawsuits between JRC and the state, parents and guardians of JRC students played a significant role in ensuring the defeat of such measures. Year after year, legislators such as Senator Brian Joyce from Canton would file anti-aversives bills, only to have parents show up at hearings on the issue to tell how electric shock and other aversives had saved their children's lives. In some cases, JRC students themselves would be brought to testify, wearing the GED while they told the legislature how it and other aversives had saved or improved their lives. JRC has also brought Brandon Sanchez – the same Autistic person who was shocked 5,000 times in a single day, and whose uncle Jeffrey Sanchez is a state representative – to hearings to show people the kind of behaviors, and students, it attempts to treat. As a result of this, Representative Sanchez has been a strong, and in fact a formidable, opponent of efforts to pass laws banning the use of aversives.

It wasn't until 2006 that JRC and its use of aversives faced significant public outcry and governmental opposition again. This began with a lawsuit, filed by Evelyn Nicholson on behalf of her son Antwone, both against JRC and against his local school district in his home state of New York for placing him at the facility, over its misuse of the GED. In one instance in particular, JRC staff told Antwone that they were "going to hang [him] up like Jesus Christ" for refusing to get ready for bed when he was told to, and proceeded to shock him when he was in the shower. Evelyn decided to take action, removing Antwone from the program and eventually filing the lawsuit, after Antwone called her from JRC and told her that he no longer believed that she loved him for letting JRC hurt him so badly.

While the Nicholsons' lawsuit was eventually dismissed on the grounds that Evelyn had initially given consent for JRC to electrically shock Antwone, in the mean time, the New York State Education Department responded to the family's allegations by conducting an investigation. After making two site visits to JRC, one announced and one unannounced, the investigators released a report that mirrored the California Department of Social Services' 1982 complaint in the extent to which aversives were used and in fact abused. In addition to its often-quoted reference to students being shocked for "nagging, swearing, and failing to maintain a neat appearance," it discussed JRC's punitive use of long-term mechanical restraint and food deprivation, and reported that JRC was using the same so-called behavioral rehearsal lessons that it had more than 20 years before. On top of this, the report contained highly disturbing findings about how these methods were used and in fact how the program was run, such as how staff would purposefully set students up by administering unfair punishments and would then further punish those students who made use of the school's official complaint process in protest. The investigators expressed serious concern not only for students' mental health, in that some of the students showed signs of post-traumatic stress disorder and depression, but also for their physical safety, writing that JRC's food deprivation programs put students at risk of malnutrition and that none of its shock devices were approved by the Food and Drug Administration.

As a result of these findings, New York passed emergency regulations that banned its students from being sent to any program, in or out of state, that used aversives. However, once again, parents came to JRC's defense, suing the state education department, counter-intuitively, on the basis of disability and other civil rights statutes. Once again, they were victorious, with a trial court preventing the enforcement of the regulations. Although the lawsuit has continued through a series of appeals, through which most of the parents' claims have been dismissed, New York continues to send students to JRC and fund their placement there.

The following year, an incident at JRC further strengthened the opposition to its methods and continued existence. In one of JRC's group homes, staff woke two students up in the middle of the night by shocking them, and proceeded to shock them a combined total of more than one hundred times – with one of the boys receiving 77 shocks – on the order of a prank caller, himself a recently escaped JRC student, who was posing as a senior member of staff. While the people who administered the shocks were confused as to why the caller was ordering the shocks in the absence of any target behaviors, they followed these orders unquestioningly, even as the students offered up no resistance and in fact tried to make it clear that they were not doing anything wrong. In spite of JRC staff initially dismissing the students' complaints of pain from having been repeatedly shocked, one of the students was eventually hospitalized for having first degree burns. In the aftermath of this incident, the Massachusetts Department of Early Education and Care made an official finding that the two students had been abused and neglected, and that the staff members responsible for this had received improper training in the use of the GED. They ordered JRC to keep the video footage of the incident on file for them to use as needed, but, in the months following the event, Matthew Israel had the footage destroyed, later claiming to have thought that the investigating agencies no longer needed it.

Over the next few years, the use of aversives at JRC attracted federal and international attention. In America, both the Food and Drug

Administration and the Department of Justice opened investigations into JRC's practices. Meanwhile, the United Nations declared that its use of electric shock and long-term restraint on children and adults with disabilities violated international human rights protections against torture. Still, the Massachusetts legislature failed to pass any state laws banning or regulating the shocks, and JRC continued to enjoy the support of its students' families, with Brandon Sanchez's father saying that he would rather put a bullet in his son's brain than have him go off the GED, claiming that it would be more humane.

For its part, JRC responded to this growing condemnation by using the arguments it had relied on since it had first opened. Despite the fact that the field of behavioral psychology had made significant advances in the area of positive, non-aversive methods of treatment since then, its administration and lawyers continued to tell lawmakers and the public at large that the choice for students with severe behavioral problems, or rather their parents, was between the aversives used at JRC and copious amounts of harmful psychotropic medications. Furthermore, even as JRC began to run radio ads calling for parents to send their children with truancy and academic problems, and even as they recruited students from impoverished backgrounds with minor, if any, disabilities, they insisted that it was a "school of last resort" treating the most severely aggressive and self-injurious people with disabilities in the country only after all other programs had failed them. In response to the allegations that JRC used shock and other punishments for minor and even harmless behaviors, they not only confirmed that this was the case but defended it as being as necessary as shocks for more dangerous behaviors. For instance, in his replies to some of the investigation reports, Matthew Israel justified the use of aversives in response to the target behavior of closing one's eyes by saying that a person who closed their eyes too frequently ran the risk of falling down stairs or otherwise coming to harm, and defended shocking a student for nagging by writing that this behavior was "so compulsive and frequent that it once led to caregivers at a previous placement trying to strangle him and lock him in a room."

Nonetheless (or instead perhaps unsurprisingly), opposition to JRC and its practices continued to increase. In 2011, the Massachusetts Office of the Attorney General prosecuted Matthew Israel for his role in hampering the investigation into the unprovoked use of shock on two students four years earlier. Israel, despite insisting on his having done nothing wrong, pled guilty to charges of misleading a witness and destroying evidence. As a result of this, he was forced to resign from his position as Executive Director and in fact leave JRC. The same year, the state of Massachusetts passed regulations banning the most painful and restrictive aversives, including those used at JRC. However, it attempted to avoid further controversy by carving out an exception for the use of aversives on students whose treatment plans already included them, effectively doing nothing to protect them against continuing abuse.

Finally, in 2012, the public saw what JRC does to people like disabilities, through proof that was irrefutable and impossible to ignore. This came to light in the form of a video, shown to a jury and news cameras as part of a lawsuit against JRC after being suppressed by the request of JRC's attorneys for eight years, of a young Autistic adult named Andre McCollins being restrained and shocked 31 times over the course of seven hours at the program. The footage begins with Andre sitting calmly in his chair while JRC staff asks him to take off his jacket. He doesn't move to take it off, and suddenly, he's screaming in pain from a shock, and he gets off the chair to hide under his desk. The staff members in the room drag him out, and five of them hold him down, meanwhile shocking him for tensing up and screaming in fear and pain. Later in the tape, he's shown strapped facedown to a four-point restraint board, yelling out, "No! No! No! No! Help me! Help, help, help, help, help! HELP!" before screaming in pain, and a buzzing sound in the background makes it clear that he's been shocked again.

The outcry, this time not just by disability rights advocates but by the public at large in Massachusetts and around the world, was enormous. Nearly a quarter of a million people petitioned the Massachusetts state legislature to ban the shocks after seeing what happened to Andre

McCollins, and indeed JRC opponents in the Massachusetts Senate renewed their attempts to pass a total ban on all painful and restrictive aversives. On the same day that a hundred people gathered in protest in front of the Massachusetts State House and the JRC itself, the United Nations condemned JRC for its torture of people with disabilities a second time and demanded that the U.S. government investigate and take action to stop it.

Still, as of writing this, JRC is still open, and continues to shock, restrain, starve and otherwise abuse approximately one hundred of its students – many if not most of them Autistic or otherwise disabled – in the name of treatment and under the protection of the law. Despite all the information that exists to show why JRC should be closed and its methods banned, many people, including politicians, journalists and treatment professionals, refuse to take an outright stance against them even where that stance could very well make enough of an impact to accomplish either or both of these things. They insist that there must be two, and thus two equally valid, sides to every story, and continue to give JRC and its supporters a forum to make the same arguments, untrue as they always were, that they've made for forty years. They assume that doctors, parents and other caretakers who deal with people with disabilities know best, and thus what they do to, or agree to on behalf of, people with disabilities must be necessary. They take it for granted that people with disabilities' dangerous behaviors are incomprehensible and thus must be managed rather than understood, and are then willing to have that principle extended to everything else a supposedly dangerous person with a disability does.

Even now, they call what JRC does treatment. That's why it still happens.

Shain Neumeier is an Autistic person with physical disabilities, is a graduate of Suffolk University Law School, and is in the process of becoming an attorney. Shain is a survivor of coercive medical and mental health treatment, and as a result has a special interest in (shutting down) abusive residential treatment facilities for youth and people with disabilities. Shain has worked with organizations including the Autistic Self Advocacy Network, the Community Alliance for the Ethical Treatment of Youth and Occupy the Judge Rotenberg Center in order to help end torture in the name of treatment, at JRC and elsewhere.

REFERENCES

Laurie Ahern & Eric Rosenthal, Mental Disability Rights International, Torture Not Treatment: Electric Shock and Long-Term Restraint in the United States on Children and Adults with Disabilities at the Judge Rotenberg Center (2010).

Fredda Brown & Dina A. Traniello, The Path to Aversive Interventions: Four Mothers' Perspectives, 35 Research & Practice for Persons with Severe Disabilities 128 (2010).

Polyxane Cobb, A Short History of Aversives in Massachusetts (2005).

Department of Social Services, State of California, Complainant's First Amended Accusation/Statement of the Issues, In the Matter of the Accusations Against the Behavioral Research Institute of California, No. L230-1278 (29 January 1982).

Jennifer Gonnerman, Mother Jones Magazine, *School of Shock* (20 August 2007).

Matthew Israel, Ph.D., Behavioral Skin Shock Saves Individuals with Severe Behavior Disorders from a Life of Seclusion, Restraint and/or Warehousing As Well as the Ravages of Psychotropic Medication: Reply to the MDRI Appeal to the U.N. Special Rapporteur on Torture (2010).

Judge Rotenberg Center, JRC Responses to Allegations in NYSED June 9, 2006 Report (2006).

Paul Kix, Boston Magazine, *The Shocking Truth* (July 2008).

Massachusetts Department of Early Education and Care, Investigation Report, Incident # 49037 (1 November 2007).

Shain Neumeier, Autistic Self Advocacy Network, *The Judge Rotenberg Center on Trial* (April 2012).

New York State Department of Education, Observations and Findings of Out-of-State Program Visitation: Judge Rotenberg Educational Center (2006).

Settlement Agreement, *Behavioral Research Inst. v. Leonard*, No. 86E-0018-GI at *16 (Mass. Sup. Ct. Jan. 7, 1987)

Joseph Shapiro, *No Pity: People with Disabilities Forging a New Civil Rights Movement* (1993).

Rhetoric

Why I Dislike "Person First" Language

by Jim Sinclair

I am not a "person with autism." I am an **autistic person.** Why does this distinction matter to me?

> *1) Saying "person with autism" suggests that the autism can be separated from the person. But this is not the case. I can be separated from things that are not part of me, and I am still be the same person. I am usually a "person with a purple shirt," but I could also be a "person with a blue shirt" one day, and a "person with a yellow shirt" the next day, and I would still be the same person, because my clothing is not part of me. But autism **is** part of me. Autism is hard-wired into the ways my brain works. I am autistic because I **cannot** be separated from how my brain works.*

> *2) Saying "person with autism" suggests that even if autism is part of the person, it isn't a very important part. Characteristics that are recognized as central to a person's identity are appropriately stated as adjectives, and may even be used as nouns to describe people: We talk about "male" and "female" people, and even about "men" and "women" and "boys" and "girls," not about "people with maleness" and "people with femaleness." We describe people's cultural and religious identifications in terms such as "Russian" or "Catholic," not as*

"person with Russianity" or "person with Catholicism." We describe important aspects of people's social roles in terms such as "parent" or "worker," not as "person with offspring" or "person who has a job." We describe important aspects of people's personalities in terms such as "generous" or "outgoing," not as "person with generosity" or "person with extroversion." Yet autism goes deeper than culture and learned belief systems. It affects how we relate to others and how we find places in society. It even affects how we relate to our own bodies. If I did not have an autistic brain, the person that I am would not exist. I am autistic because autism is an **essential** *feature of me as a person.*

3) Saying "person with autism" suggests that autism is something bad — so bad that is isn't even consistent with being a person. Nobody objects to using adjectives to refer to characteristics of a person that are considered positive or neutral. We talk about left-handed people, not "people with left-handedness," and about athletic or musical people, not about "people with athleticism" or "people with musicality." We might call someone a "blue-eyed person" or a "person with blue eyes," and nobody objects to either descriptor. It is only when someone has decided that the characteristic being referred to is **negative** *that suddenly people want to separate it from the person. I know that autism is not a terrible thing, and that it does not make me any less of a person. If other people have trouble remembering that autism doesn't make me any less of a person, then that's their problem, not mine. Let them find a way to remind themselves that I'm a person, without trying to define an essential feature of my personhood as something bad. I am autistic because I* **accept and value** *myself the way I am.*

(A version of this essay appeared previously on jimsinclair.org in 1999.)

Throw Away the Master's Tools: Liberating Ourselves from the Pathology Paradigm

by Nick Walker

I believe that the widespread and lasting empowerment of Autistic people hinges upon our ability to make an internal paradigm shift, and to propagate that shift as widely as possible. Such a paradigm shift is already happening in some parts of the Autistic community, but for the most part it's not yet recognized that it *is* a paradigm shift, or exactly what that means.

My academic career involves the study of paradigm shifts, so I figured I'd share a few of my thoughts on the matter, in the hope that they might be of some use to other members of the Autistic community in the ongoing work of shifting the public discourse around Autism, or in the more personal ongoing work of self-empowerment and self-liberation. I promise to do my best not to bore you with a whole lot of academic jargon.

First Things First: What's a Paradigm?

Even if you haven't encountered it in an academic context, you've probably heard the term *paradigm* before, because it's annoyingly over used by corporate marketers these days to describe any new development they're trying to get people excited about: *A new paradigm in wireless technology! A new paradigm in sales hyperbole!*

As a great Spanish diplomat once put it, I do not think it means what they think it means. A paradigm is not just an idea or a method. A paradigm is a set of fundamental assumptions or principles, a mindset or frame of reference that shapes how one thinks about and talks about a given subject. A paradigm shapes the ways in which one interprets information, and determines what sort of questions one asks and how one asks them. A paradigm is a lens through which one views reality.

Perhaps the most simple and well-known example of a paradigm shift comes from the history of astronomy: the shift from the *geocentric paradigm* (which assumes that the Sun and planets revolve around Earth) to the *heliocentric paradigm* (Earth and several other planets revolve around the Sun). At the time this shift began, many generations of astronomers had already recorded extensive observations of the movements of planets. But now all their measurements meant something different. All the information had to be reinterpreted from an entirely new perspective. It wasn't just that questions had new answers – the questions themselves were different. Questions like "What is the path of Mercury's orbit around Earth?" went from seeming important to being outright nonsense, while other questions, ones that had never been asked because they would have seemed like nonsense under the old paradigm, suddenly became meaningful.

That's a true paradigm shift: a shift in our fundamental assumptions; a radical shift in perspective that requires us to redefine our terms, recalibrate our language, rephrase our questions, reinterpret our data, and rethink our concepts and methods.

The Pathology Paradigm

In regard to Autism (and human neurological variation in general), the dominant paradigm in the world today is what I refer to as the *pathology paradigm.* The new, emergent paradigm — the paradigm to which we need to shift, if we want to bring about widespread and lasting empowerment of Autistics — I refer to as the *neurodiversity paradigm.*

A paradigm can often be boiled down to a few basic principles, although those principles tend to be far-reaching in their implications and consequences. The principles of a widely dominant sociocultural paradigm like the pathology paradigm usually take the form of *assumptions* — that is, they're so widely taken-for-granted that most people never consciously reflect upon them or articulate them (and sometimes it can be a disturbing revelation to hear them plainly articulated).

The pathology paradigm ultimately boils down to just two fundamental assumptions:

1. There is one "right," "normal," or "healthy" way for human brains and human minds to be configured and to function (or one relatively narrow "normal" range into which the configuration and functioning of human brains and minds ought to fall).
2. If your neurological configuration and functioning (and, as a result, your ways of thinking and behaving) diverge substantially from the dominant standard of "normal," then there is "Something Wrong With You."

It is these two assumptions that define the pathology paradigm. Different groups and individuals build upon these assumptions in very different ways, with varying degrees of rationality, lunacy, fearfulness, or compassion – but as long as they share those two basic assumptions, they're still operating within the pathology paradigm (just as ancient Mayan astronomers and 13th Century Islamic astronomers had vastly different conceptions of the cosmos, yet both operated within the geocentric paradigm).

The psychiatric establishment that classifies Autism as a "disorder"; the "Autism charity" that calls Autism a "global health crisis"; Autism researchers who keep coming up with new theories of "causation"; wing nuts who believe that Autism is some form of "poisoning"; anyone who speaks of Autism using medicalized language like "symptom," "treatment," or "epidemic"; the mother who thinks that the best way to help her Autistic child is to subject him to Behaviorist "interventions" intended to train him to act like a "normal" child; the "inspiring" Autistic celebrity who advises other Autistics that the secret to success is to try harder to conform to the social demands of non-Autistics... *all* of these groups and individuals are operating within the pathology paradigm, regardless of their intentions, or how nice they are, or how much they might disagree with one another on various points.

The Neurodiversity Paradigm

Here's how I'd articulate the fundamental principles of the neurodiversity paradigm:

1. Neurodiversity — the diversity of brains and minds — is a natural, healthy, and valuable form of human diversity. There is no "normal" style of human brain or human mind, any more than there is one "normal" race, ethnicity, gender, or culture.
2. All of the diversity dynamics (e.g., dynamics of power, privilege, and marginalization) that manifest in society in relation to other forms of human diversity (e.g., racial, cultural, sexual orientation, and gender diversity) also manifest in relation to neurodiversity.

The Master's Tools Will Never Dismantle the Master's House

At an international feminist conference in 1979, the poet Audre Lorde delivered a speech entitled "The Master's Tools Will Never Dismantle the Master's House." In that speech, Lorde, a Black lesbian from a working-class immigrant family, castigated her almost entirely white and affluent audience for remaining rooted in, and continuing to propagate, the fundamental dynamics of the patriarchy: hierarchy, exclusion, racism, classism, homophobia, obliviousness to privilege, failure to embrace diversity. Lorde recognized sexism as being part of a broader, deeply-rooted paradigm that dealt with all forms of difference by establishing hierarchies of dominance, and she saw that genuine, widespread liberation was impossible as long as feminists continued to operate within this paradigm.

"What does it mean," Lorde said, "when the tools of a racist patriarchy are used to examine the fruits of that same patriarchy? It means that only the most narrow perimeters of change are possible and allowable. [...] For the master's tools will never dismantle the master's house. They may allow us temporarily to beat him at his own game, but they will never enable us to bring about genuine change."

The master's tools will never dismantle the master's house. To work within a system, to play by its rules, inevitably reinforces that system, whether or not that's what you intend. Not only do the master's tools never serve to dismantle the master's house, but any time you try to use the master's tools for *anything,* you somehow end up building another extension of that darned house.

Lorde's warning applies equally well, today, to the Autistic community and our struggles for empowerment. The assumption that there is Something Wrong With Us is inherently disempowering, and that assumption is absolutely intrinsic to the pathology paradigm. So the "tools" of the pathology paradigm (by which I mean all strategies, goals, or ways of speaking or thinking that explicitly or implicitly buy into the pathology paradigm's assumptions) will never empower us in the long run. Genuine, lasting, widespread empowerment for Autistics can only be attained through making and propagating the shift from the pathology paradigm to the neurodiversity paradigm. We must throw away the master's tools.

The Language of Pathology vs. the Language of Diversity

Because the pathology paradigm has been dominant for some time, many people, even many who claim to advocate for the empowerment of Autistic people, still habitually use language that's based in the assumptions of that paradigm. The shift from the pathology paradigm to the neurodiversity paradigm calls for a radical shift in language, because the appropriate language for discussing medical problems is quite different from the appropriate language for discussing diversity. The issue of "person-first language" is a good basic example to start with (others more eloquent than myself, like Jim Sinclair and Lydia Brown, have already written extensively on this particular topic, and their writings are readily available on the Internet, so I'll keep this brief).

If a person has a medical condition, we might say that "she has cancer," or she's "a person with allergies," or "she suffers from ulcers." But when a person is a member of a minority group, we don't talk about their minority status as though it were a disease. We say "she's Black," or "she's a lesbian." We recognize that it would be outrageously inappropriate – and likely to mark us as ignorant or bigoted – if we were to refer to a Black person as "having negroism" or being a "person with negroism," or if we were to say that someone "suffers from homosexuality."

So if we use phrases like "person with Autism," or "she has Autism," or "families affected by Autism," we're using the language of the pathology paradigm – language that implicitly accepts and reinforces the assumption that Autism is a problem, a Something-Wrong-With-You. In the language of the neurodiversity paradigm, on the other hand, we speak of neurodiversity in the same way we would speak of ethnic or sexual diversity, and we speak of Autistics in the same way we would speak of any social minority group: *I am Autistic. I am an Autistic. I am an Autistic person. There are Autistic people in my family.*

These linguistic distinctions might seem trivial, but our language plays a key role in shaping our thoughts, our perceptions, our cultures, and our realities. In the long run, the sort of language that's used to talk about Autistics has enormous influence on how society treats us, and on the messages we internalize about ourselves. To describe ourselves in language that reinforces the pathology paradigm is to use the master's tools, in Audre Lorde's metaphor, and thus to imprison ourselves more deeply in the master's house.

I Don't Believe in Normal People

The concept of a "normal brain" or a "normal person" has no more objective scientific validity – and serves no better purpose — than the concept of a "master race." Of all the master's tools (i.e., the dynamics, language, and conceptual frameworks that create and maintain social inequities), the most powerful and insidious is the concept of "normal people." In the context of human diversity (ethnic, cultural, sexual, neurological, or any other sort), to treat one particular group as the "normal" or default group inevitably serves to privilege that group and to marginalize those who don't belong to that group.

The dubious assumption that there's such a thing as a "normal person" lies at the core of the pathology paradigm. The neurodiversity paradigm, on the other hand, does not recognize "normal" as a valid concept when it comes to human diversity.

Most reasonably well-educated people these days already recognize that the concept of "normal" is absurd and meaningless in the context of racial, ethnic, or cultural diversity. The Han Chinese constitute the single largest ethnic group in the world, but it would be ridiculous to claim that this makes Han Chinese the "natural" or "default" human ethnicity. The fact that a randomly-selected human is statistically far more likely to be Han Chinese than Irish does not make a Han Chinese more "normal" than an Irishman (whatever that would even mean).

The most insidious sort of social inequality, the most difficult sort of privilege to challenge, occurs when a dominant group is so deeply established as the "normal" or "default" group that it has no specific name, no label. The members of such a group are simply thought of as "normal people," "healthy people," or just "people" — with the implication that those who aren't members of that group represent deviations from that which is normal and natural, rather than equally natural and legitimate manifestations of human diversity.

For instance, consider the connotations of the statement "Gay people want the same rights as heterosexuals," versus the connotations of the statement "Gay people want the same rights as normal people." Simply by substituting the word *normal* for *heterosexual,* the second statement implicitly accepts and reinforces heterosexual privilege, and relegates gays to an inferior, "abnormal" status.

Now imagine if terms like *heterosexual* and *straight* didn't exist at all. That would put gay rights activists in the position of having to say things like "We want the same rights as normal people" – language that would reinforce their marginal, "abnormal" status and thus undermine their struggle. They'd be stuck using the master's tools. If terms like *heterosexual* and *straight* didn't exist, it would be necessary for gay rights activists to invent them.

This is why an essential early step in the neurodiversity movement was the coining of the term *neurotypical. Neurotypical* is to *Autistic* as *straight* is to *gay.* The existence of the word *neurotypical* makes it possible to have conversations about topics like neurotypical privilege. *Neurotypical* is a word that allows us to talk about members of the dominant neurological group without implicitly reinforcing that group's privileged position (and our own marginalization) by referring to them as "normal." The word *normal,* used to privilege one sort of human over others, is one of the master's tools, but the word *neurotypical* is one of *our* tools — a tool that we can use *instead of* the master's tool; a tool that *can* help us to dismantle the master's house.

The Vocabulary of Neurodiversity

The word *neurotypical* is an essential piece of the new vocabulary of neurodiversity that's beginning to emerge — that *needs* to emerge — if we are to free ourselves of the disempowering language of the pathology paradigm, and if we are to successfully propagate the neurodiversity paradigm in our own thinking and in the sphere of public discourse.

The word *neurodiversity* itself is of course the most essential piece of this new vocabulary. The essence of the entire paradigm — the understanding of neurological variation as a natural form of human diversity, subject to the same societal dynamics as other forms of diversity — is packed into that one word.

Another useful word is *neurominority.* Neurotypicals are the majority; Autistics are a neurominority. This term was coined years ago by Jim Sinclair, one of the seminal figures in Autistic self-advocacy, who is also widely credited with coining the term *neurotypical.* As of this writing, the word *neurominority* hasn't yet caught on like *neurotypical* has. I'd like to see it come into more widespread usage, because there's a need for it; there are a lot of topics in the discourse on neurodiversity that are much easier to talk about when one has a good, non-pathologizing word for referring to all the people who aren't neurotypical (*Autistic* doesn't work as a synonym for "not neurotypical," because Autistics aren't the only people who aren't neurotypical; there are other neurological styles besides Autism that are currently marginalized and poorly accommodated by the dominant culture).

Terms like *neurodiversity, neurotypical,* and *neurominority* allow us to talk and think about neurodiversity in ways that don't implicitly pathologize us. As we cultivate Autistic community and interact with other neurominority communities, and as we continue to generate writing and discussion on issues of relevance to us, more new language will emerge. Already, we've generated terms like *stim* and *loud hands* to describe important aspects of the Autistic experience. And in my own academic work, my studies of cross-cultural competence (the ability to interact and communicate skillfully with people from multiple cultures) have led me to develop the term *cross-neurotype competence,* a term that I hope will catch on in certain circles.

It's also my hope that the terms *neurodiversity paradigm* and *pathology paradigm* will catch on and come into widespread usage. In the interest of clarity, it's useful to make the distinction between *neurodiversity* (the phenomenon of human neurological diversity) and the *neurodiversity paradigm* (the understanding of neurodiversity as a natural form of human diversity, subject to the same societal dynamics as other forms of diversity). And having a name for the pathology paradigm makes that paradigm much easier to discuss, recognize, challenge, and deconstruct (and eventually dismantle).

Words are tools. And as we recognize that the master's tools will never dismantle the master's house, we are creating our own tools, which can help us not only to dismantle the master's house, but to build a new house in which we can live better, more empowered lives.

Outposts in Your Head

It breaks my heart when so many of the Autistic people I meet speak of themselves and think of themselves in the language of the pathology paradigm, and when I see how this disempowers them and keeps them feeling bad about themselves. They've spent their lives listening to the toxic messages spread by proponents of the pathology paradigm, and they've accepted and internalized those messages and now endlessly repeat them in their own heads.

When we recognize that the struggles of neurominorities largely follow the same dynamics as the struggles of other sorts of minority groups, we recognize this self-pathologizing talk as a manifestation of a problem that has plagued members of many minority groups – a phenomenon called *internalized oppression.*

A contemporary of Audre Lorde's, the feminist journalist Sally Kempton, had this to say about internalized oppression: "It's hard to fight an enemy who has outposts in your head."

The task of liberating ourselves from the master's house begins with dismantling the parts of that house that have been built within our own heads. And *that* process begins with throwing away the master's tools so that we stop inadvertently building up the very thing we're trying to dismantle.

Throwing Away the Master's Tools

Once we recognize that the foundation of the pathology paradigm — the fictive concept of "normal people" — is a fundamental element of the master's toolkit, it becomes a lot easier to identify and rid ourselves of the master's tools. All we need to do is take careful stock of our words, concepts, thoughts, beliefs, and worries, and see whether they still make sense if we throw out the concept of "normal," the concept that there's one "right" way for people's brains and minds to function.

Once we've thrown away the concept of "normal," neurotypicals are just members of a majority — not healthier or more "right" than the rest of us, just more common. And Autistics are a minority group, no more intrinsically "disordered" than any ethnic minority. When we realize that "normal" is just something a bunch of people made up, when we recognize it as one of the master's tools and toss it out the window, the idea of Autism as a "disorder" goes out the window right along with it. Disordered compared to what state of order, exactly, if we refuse to buy into the idea that there's one particular "normal" order to which all minds should conform?

Without the fictive reference point of "normal," functioning labels – "high-functioning Autism" and "low-functioning Autism" – are also revealed to be absurd fictions. "High-functioning" or "low-functioning" compared to *what?* Who gets to decide what the proper "function" of any individual human should be?

In the pathology paradigm, the neurotypical mind is enthroned as the "normal" ideal against which all other types of minds are measured. "Low-functioning" really means "far from passing for neurotypical, far from being able to do the things that neurotypicals think people should do, and far from being able to thrive in a society created by and for neurotypicals." "High-functioning" means "closer to passing for neurotypical." To describe yourself as "high-functioning" is to use the master's tools, to wall yourself up in the master's house – a house in which neurotypicals are the ideal standard against which you should be measured, a house in which neurotypicals are always at the top, and in which "higher" means "more like them."

If we start from the assumption that neurotypicals are "normal," and Autistics are "disordered," then poor connections between neurotypicals and Autistics inevitably get blamed on some "defect" or "deficit" in Autistics. If an Autistic can't understand a neurotypical, it's because Autistics have empathy deficits and impaired communication skills; if a neurotypical can't understand an Autistic, it's because Autistics have empathy deficits and poor communication skills. All the frictions and failures of connection between the two groups, and all the difficulties Autistics run into in neurotypical society, all get blamed on Autism. But when our vision is no longer clouded by the illusion of "normal," we can recognize this double standard for what it is, recognize it as just another manifestation of the sort of privilege and power that dominant majorities so often wield over minorities of any sort.

Life Beyond the Pathology Paradigm

A paradigm shift, as you may recall, requires that all data be reinterpreted through the lens of the new paradigm. If you reject the fundamental premises of the pathology paradigm, and accept the premises of the neurodiversity paradigm, then it turns out that you don't have a disorder after all. And it turns out that maybe you function exactly as you ought to function, and that you just live in a society that isn't sufficiently enlightened to effectively integrate people who function like you. And that maybe the troubles in your life have not been the result of any inherent wrongness in you. And that maybe everything you've heard about Autism is open to question, and that your true potential is unknown and is yours to explore. And that maybe you are, in fact, a thing of beauty.

When you've thrown away all of the master's tools, when you've dismantled all of the enemy outposts and all of the pieces of the master's house that were in your head, when you've freed your mind from the influence of the pathology paradigm, you can look at yourself and know that on the deepest, most fundamental level, there is nothing wrong with you. Sure, you've been damaged in the course of living. Life damages everyone, some more than others, starting very early. But healing from damage gets easier once you know that underneath it all, there is a True Self that has been there from the start and will always be there – a True Self that is beautiful, and that is always waiting to shine forth in unexpected moments of grace. A True Self that never had anything wrong with it, that is worthy of infinite love, that is whole, and perfect, and Autistic.

Killing Words

by Zoe Gross

Let me present to you a sequence of events.

On March 6, 2012, a 22-year-old autistic man named George Hodgins was murdered in Sunnyvale, California. His mother, Elizabeth, pulled out a gun, shot him point-blank, and then killed herself.

In the following days and weeks, journalists wrote about George Hodgins' murder. In their articles they called him "low-functioning and high maintenance" and called Elizabeth Hodgins "a devoted and loving mother." They sought out quotes from other parents of autistic children, who normalized the crime by saying things like "every mother I know who has a child with special needs has a moment just like that."

People came to comment on these articles. They said that they felt sympathy for the mother. They called her George's "guardian angel." They said no one should judge her unless they had walked in her shoes. They said that it wasn't wrong because he was autistic, and autistic children are hell to raise. They said that it wasn't wrong because she was obviously responding to a lack of services. (In fact, she had refused services.) They said that it wasn't wrong because he was disabled, so his life couldn't have been very good anyway.

On March 8, 2012, Robert Latimer went on television to talk about how loving and compassionate it was when he gassed his disabled daughter Tracy. He called for "euthanasia"—the murder of disabled children by their parents—to be legalized in Canada. A woman who appeared with him agreed. She has two disabled children who she would like to kill, but she can't because it is against the law. No opposing viewpoints were presented.

On March 17, 2012, the Autism Society released a statement about "the tragic story of Elizabeth Hodgins", which "...shows that high stress on parents is very common in the autism community." The statement, signed by both Autism Society presidents, blamed her actions on a lack of services. They also noted that "the divorce rate among parents with a child with autism is as high as 70 percent due to the pressure" (this is actually a myth that was debunked in 2010). They never even mentioned George's name.

On March 31st, 2012, Patricia Corby drowned her 4 year old autistic son Daniel in the bathtub, in San Diego, California.

***

We need to start looking at these murders as copycat crimes, which are encouraged when murders of disabled people receive positive press coverage. Just as Katie McCarron's murder followed "Autism Every Day," Daniel Corby's murder follows George Hodgins' murder, and subsequent media coverage which excused, explained away, or even promoted the murder of disabled people by our parents.

When journalists call murderers "loving and devoted parents," when television shows give Robert Latimer airtime, when parents normalize murder by saying that all special-needs parents have murderous thoughts, the result is an environment in which these murders are seen as acceptable. Media coverage like this sends a message that homicide is a normal, understandable response to any discomfort one might experience while parenting a disabled child, and we can't pretend that other parents of disabled kids aren't hearing that message.

***

Let me present to you a sequence of events.

If you wrote an article about George Hodgins' murder, or if you gave a quote for one, or if you covered it on television, or if you blogged about it, or if you commented on it,

and

if you said that no one should "judge" the murder as wrong,

if you said that Elizabeth Hodgins was "driven to murder" by George's autism or by "lack of services,"

if you called the murder "understandable,"

if you said "it wasn't a murder, it was a mercy killing,"

if you said "all parents of special-needs children have felt this way,"

please take a minute to wonder if Patricia Corby heard you.

(A version of this essay previously appeared on illusionofcompetence.blogspot.com on April 10th, 2012.)

Disability Catch-22s

by Zoe Gross

So here are some things a lot of people don't know about me:

About twice a month I walk in front of a moving car by accident. About twice a month I choke while drinking.

Here's another interesting thing: when I try to talk about autism, and why I as an autistic person should have a voice in the discussion of autism, some non-autistic parents and professionals get mad at me. They say, "You're a college student, you clearly don't have the same kinds of problems that someone with Real Autism does. Your autism must be so mild that you are irrelevant to this conversation." And then they start talking about what Real Autism looks like, often referencing their own children. They'll say things like "My kid has Real Autism that is so very real, he is unaware of dangers and might wander into the street and get hurt!" or "I worked with this little girl who had Real Autism, and she was a choking risk because she had difficulty swallowing!" And then they say "Clearly, these things never happen to you, because you can write a research paper."

I don't understand the ideas people have about disability sometimes.

Like, obviously not all autistic people are the same and our disability affects us all a bit differently. But at the same time I find it frustrating that when disabled people try to advocate for ourselves, we are often immediately dismissed as "not disabled enough" just by virtue of the fact that we have opinions we want to express. This doesn't just happen in discussions about autism – I've seen people with all kinds of disabilities be accused of being "not disabled enough for your opinion to count" when they start talking about their rights.

So today I was in Starbucks spitting coffee on myself and coughing, and people were asking me if I was okay and I wanted to say "I'm fine, this happens all the time," but I couldn't really breathe enough to talk. And what I was thinking about, as I recovered from my accidental attempt to breathe frappucino, was how angry it makes me that so many non-disabled people consider disability a moveable goalpost.

Because here's the thing: the same person who will argue that disabled people locked up in institutions need to be there because they might walk in front of a car or choke on food or water, will then turn to me and say that even though I have these experiences fairly regularly, I'm not Really Disabled, and they can tell because I don't live in an institution.

Can you spot the catch-22?

(A version of this essay appeared previously on aapdinterns.blogspot.com in 2012.)

Like A Person

by Amanda Forest Vivian

My post yesterday was supposed to be about something else, but I got distracted by the fact that in high school my homosexuality created "special needs" that I had to advocate for. I think it's a funny story and also shows that, while disability is real, many of the worst aspects of having a disability aren't innate to being disabled.

My friend Niyatee said that she interacts with me as though I don't have AS, and she wondered if that was ableist. I don't think it is. At the same time, I like that she thought of it and doesn't buy the idea that people with disabilities, or any difference, should be treated "like everyone else". The "like everyone else" model actually puts a lot of pressure on people who are different to reduce their difference to one very measurable, non-threatening thing, and be "like everyone else" otherwise. For example, for my teenage self, homosexuality couldn't just be as simple as having a girlfriend or wife in the future while a boyfriend or husband was in everyone else's. Because I was attracted to girls, it affected many aspects of how I related to my peers. I ended up feeling like a failure because I couldn't keep my homosexuality "to myself," as I saw it. It was messy. It spilled out into other people's lives.

There probably are lesbian teenagers who have completely asexual friendships with straight girls. Similarly, there are disabled people whose only difference from non-disabled people is that they are in a wheelchair; and while it's hard to find an ASD example of a "like everyone else" disabled person, there is probably someone out there who has developed good social skills and doesn't have trouble with routines and obsessions, but has to use typing to communicate. If you can accept that this person types, you're good, otherwise you can treat them like... well, you know.

One of my favorite books contains the gloriously inarticulate sentence, "Mike needed to treat Randall like an autistic person. But he also needed not to treat him that way." The book, *Send in the Idiots* by Kamran Nazeer, and Mike and Randall, are all based on a real couple. Mike was great at advocating for Randall when people tried to bully and manipulate him, but he also patronized Randall, overestimating his guilelessness and dismissing his poetic talent as a savant skill. While Mike was admirably attuned to Randall's impairments, he didn't recognize the parts of Randall that didn't fit a stereotype. To supplement Nazeer's incoherence with my own, the best way to treat other people is always "like a person". Not like everyone else. Not like a gay person or a disabled person or a person of color.

My school treated me like everyone else in a way that was damaging. But on the other hand, what would it have meant for my school to treat me "like a gay person?" I guess, based on my dancing and changing problems, you might institute a system where gay students are classified as the "third sex" as we were considered to be in the early twentieth century. It would not be standard practice for gay students to change with the same gender; you would set aside another room. If the atmosphere was especially puritanical (the type of school that doesn't allow boys in girls' residential halls, for example), you would have to set aside more rooms depending on how many gay students there were, with one gay boy and one lesbian changing in each changing room so there was no possibility of misconduct.

I have a feeling that if a school did this, it would be seen as a bad thing by almost everyone. Conservatives would complain that the school was recognizing an "alternative lifestyle," while liberals might protest

that it treated gay people like another species. I would have liked it —
after all, it's a policy tailored to fit my teenage self —Y but other gay
kids would have been embarrassed that it was made into such a big
deal. And of course the policy doesn't mention bisexual or questioning
students, who would presumably make up a "fourth sex" not allowed
to change with anyone. My school ignored the ways same-sex-
attracted students were different, but the third and fourth sex system
overestimates it, and assumes that all SSA students are different in the
same way.

Actually, putting aside the fact that my school treated me like everyone
else in a way that caused special needs, once I actually *had* those
special needs, certain teachers did a great job treating me like a
person. As I mentioned in the previous post, Mrs. M. either understood,
or didn't understand but respected, why I had so much anxiety about
dancing with girls. She was also supportive when I dealt with my self-
consciousness in idiosyncratic ways, like refusing to workshop my
plays until my classmates had signed a contract saying they
understood that it was natural for a gay person to write plays about
gay people, and that they wouldn't be surprised or judgmental when
that plot element appeared. As has probably been obvious, my gay
person special needs were completely interconnected with my
Asperger's special needs, which my teachers were equally sensitive to
even though not all of them knew about my diagnosis. I didn't have to
invoke a label for Mrs. G. to believe me and help me when I explained
that I couldn't learn a dance by watching other people do it. I almost
think it was better without a label, because it meant that Mrs. G. didn't
think of a book or movie about autism, but just helped me with the
specific problem that I had.

My friend John doesn't believe I have Asperger's. He says that I seem
normal and people are overdiagnosed with trendy disorders. But he
doesn't make a big show of being amused or baffled by the way I talk,
which is something annoying that most people do when they don't
know I have AS. This summer, John and I planned to meet in New York
City, and based on what he already knew about me, he assumed I

would have trouble taking the subway. He offered to take an unnecessary ride so he could find me at the train station and I wouldn't have to take the subway alone. This is a really good example of knowing and thinking about someone's challenges, without making a big deal out of how they are different. And I couldn't care less if John thinks I have Asperger's, because he treats me like a person.

One of the first times I talked to Niyatee, she kept saying how she liked the way I talked because "you just say things straight out". I said that I wished everyone liked it. I actually didn't, because it made it hard to write emails to professors or prospective employers. Then Niyatee said she felt embarrassed because she'd forgotten that I had Asperger's and had assumed I talked the way I did on purpose. This is the only time that she ever needed to consciously think about my AS, and because that was more than a year ago, she thinks it means she might be treating me "like everyone else." But actually, all it means is that when she finds out things about me she just finds them out, and doesn't feel the need to divide them into piles called Amanda and Asperger's, which is good, because those are really difficult piles to make and it also doesn't matter.

(A version of this essay previously appeared on adeepercountry.blogspot.com on September 27th, 2009.)

Why No One Counts

by Amanda Forest Vivian

Something I've noticed: a person with a disability having a conversation about the value of people with disabilities (which you can call whatever you want, but usually something more tactful than "the value of people with disabilities") can never actually be disabled.

The reason this is true is pretty obvious!

Someone who is talking about how reasonable it is for a parent to not want a kid with a disability, or how it's wasteful for kids with disabilities to get the best possible education, or how they'd never date a person with a disability, isn't thinking of fully formed and complicated disabled people.

They're not saying it's reasonable not to want a blind kid who becomes an anarchist and can't go to a family gathering without getting in fights with your more conservative relatives. If they say the word *blind*, they're usually referring to a kind of blindness that doesn't actually exist--a kind that is not attached to a real person.

This is why people who believe things like that can care about you even if you are disabled. You actually are other stuff besides a disability floating in space, so you don't resemble their version of a disabled person.

So, you know, someone is talking about how super hard it is to have a kid with autism or Down Syndrome or cerebral palsy and how much sense it makes for people not to want that. And you're like, "But I have autism, it makes me feel bad when you say that, aren't we friends?"

"Well, you have to admit your autism is different. I wouldn't mind having a kid like YOU."

Well, duh, because I wrote you letters, and you told me my hair color is uneven, and we eat Oreos together, you eating the cookie sides while I scrape out the paste with my teeth.

But you have to admit that the way you talk about disabled people, you never let them far enough in your mind to know if they would write you letters too.

(A version of this essay appeared previously on adeepercountry.blogspot.org on November 28th, 2011.)

Passing As Ethics: A Primer

by Amanda Forest Vivian

Passing as Ethics.

So, passing as ethics is a term I invented and I use it a lot. It's at the core of a lot of the stuff I write. In retrospect, I wish I had said "passing as functioning" or "passing as cure" because I think that would be more inclusive and cover more ground. Originally I thought that passing as ethics only happened to people with autism, but as I learned more I found out that it was more pervasive than I could ever have imagined.

Here are some passing as ethics values. I'm mostly writing this as if a professional is saying it, but disabled people can totally feel most of this stuff about themselves and I certainly did for a long time. I think it's a very basic part of life for most people.

1. It is better for a person with a physical disability to walk without any visible mobility aids than it is to use a wheelchair, crutches, or cane—even if the person finds it painful or tiring to walk unaided, and/or is in danger of falling.

2. If someone's disability causes them to have an unusual gait, this is a problem, and it would be an improvement if their gait could be changed to look more normal, even if this didn't make the person walk any faster or more easily.

3. Habits that mark someone as a person with an intellectual disability or autism, such as flapping hands, are inherently bad, and people who do them should be trained not to do them.

4. If there is a conflict between someone with autism and someone without autism, it's the person with autism's fault. If a person with autism gets bullied, this is evidence of why #3 is true; if no one had been able to tell they had autism, this wouldn't have happened.

5. If someone misunderstands a person with autism, it is because the person with autism didn't express themselves right.

6. Deaf and hard-of-hearing people should learn to lip-read. Hearing people need not learn sign language.

7. So basically, people with disabilities should always try to communicate in a way that is comfortable for people without disabilities, even if it makes the people with disabilities uncomfortable.

8. To sum up, any habit, style of movement, facial expression, interest, feeling, word choice, way of pronouncing words, way of sitting, way of communicating, okay you get the idea, that is commonly associated with disabled people is
   a. the opposite of success, and must be destroyed to improve someone's "functioning"
   b. morally wrong in some cases--that is, the person who is doing the behavior that's associated with disability becomes automatically wrong in any conflict

9. If someone who used to look like they had a disability now doesn't look like they have a disability (to most people), then they are recovered/cured (no matter how negatively it affects them to hide their disability, and no matter how many less visible aspects of their disability continue to affect them).

10. Don't kill yourself after reading #1-9 because people will just think you killed yourself because it was so depressing to be disabled.

(A version of this essay previously appeared on adeepercountry.blogspot.com on December 1st, 2010.)

I'm Spasticus Autisticus

by Amanda Forest Vivian

I am a big, big lover of this song and I was going to just post it on Facebook as my reasonably uninvolved observance of Autism Acceptance Day. But I happened to find an interview with Ian Dury about the song, which disappointedly ended with him sort of apologizing for mentioning autism and saying it's probably "frightening" for parents. I never thought a dead guy could stomp on my heart so hard, but it was the 80s and there wasn't even what there is now in terms of Autistic-identified people who could have told him not to apologize. So I forgive you Ian Dury, like I could ever be mad at you for long.

The main thing about the interview was that he confirmed my gut interpretation of the song, which is what I really want to talk about here.

"On the single bag there's what's supposed to be an explanatory note, which is about my tribe being...knowing our racial creed and paying no heed to such things...it can be rich or poor, disablement can get anybody. It was really about Spasticus being a slave who wished to be free, and I put at the bottom 'We too are determined to be free.' And it's based on - the idea of Spasticus is based on a film called *Spartacus,* which had Kirk Douglas in it, and at the end bit, they say 'Which one of you is Spartacus,' you know--'I'm Spartacus,' then they all go 'I'm Spartacus,' and they hung everybody that confessed."

I've been moving away a lot from identifying as Autistic, and probably not for good reasons, but just because I know professionals are on a mission to take it away from as many people as they can. And it's hard for me to want to hold onto it when every time I tell anyone I have autism they seem determined to interrogate and confound the reality of my disabled life. So I've retreated into just being 'slow and crazy', which are words that are available for all people at no charge, or 'charger'. If I'm feeling a little more political, I use old words like 'feebleminded' or very new words like 'headcrip' — again none of these words are technical terms, and aesthetically and emotionally, that's a big part of their appeal.

But this worries me the same way the word queer has sometimes worried me. The problem with only identifying with something vaguely and choosing the word for your identity aesthetically is that there's strength in community, identity, and numbers, and if everyone is called something else it's hard to find and hold onto each other, to support each other and try and work together for the things that will benefit people like us.

I have always thought that one of the worst disadvantages disabled people face is how few disabled people there are. Don't get me wrong, there are shitloads of wheelchair users, people with learning disabilities and developmental disabilities and mental handicaps, deaf and blind people and hard of hearing people and people with low vision, people who use crutches and canes, people who don't use anything but have to live differently because they live with chronic illnesses, and you know, you know a lot of people like this, and you can think of all the kinds of "people like this" I have neglected to mention.

But that's all we mostly are — people like this.

I've said there are two kinds of disability and you end up fighting yourself with either one. A person is stigmatized as disabled, seen as unworthy of the things he wants from life, and has to prove himself non-disabled in order to be his own person, no matter how much he may harm himself in the process by doing things he can't do. Or a person isn't considered disabled and has to do things she can't do because everyone expects her to do them and there is no support. It's a trap either way.

In both ways a disabled person is fighting not to be disabled. The second person might have a nostalgia for the stigmas and stereotypes of "visible" disability, because it seems better than getting no support or recognition, but ultimately she feels too guilty to try and get those things. Holy shit I'm tired. What I'm trying to say is, what do disabled people think about themselves?

Basically: they do not think they are disabled.

They either think of it as something they have "overcome" or "risen above" with their accomplishments or just their personality, or they think of it as something nasty and rude to mention, or they think of it as something they don't deserve to claim because their disability isn't real or isn't that bad, or they think of it as a word that if they used it about themselves would indicate that they're sad, that they're giving up.

This has real practical effects on "people like us," this nameless population. We're so fucking short on disabled writers, disabled scholars, disabled teachers, disabled staff, disabled activists, disabled doctors (imagine the DSM being written primarily by doctors with mental disabilities); we're so fucking short on people who have an identity and loyalty to other disabled people. Because we all think the word disabled is bad for us! We all throw it away, and when we do that we have nothing because we only have ourselves and whatever word we have for ourselves — not disabled, just different; not disabled, just has trouble walking; just crazy, just stupid, just slow — just perfectly individual and unique and alone. But our people need armies and bodies of work.

If I was going to start one organization to help disabled people, its focus would be to help kids with disabilities meet adults who identify as disabled. I've thought this for a year or two and I don't think I have the skillset for that kind of thing, but it does pull on me sometimes because it's not that people like us aren't talented and tender and brave, but that we all hang separately.

Anyway. "I'm Spasticus Autisticus" is what I'm trying to say.

(A version of this essay previously appeared on adeepercountry.blogspot.com on April 1st, 2012.)

Connecting Dots

by Bev Harp

Somebody calls autism a tragedy. Somebody kills an autistic person. Somebody doesn't see how these two events are connected. I try to explain. I try harder. It happens again and again and again and somebody 'splains it away.

The topic here is devaluation. When it becomes commonplace to pair the words autism and tragedy, the pairing seeps deep down into the collective mind. When the puzzle piece becomes the recognized symbol for autism, the message comes over and over that there is something unfinished about the person. Something mysterious that the general public cannot be expected to understand. Now when someone hears "autism," tragedy echoes in the background. Puzzlement reverberates. This one is not like the others. This one is out of our range of understanding and compassion.

Somebody calls my request for respectful language and symbolism "political correctness." Although this respect exists barely anywhere, it is portrayed as enforced, and therefore something that must be rebelled against. Somebody gets the bright idea to light buildings up blue for awareness. Everybody is more aware of the tragedy and the mystery and otherness. Nobody asks autistic people what this might mean for their futures.

She wants a job, but the employer has heard that people like her are prone to violence. She wants to live on her own, but she carries the luggage stickered with claims of eternal childhood and helplessness. She needs a communication device, but someone knows this is pointless because she is empty. Someone has *heard* things. Out of frustration, she bangs her head. Somebody takes this as evidence, now she is locked away.

Somewhere else, another child has been diagnosed with autism. He is forced to drink bleach, drowned in a bathtub, or smothered to death. This is the true meaning of tragedy. The voices are crying for understanding, not for the murdered but for their killers. The difficult, difficult lives they have led, autism is to blame. A puzzle piece is affixed to another bumper, the enigma of autism advertised, along with the pleas for an end to it, spewing out into the air as someone else drives on into the darkness.

This post is offered for Blogging Against Disablism Day in honor of Katie McCarron (2002-2006).

(A version of this essay appeared previously on aspergersquare8.blogspot.com on May 1st, 2012.)

Metaphor Stole My Autism: The Social Construction of Autism as Separable from Personhood, and its Effect on Policy, Funding, and Perception

by Zoe Gross

"We are fighting against autism." "He is behind the wall of autism." "Autism stole my child." As Autism Spectrum Disorders have become a subject of public fascination, these metaphors have become commonplace.

Why is autism spoken of so metaphorically, compared to other conditions? According to Susan Sontag, one reason could be because its cause is unknown. Sontag writes that when people do not understand how a condition works, they are more likely to build metaphors around it:

> The fantasies inspired by TB in the last century, by cancer now, are responses to a disease thought to be intractable and capricious – that is, a disease not understood – in an era in which medicine's central premise is that all diseases can be cured. Such a disease is, by definition, mysterious. (Sontag, 5)

Stigmatized conditions also lend themselves to metaphorical language, and autism has acquired a great deal of stigma as awareness of the condition has risen. In his article "AIDS and Stigma," Gregory Herek lists four conditions that contribute to societal stigma against a particular condition. Two of these apply to autism: "Greater stigma is associated with illnesses and conditions that are unalterable or degenerative," and "A condition tends to be more stigmatized when it is readily apparent to others – when it actually disrupts a social interaction or is perceived by others as repellent, ugly, or upsetting" (Herek, 128-129). Autistic people often behave in ways that deviate from societal norms, and this can indeed cause non-autistic people to become quite upset. One response to this feeling of being unsettled by people with a certain condition is "giving the thing a name that belongs to something else" – in other words, constructing metaphors around a condition (Sontag, 93).

Sontag explains the relationship between stigma and metaphor this way: "Any important disease whose causality is murky, and for which treatment is ineffectual, tends to be awash in significance. First, the subjects of the deepest dread... are identified with the disease. The disease itself becomes a metaphor" (Sontag, 58). Although autism is not a disease, it is similarly awash with significance today, and many scientists and laypeople alike have become obsessed with the search for its cause. This paper will explore the ways in which autism has become associated with "the subjects of deepest dread" in our society, through several types of metaphor, which construct autism as an entity separable from autistic people.

Military Metaphors

One of the most popular metaphoric constructions of autism is the military metaphor. Sontag analyzed the military metaphor in another context when she wrote, "The controlling metaphors in descriptions of cancer are, in fact, drawn... from the language of warfare; every physician and every attentive patient is familiar with, if perhaps inured to, this military terminology" (Sontag, 64). This can be seen in the commonly-used phrase "she is battling cancer" (or, in the case of an obituary, "he lost his battle with cancer"). The military metaphor is just as ubiquitous in the discourse of autism; autism is constructed as a militarized force besieging an otherwise-normal child.

This way of thinking is reflected in the names of organizations such as Fighting Autism and Defeat Autism Now, and in the discourse of "warrior moms" popularized by the anti-vaccine celebrity Jenny McCarthy and her followers. It can be heard in the "I am Autism" advertisement produced for Autism Speaks, in which a parent, addressing "autism" directly, says: "I am a parent riding toward you, and you can push me off this horse time and time again, but I will get up, climb back on, and ride on with the message... We are a community of warriors" ("I am Autism" transcript). This image of the parent as a knight on horseback is embedded within an orgy of autism-as-separable metaphors. The end result is a portrait of autism not as a neurotype, but as some sort of monstrous force, clashing on a metaphorical battlefield with a cavalry of "warrior moms."

Sontag points out that cancer is thought of as being at war not only with individual patients, but with an entire nation. She writes that "the disease itself is conceived as the enemy on which society wages war. More recently, the fight against cancer has sounded like a colonial war – with similarly vast appropriations of government money" (Sontag, 66). When autism is described in a militaristic way, it is exclusively this second, nation-wide type of war being described. As with all autism-as-separable metaphors, autistic people are not considered to have the agency to take up arms against their own condition – the war is fought by non-disabled relatives, professionals, and organizations. This war, too, has involved "appropriations of government money" in the form of the Combating Autism Act, a law which reflects the military metaphor in its title.

Sontag points out the pitfalls of the military metaphor in her writing. She argues that, by invoking enemies and warfare, "military metaphors contribute to the stigmatizing of certain illnesses and, by extension, of those who are ill" (Sontag, 99). Sontag's point that stigma against a condition will be applied to people with that condition is even more true of autism, which is both congenital and pervasive.

Kidnapping Metaphors

"We have your son. We will make sure that he will not be able to care for himself or interact socially as long as he lives. This is only the beginning. – Autism" (Kaufman)

This is the text of one advertisement from the Ransom Notes Campaign, a series of advertisements created for the NYU Child Study Center in 2007. (See Appendix 1 for pictures of the Ransom Notes advertisements.) Using the tagline "don't let a psychiatric disorder take your child," the Ransom Notes Campaign sought to galvanize parents to seek treatment for their children. In order to do so, the campaign relied on another kind of metaphor which presents autism as separable from the autistic person: the kidnapping metaphor.

Kidnapping metaphors portray autism as a body-snatcher, holding an otherwise-normal child hostage. Many parents invoke this metaphor when describing their own experiences, with laments such as "autism took my child away from me." Obviously their children are still physically present – the implication of the kidnapping metaphor is that autistic children were born neurotypical, but these non-disabled children were "stolen away" by the onset of their autism symptoms. This metaphor is popular among people who believe that vaccines cause autism. For example, the name of Jenny McCarthy's organization, Generation Rescue, refers to using biomedical approaches to "rescue" children who have been abducted by autism.

The kidnapping metaphor is also central to the advertisement "I am Autism," in which the anthropomorphized character of "autism" declares its nefarious intentions:

> I am autism. I'm visible in your children, but if I can help it, I am invisible to you until it's too late. I know where you live.

And guess what? I live there too... I speak your language fluently. And with every voice I take away, I acquire yet another language. I work very quickly... I have no interest in right or wrong. I derive great pleasure out of your loneliness. I will fight to take away your hope. I will plot to rob you of your children and your dreams. ("I am Autism" transcript)

"Autism" in this advertisement speaks like a super villain, using buzz words relating to kidnapping, child molestation, and crime. "I know where you live" is a classic threat; phrases like "every voice I take away" and "I will plot to rob you of your children" call to mind images of chloroform-laden rags and cars speeding away into the night. By using this language, "I am Autism" taps into common fears: any parent would dread the idea of their child being abducted by a kidnapper.

Barrier Metaphors

Seen through the lens of the barrier metaphor, autism is a physical obstacle which stands between an otherwise-normal child and the world around them. This is one of the oldest metaphors for autism. In 1967, a little more than 20 years after Leo Kanner coined the term "autism" to describe a set of symptoms in children, psychologist Bruno Bettelheim published *The Empty Fortress: Infantile Autism and the Birth of the Self*. Bettelheim believed that "refrigerator mothers" caused autism in their children. His version of the barrier metaphor was particularly extreme. By referring to autistic children as "empty fortresses," Bettelheim implied that an autistic child was no longer a person at all – all that remained was the "fortress" of autism, the defense created by the now-vanished child against their mother's cruelty.

More modern incarnations of the barrier metaphor offer a more "hopeful" spin: inside the barrier of autism, an otherwise-normal child waits for contact from the outside world. It is common to hear that autistic children are "in their own world of autism," or that autism is a wall, pane of glass, or shell which surrounds the child. The interesting thing about this construction is that autism is not spoken of as being *in* the child at all – instead, the (presumably non-disabled) child is within autism. In Autism Speaks' advertisement "I am Autism," a mother challenges the anthropomorphized disability by asking it: "You think that because my child lives behind a wall, I am afraid to knock it down with my bare hands?" ("I am Autism" transcript)

Similarly, practitioners of the Son-Rise Program (a scientifically unproven therapy method involving imitating an autistic child's behaviors) claim that their therapy works because it allows them to "enter the world" of autistic children and "bring them back into our world." The parent testimonials on the Son-Rise website use this metaphor enthusiastically. One mother found that Son-Rise "offered her the opportunity to join into Anthony's world." Former patient Anna is described as having been "very much in her own world" before being given Son-Rise therapy, and little Griffen was brought into the program after having "regressed into his own world when he was two years old" ("Son-Rise Parents Share Their Stories"). In the Son-Rise literature, as well as in "I am Autism," autism is not a disability at all, but a place where an otherwise-normal child is trapped, waiting to be set free.

Death Metaphors

In "AIDS and Stigma," Herek notes that "Greater stigma is associated with illnesses and conditions that are unalterable or degenerative… Being diagnosed with such a disease is often regarded as equivalent to dying" (Herek, 128). Autism is indeed an unalterable condition, and many people have spoken about it metaphorically in ways that refer to this perceived equivalency. These metaphors construct autism as death, or a fate worse than death, for an otherwise-normal child.

An extreme example of this metaphorical thinking is the blog Lives Lost to Autism, which features the tagline, "for many, autism can be deadly" (*Lives Lost to Autism*). The function of this website is to relay news stories involving the deaths of autistic people, and reinterpret them as "lives cut short by autism." Given that autism is not fatal, the actual causes of death in these cases vary from accidental drowning to abuse and neglect. The message of the website is, essentially, that the death of any autistic person is caused by autism. Autism becomes an almost mystical force, a sort of bad luck charm which attracts death, from various causes and in various incarnations. And if these deaths are caused by autism, then the way to stop future deaths is not to prevent accidental drowning and institutional neglect, but to prevent or "cure" autism. This idea of autism as death, and "cure" as life-saving intervention, is reflected in the advertisements of the Son-Rise Program, whose practitioners claim to be able to "recover" children from autism. Son-Rise materials often bear the tagline, "Autism doesn't have to be a death sentence." By this they mean that autism need not be life-long – they offer "recovery" from autism, which through the lens of this metaphor is reinterpreted as salvation from death.

Other incarnations of the autism-as-death metaphor are more commonplace. One ubiquitous bit of metaphor is the use of the word "grieving" to describe the feelings of parents processing their child's diagnosis. Autism Speaks, the largest American autism charity, uses this language frequently, including in its advice to parents of newly-diagnosed autistic children. On a webpage entitled "Autism & Your Family," the organization tells parents: "You want your child to get better so much you may feel some of the stages commonly associated with grieving" ("Autism & Your Family"). The article then lists a modified version of the Kübler-Ross stages of grief; for parents of living autistic children, these stages are apparently shock, sadness, anger, denial, loneliness, and acceptance. Autism Speaks encourages parents to "mourn some of the hopes and dreams they held for their child," to fully feel their "loss" and "outrage." The language used here is very similar to the language of literal bereavement – consciously so, given the "stages of grief" approach.

The metaphorical connection between autism and death has been made explicit many times. It is common for parents to "mourn" their living autistic children, but some parents take the metaphor further, expressing a desire to trade their child's autism for a life-threatening illness. In 2008, one couple published a book entitled "I Wish My Kids Had Cancer." More famously, J.B. Handley, a co-founder of Generation Rescue, declared: "Most parents I know will take measles over autism" (Gardiner). The autism-as-death metaphor is so widespread that recently, after one parent published a book in which he declared he felt no need to mourn for his autistic son, another parent publicly accused him of lying:

> I'm still bristling over the whole assertion that he never needed to mourn. If that's really true — and if I get to the end of the book and he's still never for one moment had a bit of grief over the cognitive dissonance between what he expected and what he got — then he's a lot more self-actualized than I am, and I tip my hat to him. But as a fellow autism parent, I can't help feeling that a piece of this story was brushed aside because it didn't fit the feel-good theme (Belkin).

Consequences of autism-as-separable metaphors

In her introduction to *AIDS and its Metaphors*, Susan Sontag explained her opposition to metaphorical language around illness. She wrote that:

> the metaphoric trappings that deform the experience of having cancer have very real consequences: they inhibit people from seeking treatment early enough, or from making a greater effort to get competent treatment. The metaphors and myths, I was convinced, kill. (For instance, they make people irrationally fearful of effective measures such as chemotherapy, and foster credence in thoroughly useless remedies such as diets and psychotherapy.) (Sontag, 102)

Metaphors which construct autism as separable from the personhood of autistics have a similar effect. These metaphors can lead to dangerous treatment. Some parents and doctors, convinced that autism is separable from the personhood of autistics, will do terrible things to "get the autism out" of their children or patients. Like Sontag's credulous cancer patients, they swear by autism "remedies" that are not only useless, but potentially deadly.

Death metaphors specifically can lead to this sort of treatment. If parents think of their autistic children as dying, dead, or terminally ill, they will be more likely to try risky and unproven "therapies" to try to "save" them. A recent fad "treatment" for autism was the testosterone-lowering drug Lupron, which is sometimes used to chemically castrate sex offenders. Dr. Mark Geier, whose license to practice medicine was recently suspended, popularized the use of Lupron based on his theory that autism is caused by mercury in vaccinations. Geier found a market among parents who were undeterred by the lack of proof for this causation theory or for Lupron's efficacy as a treatment for autism. These people were willing to subject their children to a treatment which involves regular, painful injections and can "disrupt normal development, interfering with natural puberty and potentially putting children's heart and bones at risk" (Tsouderos). Metaphors which treat autism as a kind of terminal illness encourage this behavior – parents will try anything to save the life of a dying child, even if the long-term consequences are severe. In the case of terminal illness, this approach makes some sense, because coping with complications from a medical treatment is better than death. It does not, however, make sense to take this no-holds-barred approach to the treatment of a stable and non-harmful disability such as autism.

As Susan Sontag pointed out, the military metaphor can also have dangerous consequences. Sontag writes: "It is not desirable for medicine, any more than for war, to be 'total'... The body is not a battlefield. The ill are neither unavoidable casualties nor the enemy. We – medicine, society – are not authorized to fight back by any means whatever" (Sontag, 183). Sontag was speaking of life-threatening diseases such as cancer and AIDS, but many have taken this "total war" approach to autism as well. In 2005, a five-year-old boy named

Abubakar Nadama died while being given intravenous chelation. Chelation is an approved treatment for heavy metal intoxication, but carries grave risks and is not approved for use in the treatment of autism. In fact, Nadama's mother brought him to the United States from England to receive the "therapy," because chelating autistic children is illegal in the UK. Nadama's death did not dissuade proponents of chelation in the US, however: advocates of "biomedical treatment" continue to urge parents to subject their children to chelation (Mnookin, 263-264). To these anti-vaccine activists, who operate according to the military metaphor, Abubakar Nadama is not a victim of medical incompetence or child abuse, but a casualty in the war against autism.

Metaphors surrounding autism have also affected policy. In "AIDS and Stigma," Gregory Herek explains that stigma against a condition can affect government spending and policy around that condition and cause funds to be allocated less wisely:

> The politics of AIDS stigma have repeatedly hindered society's response to the epidemic... Extensive resources that might otherwise have gone to prevention instead were needed to respond to coercive AIDS legislation whose purpose was primarily to stigmatize and punish PWAs [people with AIDS]... Indeed, some commentators have argued that stigma is the root cause of the HIV epidemic in the United States. (Herek, 130)

The article points out that stigma has negatively affected policy decisions around HIV/AIDS: for example, the fact that HIV/AIDS is constructed as a "deserved" illness means that many governmental and non-profit organizations have been unwilling to allocate resources to proven HIV-prevention programs such as needle exchange and sex education.

Stigma and metaphoric constructions of autism have also had a negative impact on the allocation of funding. Since autism is constructed as both a separable trait and a terrible one, many non-autistic people have become obsessed with removing it – if not from individual autistic people, then from the human species as whole. As a result, our society's first priority with regard to autism is finding a cure or means of prevention, as opposed to creating an inclusive environment for people on the autism spectrum. This is reflected in government policy and in the availability of funds for various initiatives. The Inter-Agency Autism Coordinating Committee reported that in 2009, 32% of autism-related research dollars went   to research which focused on determining the cause and prevention of autism. In contrast, only 3% went to research geared toward improving services for people on the spectrum, and less than 1% went to studying the needs of autistic people across the lifespan. ("2009 IACC Autism Spectrum Disorder Research Portfolio Analysis Report"). (See Appendix 2 for a graph from the IACC's report.)

Research which seeks to improve autistic people's quality of life is called "until-then research" by some scientists working in the field of autism. This refers to the idea that curing or preventing autism is priority number one in autism research – anything else will only be temporarily meaningful. Thus, we can see that the idea of autism as separable has affected spending on autism research, leading to the under-funding of research into quality of life. It is revealing that these disparities are at least partially the result of the way resources are allocated by the Combating Autism Act, which has an autism-as-separable metaphor in its title.

Finally, the idea of autism as separable from autistic people has lead professionals and parent-advocates to disregard the priorities and perspectives of Autistic people themselves. Many on the autism spectrum would prefer to see initiatives funded which would foster the inclusion of autistic people in society – for instance, job coaching, de-institutionalization, personal assistance for those who require it, and greater access to methods of Alternative and Augmentative Communication (AAC). However, many of the metaphors which surround autism foster the exclusion of Autistic people by portraying us as non-entities – corpses, empty shells – or as beings without agency, awaiting rescue. These metaphorical constructions of autism do not encourage non-disabled people to take Autistic opinions seriously; they only increase the stigma associated with autism in our society. As long as people prefer to think of autism as a kidnapper, a killer, a barrier, or an opposing army, as opposed to merely another aspect of personhood, Autistic people will not be truly accepted.

Appendix 1: Advertisements from the Ransom Notes Campaign

We have your son.

We will make sure he will
not be able to care for
himself or interact socially
as long as he lives.

✳This is only the beginning.

                                    Autism

Appendix 2: 2009 NIH-ARRA ASD Research Funding by Topic

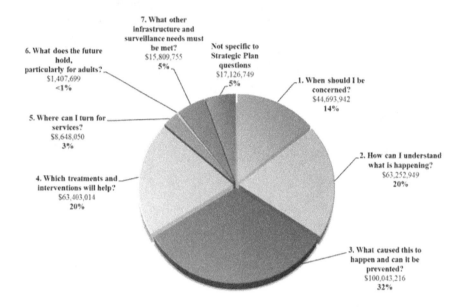

Source: 2009 IACC Autism Spectrum Disorder Research Portfolio Analysis Report

Works Cited

"2009 IACC Autism Spectrum Disorder Research Portfolio Analysis Report." Inter-Agency Autism Coordinating Committee. Accessed October 2, 2011. http://iacc.hhs.gov/portfolio-analysis/2009/index.shtml

"Autism Speaks 'I am Autism' Ad Transcript." *The Autistic Self-Advocacy Network*. Published September 23, 2009. Accessed September 20, 2011. http://www.autisticadvocacy.org/modules/smartsection/item.php?itemid=58

"Autism & Your Family." Autism Speaks Inc. Accessed October 1, 2011. http://www.autismspeaks.org/what-autism/autism-your-family

Belkin, Lisa. "Autism, One Parent to Another." *New York Times*. September 7, 2011. Accessed September 30, 2011. http://parenting.blogs.nytimes.com/2011/09/07/autism-one-parent-to-another/

Harris, Gardiner. "Measles Cases Grow in Number, and Officials Blame Parents' Fear of Autism." *New York Times*. August 21, 2008. Accessed October 1, 2011. http://www.nytimes.com/2008/08/22/health/research/22measles.html

Herek, Gregory M. "AIDS and Stigma." *The Sociology of Health & Illness: Critical Perspectives*, 8th edition. Ed. Conrad, Peter. New York: Worth Publishers, 2009, 126- 134.

Kaufman, Joanne. "Ransom-Note Ads About Children's Health Are Canceled." *New York Times*. December 29, 2007. Accessed

September 25, 2011.
http://www.nytimes.com/2007/12/20/business/media/20child.html

Lives Lost to Autism. Accessed September 20, 2011.
http://liveslosttoautism.blogspot.com/

Mnookin, Seth. *The Panic Virus: A True Story of Medicine, Science, and Fear.* New York: Simon & Schuster, 2011.

"Son-Rise Parents Share Their Stories." Autism Treatment Center of America. Accessed October 2, 2011.
http://www.autismtreatmentcenter.org/autism-education

Sontag, Susan. *Illness as a Metaphor* and *AIDS and its Metaphors.* New York: Picador, 1990.

Tsouderos, Trine. "'Miracle drug' called junk science: Powerful castration drug pushed for autistic children, but medical experts denounce unproven claims." *Chicago Tribune.* May 21, 2009. Accessed October 1, 2011.
http://www.chicagotribune.com/health/chi-autism-lupron-may21,0,242705.story

Why Autism Speaks Hurts Us

by Amy Sequenzia

When I was little and started to type, I was saying things like "life with autism is insanity." I didn't recognize autism as an important part of who I am and I was only repeating what I heard. My parents were supportive of my typing and loved me deeply. But they also were told that I could never be happy as long as I "had" autism. The efforts, "experts" said, from families and advocates, should be towards supporting research to find a cure.

That was a long time ago. At some point in my life, I started thinking for myself and accepting autism as the most important part of my personality. I am autistic and that's who I am. It wasn't easy and it was bumpy. But if today I am accepted by a growing number of people, if more people read and value what I write, it is because I accepted myself as I am. And I am a proud autistic woman!

I do not have the advocacy organizations of my younger years to thank for that. Back then, they proclaimed in their names that they would "defeat" and "cure" autism — NOW! They were saying that I had to be defeated, cured from a terrible condition, exterminated. They never paused to think that I, and other autistics, did not really want to be discarded as undesirable. And it is scary when people keep saying that we don't deserve to be here.

Today things seem to be even worse. Even for me, although I have found my place and my voice. My family and close friends have accepted me as autistic, but the challenges I face are made worse by the negativity Autism Speaks and their followers link with being autistic. Things are worse because those organizations that once wanted to see me gone today follow the lead of Autism Speaks.

Autism Speaks is a powerful organization, with support of many celebrities and easy media access. I believe most of the celebrities that help making Autism Speaks so recognizable don't have an understanding of what autism is. They probably want to help and they buy into the picture of despair spread by Autism Speaks.

The same is true for the thousands of people going to "autism walks" and donating money to Autism Speaks. They don't know, or refuse to acknowledge, that the message they are supporting is that society should fear and segregate their children; they don't know, or refuse to acknowledge, that all the money raised will not be used to help their children with education, services or accommodations that can make navigate the world a little easier for their children; they don't know, or refuse to acknowledge, that a lot of the money is used to advertise their children as burdens, as people society should shun, isolate and eventually eliminate.

We autistics know this well and, with our allies, have been very vocal about the damages Autism Speaks is doing to our lives and to our future. I keep thinking about my life. Accepting myself was a difficult and long process. My self-esteem was low and I did not have consistent support. People in my life were torn between believing the messages of despair and gloom, and seeing me as a whole person – disabled and different, but not less.

Eventually, we were able to move forward in our process and this is my point: I cannot avoid thinking that it could have been easier, that time would not have been lost and that I could have had many opportunities — now gone – in my life if my family had been offered more support instead of being told I was too defective and that my only chance to be a "real person" was if I could be fixed.

But I am here today, speaking out, despite the predictions of a lesser life. If organizations like Autism Speaks were really thinking about us, they would stop spreading fear of autism and they would start talking to us, the only true experts on autism. They would then help us achieve the goal to cure what really needs to be cured: the false assumptions of what life as an autistic person is, what life with an autistic person is.

And I mean talking to all of us. I, for example, am one of the adults Autism Speaks considers helpless and a burden to society. I am said to be a tragedy for my family, although I am not and Autism Speaks cannot tell my family how they should feel about me. I can give the so-called "experts" valuable information about how to better help me with the difficulties I face.

Autism Speaks hurts us when families of newly diagnosed autistic children have their energy drained by the negative messages they get from that organization. The fear and the bleak future is all they get. They start resenting the child in front of them and they start hoping for a "better," "non-defective" child. They waste their energy trying to fix what is not broken, what is simply different. And the autistic individuals are silenced, with an uneasy feeling that we are disappointing to the people we love, that no matter how much we try, we will never be good enough, ever.

If the messages and information they get come from Autism Speaks, they never see autistics that are happy, accomplished, successful and thriving, as autistics, in our own way; or the families that are not suffering, despairing, afraid of the future or depressed because a child is autistic; they don't see that, fear replaced by acceptance, no longer makes sense. When more families accept autism, they work for the rights of every autistic. And this is a good goal.

Autism Speaks hurts us when they use all their resources trying to make us look like not good enough for society. We need to fight for acceptance, so that families, allies, educators and policy makers can re-direct their energy to what is uniquely important to each autistic child and adult, so that we can all thrive, in our own pace, in our own way.

No burden, no tragedy, no fear, no despair. Those concepts come from Autism Speaks, an organization that never listened to autistics, and is not interested in listening to us. They don't have the insight, the expertise and ultimately, the right to direct the conversation about autism. This right belongs to us and we are the only ones who can decide who our allies are, who can speak on our behalf.

(A version of this essay previously appeared on thinkinclusive.us on May 23rd, 2012.)

How Indistinguishability Got Its Groove Back

by Amanda Forest Vivian

How Indistinguishability Got Its Groove Back, part 1

My first writing about disability was about an ABA school that I interned at when I was 20, which was a very ableist and passing-obsessed environment. Being in that environment I was forced to confront things I'd tried not to think about.

I remember when I first started writing about this kind of thing I was very careful to say that I wasn't anti-ABA and thought ABA could be really helpful and useful. I've kind of dropped that whole thing, not because I'm against behaviorism—I arguably am a behaviorist—but because I guess I am against any school or therapist who identifies as "ABA." ABA is technically a way of teaching, not what is taught, but it has historically been associated with physical punishment and it still is very much associated with passing. So, I tend to make certain assumptions about anyone who identifies with the label ABA without trying to apologize for or justify it.

Recently my dad was trying to convince me to work at a very old, famous ABA program, because of the benefits. When I pointed out that the person the program is named after used to give electric shocks to children to stop them from flapping their hands, my dad told me that he had researched this on the Internet and "they don't do that anymore." But this isn't enough for me.

It's not enough for professionals to refrain from the most obviously abusive practices, especially if they identify themselves with the doctor who introduced those practices. If you're going to work in an area that has that kind of history, you have to address that history. It's not enough to just stop hitting kids because you shouldn't hit kids— you have to think about *why* people like you were hitting kids in the first place and how they got to a point where they decided it was okay, and how you might end up getting to a similar point.

2. How Indistinguishability Keeps Its Groove

I'm sorry to mix metaphors because I often compare zombies to people like me (unusual gait, does the same things a lot, often judged to be better off dead) but let's focus on some different aspects of the zombie and swivel that image over to another group of people: staff.

How did you get your groove back? Well, indistinguishability, you never really lost it, and that's what scares me. Maybe this is a failure of mine because how can I be more scared by a difference of opinion than I am by more obviously bad things, like violence? I'm not sure. I know I find vampires pretty unterrifying when they're sadistic, but zombies are unbearable because they don't even know or choose the crimes they commit. There's nothing to explain.

So what I'm trying to do is explain. Not why I'm against indistinguishability, cause I have, but why it seems so stupid when I say that, like I'm against electricity. People respond with the most ill-thought-out support, and it doesn't matter at all. "But flapping your hands is against social norms and kids need to learn to follow social norms!" Across the country, kindergarteners are told to be yourself and do the right thing even if it makes you stand out—except when it comes to this one group of little kids. "But other kids will notice that they're different and exclude them!" Okay, just like when kids are bullied for race or religion their teachers start training them to look like white Protestants. Maybe you're thinking people can't pretend to be white, but some people can—and besides, good luck convincing his peers that a kid who can't talk isn't disabled, even if he keeps his hands by his sides.

This is a completely meaningless argument though because anyone who defends a point so weakly has already won. Even if someone says, "Yeah, I guess you're right," it's like some interesting philosophical discussion about unicorns. Intelligent input darling, now let's go back to our day job where we kick horses in the face for having horns when they shouldn't.

"Hey hold on," you may be saying, "I'm not kicking anyone in the face! I'm just writing a behavior plan where if Erica talks about unicorns too much she doesn't get dessert."

That's cool but a lot of disabled people have had to live with this stuff longer than you have, and it kind of feels like being kicked in the face.

"Aw, but it doesn't feel that way to me."

That's because it's your job. Everyone's job feels normal to them. Our government likes to pretend that Abu Ghraib happened because Lynndie England is a bad person, but she just had a work environment where she thought it was normal to act a certain way. I know this is an aggressive comparison, but there isn't a point of wrongness where the things that you're doing suddenly feel wrong. I feel that if people were more aware of the broad spectrum of things that can feel normal when it's your job, it would be possible to engage them in real conversation about what they do.

3. How you learn how things are done

My dad told me that most parents wouldn't understand my "visceral reaction" when I see indistinguishability held up as an ideal, or even as something that would be nice. As if we were talking about religion, which he dislikes, he said, "Maybe it's not important and it's not what they should want, but most people want to be normal, so they want their kids to be normal. You can't tell them their choice is wrong."

"I don't really think it's parents who make that choice," I said.

"Oh, so it's just the evil professionals making parents do what they want?"

"Well, yes." Not that I think professionals are evil—this is really about staff infection, not individuals. Lots of the infected are probably great to play Dungeons & Dragons with (more on that later) but they have a particular way of thinking about people with autism.

Parents often don't. I know how I feel about disability in general and autism in specific, because disability is a permanent part of my life. For the average person that isn't the case. Now they have a kid who has this—what do you call it? Disease? Mental illness? Neurodevelopmental condition? Well, they have this scary autism word that you see on TV. What the fuck. This is terrible. What do they do? What are they supposed to think?

It's perfectly normal, when something happens which is challenging and with which you have no experience, to look to the people around you for examples of how to respond. If your kid has autism, the people around you are often telling you that "recovery" for someone with autism is about looking non-disabled, and that this recovery is urgent, so you go along with it because you're not a fucking autism expert. You don't know how things are done.

Unfortunately, it's exactly the powerful momentum of how things are done which keeps people from thinking much about the things they are doing. Sooner or later, the parents know how things are done too.

How Indistinguishability Got Its Groove Back

Is something that might someday appear in all its parts and might not. Right now, I'm primarily interested in writing about staff infection. Spoiler alert though: the answer to "how did indistinguishability get its groove back?" is exactly that.

Or like I said before: it never really lost it.

I think there are two reasons "staff"—*very* broadly defined as doctors, teachers, therapists, aides, and a million other people—end up trying to control people with disabilities.

1. They believe people with disabilities inherently need to be controlled.

2. They get in a position of power because of the support needs of people with disabilities' and/or youth, and have the opportunity to make people with disabilities more convenient to deal with.

Whichever reason is not your reason can be used as a straw reason to support the real reason. I could give examples, but basically you know it when you see it. Doing this relates to the Harder Fallacy and Shocking Behavior and things like that.

The way indistinguishability got its groove back is that a person with power looked at a person diagnosed with autism and decided they didn't like the way person's body looked or the way the person felt about things. Or, as I say when I get angry, the way the person said no.

The person with power started trying to change the person with autism's body, or whatever they thought was wrong. The person with autism couldn't defend themselves because they couldn't talk. Or, if they could, other people felt their beliefs, opinions, and arguments were inherently weaker than those of people without disabilities.

The person with power told their co-workers or their employees or the other people in their field to do the same thing. They, by and large, did.

Occasionally, someone was bothered by it but afraid of losing their job, being seen as a pushover by their coworkers, or not being respected by other autism scientists. But most people weren't bothered. Maybe the original person with power was very charismatic and converted them. Maybe they already didn't like how the person with autism's body looked. Maybe they just didn't think about it, accepted it as part of their job, and eventually came to be a little passionate about its rightness. After all, no one was trying to change *their* bodies.

When I say this happened once, I mean that people in power make this decision about people with autism on a regular basis. Probably as you are reading this a person is deciding to be this way, and their decision will spread because it doesn't occur to many people to question it.

To some extent this is true about any decision within that dynamic. Let's say someone decided that all kids with a certain disability have to play soccer, or read Tarot cards. I think this would actually catch on to a greater degree than you would expect. But indistinguishability is such a historically popular thing for people in power to choose to force on disabled people that it has a kind of momentum. You just think about it and it's already there.

Every person in power who unthinkingly chooses or supports indistinguishability is adding to its mass. It's an army of laziness, an army (usually) of feeling safe in your body. Of being able to talk about how much you love *The Office* in between sessions of training a kid with autism not to make jokes that don't have an obvious punchline. It's easy to do pretty much anything to people with disabilities but indistinguishability has an army.

The pressure of the army makes room for more soldiers. Obviously. This has all been an excuse for a pun. The way indistinguishability got its groove back is that indistinguishability actually is a groove being worn into the fabric of society by sheer constance and bullheadedness. Have a nice day.

(A version of this essay previously appeared on adeepercountry.blogspot.com.)

Voice

Plural of Medium

by Savannah Logsdon-Breakstone

...is Media. And media is how people express and communicate. Your voice is a medium, writing is a medium, art and video and... Yes, even poking someone repeatedly or jumping up and down or twitching your eyes in a pattern can be using a medium—your body—to communicate.

Everyone can use some sort of media. Before I get protests, I'm including pushing away unwanted things, fecal smearing, and tiny behaviors as well as examples of use of media. Sometimes our method and medium is ignored or not understood, but that doesn't make it less our medium. Sometimes we can't even define exactly what we are communicating with our media yet, but it's a process. Sometimes, figuring out what we mean—communicating with ourselves—is even more a part of using media than communicating with others.

When we are given the chance to be exposed to new media, new methods of expression, we are being given access to more opportunities to find the way to get it out right. To find communication. Eventually some of us do gain access to media that other people understand our use of. We learn to speak, or sing, or make music or videos. We paint, or sew, or costume; we write, decoupage, rearrange, and stack. We learn to dance, to write, and to find a new way to get the message across so that it is heard. Some of us aren't given that chance, and some people even find that other people's media aren't for them.

When you are someone whose communication methods or media are ignored when you want them observed, it can be an opening to find a new medium to call your own. I learned to type, I gained those skills, and I suddenly had access to a much larger community than I had when speaking or shrieking or running away or stacking dolls gave me.

Indeed, the way that typing opened up writing to me was a better medium in the end for me than those I already had—my fluency writing now is better than my speaking was at the height of my verbal ability. I can use this medium, the medium of digitized writing by the hitting of keys, in times when I can't even verbally speak at all, in times where my message as a kid might have been lost in other people's reactions to my screaming wordlessly because I didn't have the right words to speak any more.

Other people find other media. Some people won't rely on their media the way I do. Some people might rely on it more.

How beautiful would a poem in just PECs, just the way they are handed, be?

Some media is painful, or dangerous, or scary—or even, in the case of Thich Quang Duc, deadly. Sometimes that can be powerful, while other times—like fecal smearing—it can be too alarming to observers and yes, dangerous, to get across anything, even your own distress. Sometimes the media we know isn't sufficient to express what we mean—is your reaction to fecal smearing to recoil, maybe even freak out, or is it to find a way to figure out if someone is constipated? (If it's the second one, I'm guessing you have a little experience with this cross media translation.)

In some cases, the solution is to find more ways to experience and express experience. Gaining new skills, or discovering alternatives.

———

Other times it might be to just let other people react to you burning soundlessly.

The first time someone walked a friend through other signals for "my butt hurts" or that that type of pain is constipation, she nearly squeezed my hand off in joy.

Sometimes, a new medium is just a great way to accomplish something that you might not otherwise be able to do. Creating a more accurate and useful AAC device—even for less—or finding an easier way to collaboratively caption videos on the web. Applying dance to practical mobility difficulties or exploring how movements can be adapted to suit all types of bodies. Crafting tools to navigate difficult sensory environments or using virtual video distribution to share a larger message.

All media, in practice, in use, building and creating access, building and creating our futures.
What does it mean to build access together? What world can we envision when we apply love and justice to our media to find a world where we honor all people, regardless of ability, and their needs?

This summer, I and others will be attending the Allied Media Conference. It's not a disability conference, or a topical conference. AMC is just brought together by people that believe that we can use a wide range of media to change the world. Within that larger vision, people with disabilities saw a vision for our justice, for a way to create access collectively.

Creating Collective Access allows us to make accessible the potential of media skill sharing, network, and vision planning that AMC promises to people who might not otherwise be able to be a part of it. PwD and our Chronically Ill brethren face access barriers beyond a lack of ramps and braille. Working together and treating access as a matter of community rather than individual "burden" allows us to be a part of building a world that includes us and the potential we can realize through media.

And in turn, we can make accessible the wider community—the world.

What does it mean to explore and honor our potentials, our media, our vision? What sort of world can we build when access is a part of what it means to build communities? When it is a natural part of the creation of change?

(A version of this essay previously appeared on crackedmirrorinshalott.wordpress.com on April 24th, 2012.)

Metaphors Are Important

by Julia Bascom

As Kimba starts talking and typing more, and as I start to develop working relationships with other students, a lot of my assignments in lifeskills have become centered around writing. Writing, being a writer (and versus being a speaker), and teaching (is this possible?) writing have thus featured heavily in my thoughts lately.

Most of my concern lies with regard to *voice*.

I am a writing snob: not because I am the most eloquent, grammatically-adept, perfectly spelled starving artist to ever grace the world with her words (ask me about my journeys with commas sometime, or my passionate love affair with fragments and run-ons), but because I am a writer. I am not *someone who writes*; I am someone for whom there is no other option. This is the difference between "I am *someone who* (hatefully, regretfully, anxiously) *talks*" and "I am *a writer*." My writing, a complete opposite to my speaking, is joy and confession and a *need* for both of these things, and I hope this is transparent.

I have talents that I'm not supposed to have: I can tell who crushes on who by how they stand, I can read strides, I can hear the tonal differences between an alto and a soprano singing the same line so clearly that to me they sing entirely different notes, and I can read through the lines and tell when a person doesn't *need* to be writing at all. That, *that* is what makes me a snob, because I cannot abide a person putting pen to paper or fingers on keys when they don't *need* to, when word choice is not as relevant and demanding and essential to them as breathing and syntax is about being *correct* and not about being *evocative*.

I am a writing snob, and some of the kids in lifeskills are my very favorite writers.

I could write pages of context about the impact of Kimba's sparse, elegant, punch-to-the-gut syntax when he told me about being made to eat out of the trash, about *spaghetti...no. Cheeseburger...no. Dogfood yes. Bad boy. Go outside. Stay in the yard.*

(Because bad boys don't get to eat food, but they do get to eat garbage, or wood covered in old lead paint, and they get put and kept outside, and this was the first time he ever sat me down and tried to tell me something, and he can use much more verbose syntactic structures but he was more concerned with making damn sure I understood exactly what had been done to him.)

I want Tanya to make a book from the story of her life she carefully encoded in her response to a picture I showed her of a balloon alone in the sky:

*The boy bought a balloon, and it was red. He was walking and holding his balloon, and then he let go because he was stretching up to the sky, and the balloon flew away. And he wanted that balloon, but it flew away and it stayed in the sky for a month and then it got struck by **lightning** and exploded. Kapow! Pieces of it everywhere. The boy bought another balloon, and he lost that one, too.*

(And the most important part of the story, she said, is that it is funny. It makes people laugh (*because he loses one balloon, and then another*). *Not the boy though.*

What about the balloons? I asked.

Probably not the balloons either, she confided.)

I imagine handing these manuscripts off to a crotchety old Honors English teacher I had, who writes a biweekly column in our local paper that makes me want to throw rotten eggs because he doesn't *need* or even really want to write, it drips through his every sentence, he just wants to stand on a box and pontificate and *evaluate*, though never himself. I imagine handing him these snapshots of my students' souls and watching his red pens slash through them. The honesty, the effect, the things they say outright as well as in silence (he had what he wanted, it disappeared, he got a replacement, that disappeared too, it's a funny story except for how it's not at all), the things these intellectually disabled children can do without even trying that he simply cannot...they wouldn't matter at all.

He would be threatened by their voice.

These students have *voice*. Interestingly, one is a selective mute and another rarely speaks above a whisper, but when they have a *story*, when they need to make you understand, they have more of a voice than almost any other writer I've read. I'll take Tanya's understated *she taught me how to play UNO* as a reason for letting her bully pretend to be her friend over the cheerful notices the teachers and secretaries send out about field-trips and costume fees or the "Rural New Hampshire And The Single Girl" column in the paper. Tanya is honest. Tanya isn't afraid to mean it.

A voice is something honest, a certain unique blend of said-and-unsaid, a particular flavor of syntax and vocabulary and control that stays with you long after you've put down the book and think you've understood everything you just read. It's arresting and affecting, and my students have it in spades. I would submit that they're really never had a choice in the matter and, given that few of them have had any practice in writing before this past month, they haven't yet had a chance for it to be beaten out of them.

(There is one student. Her mother refuses to believe she is intellectually disabled, or treat her medical problems, and insists that she must do the physically impossible and pass as normal. She is allowed to attend Special Olympics events, which her mother coaches for, as an *assistant*—she signs the other kids in and out and keeps track of scores, but she isn't allowed to compete, or smile. She writes like a caricature, like a frightened and desperate mimicry of what she is told she's supposed to sound like. She's not allowed a voice. She can't mean anything, and behind every sentence is a nervous laugh or a hiccuped sob.)

These students aren't writing novels, and they don't let their voices out outside of specific circumstances: quiet, time with their thoughts, accessible method of expression, a clear question, and so on--the sort of things every writer needs. But because they are intellectually and/or developmentally disabled, because they need help spelling or scrawling, because their syntax is alternately sparse and cluttered, because they aren't even really supposed to have thoughts let alone voice, because *different* means *harder* means *defective* means *not worth it*...because of all of that, it doesn't matter what they write or how well they write it.

(I find most publications too poorly written to bother with. I have a nightly debate concerning whether or not I should just erase everything I've written ever because it is so shitty. I want to emphasize, again, just how elitist I am about writing, how much of a snob I am, how low my expectations were when I sat down to write with them, and how much crow I've eaten this month.)

These kids are *writers*, and it doesn't matter because it's not allowed, because their writing samples will be collected and graded and judged more harshly, against higher standards, than any of my essays in AP English ever were (go ahead, read the NH Alt. Assessment Standards and see for yourself. Come into our room and watch how these kids have to prove that they're sentient on an hourly basis, and then please tell me why I still feel surprised when I see their essays *thrown in the trash*). People with no voice of their own and no belief that a lifeskills kid could ever have anything to say are the gatekeepers of who gets listened to, who gets read, and they superimpose zombie faces and stutters over Tanya's stories and say *we really need to focus on her handwriting*.

So you see, I'm supposed to teach writing, which is less a matter of direct instruction about commas and more a matter of facilitating practice in having a voice. Drawing is just looking, and singing is just hearing, and writing is just listening to your own voice. These kids need to be told, explicitly, repeatedly, *by at least one fucking person*, that they **have** voices, and they are valuable voices, and they deserve to be heard, and the first person they should want to listen to them is themselves.

It takes practice.

What I want to know is: how am I supposed to do this, and how can I justify doing this at all, when, as Kimba will be only too happy to remind you, the ones with voices just get their tongues cut out?

An Ethnography Of Robotics

by Julia Bascom

First, a story. (*A little Christmas story. I call it: the story of Schmuel. Tailor of Klimovitch.*)

*****

(The best part of the story is what I leave out.)

*****

I met a mini!Kurt the other day. He was very blonde, with intense brown eyes, but he was very particular about his hat, and his dad was Burt Hummel in all the ways that counted. I'd guess he was about four–his voice was still all exclamation points.

"I'M MATT!" he said, hiding his face from me, and then trying to run out of the waiting room. It was cool though–I don't know if I even managed a *hi*.

He was at the stage where he was still mainly echolalic, but he was learning how to store and recombine and modify phrases to work for him. I was excited for him, and almost proud, because he'd mastered two essential skills for that–swapping pronouns, and prompting other people to remember their lines. His dad, trying to bundle him into his coat, was not playing along at first.

"I'M SO CUTE!" mini!Kurt reminded him, trying to make his arms go into the right sleeves. "I'M SO CUTE!? I'M SO CUTE?"

"Yeah," Dad sighed, wrestling with the zipper. "You're cute."

"SO CUTE?"

"So cute, that's right."

Mini!Kurt, satisfied that everything was going according to plan, was ready to leave. "BYE!" he called, waving his hand backwards at me, a perfect mirror image.

I waved. Had my mind been more together, I would have flapped.

*****

Echolalia is metalanguage.

*****

Echolalia is an unexpected treasure hunt. You can be watching a bootleg musical you never thought would be any good, but turns out to be *beautiful*, and suddenly they're going up the scale singing *hot hot hot hot,* and you're back with Kimba, and he's saying *hot hot hot hot–* only he's got this elaborate metaphor about fire and anger going on right now, and here it means *I think you're mad at me, so I'm mad at you, don't touch me.*

And then you're back at your laptop, wondering when he started watching musicals and rethinking half the things you thought you knew.

*****

Echolalia is what you use when language is too much. It's just also what you use when it's not enough.

These things are not opposites.

*****

Walt knows my name, but he'd rather call me Mulan. We're on the swings, trading movie titles.

"101 Dalmations?" I offer.

"Mulan no thank you!" He chides. Considers. "Rio, with Jesse Eisenberg?"

I grin. I'd only said that once, but he'd picked up on my crush, and he offers it back to me when I am having a hard time with the conversation. I try to remember his favorite, as a peace offering. "Kung Fu Panda II, in theaters now?"

I get it right.

Months later, it will still be the best conversation of my life.

*****

Echolalia, from Echo, of Greek mythos, cursed to speak only through the words of others.

We make it work though. About the *cursed*: opinions aren't the same as facts, and no one ever asked Echo.

To be fair, no one would have listened, either.

*****

As much as I can hate words, I delight in them, too. When I'm echoing, referencing, scripting, riffing and rifting, storing and combining and recombining, patterning, quoting, punning, swinging from hyperlexic memory to synesthetic connection, words are my tangible playground.

Make me talk like you, and you'll get a bunch of syntactically sophisticated nonsense. Let me keep my memories and connections, my resonations and associations and word-pictures, and if you slow down enough, you might hear something ringing true.

These are the words I'm using right now. It's okay if you can't see the picture yet; I can't either. It's coming together though, the more I practice them.

Ethnography of robotics.
Neuropoetics.
Girls like you always get to see Ireland.
Send my love to the leprechauns.
Please don't special-episode me.
Why don't you trust me? Because, honey, you keep setting things on fire.
The first rule of tautology club is the first rule of tautology club.

I think they might be four separate pieces. The joy is how they come together.

The bestworst part is no one ever knowing.

*****

(The best part of the story is what I leave out.)

*****

I don't trust my words on my own.

That's not why I echo though.

I know it's tempting, but, listen.

*****

Or maybe I'm lying, because I'm not brave enough to explain.

Don't worry though. I know that Kimba loves musicals now, and Walt named me after a warrior.

We'll get there.

Socializing Through Silence

by Melanie Yergeau

I wish you wouldn't interpret my silence as silence.

My silence is, in fact, a compliment. It means that I am being my natural self. It means that I am comfortable around you, that I trust you enough to engage *my* way of knowing, *my* way of speaking and interacting.

When I dilute my silences with words—your words, the out-of-the-mouth and off-the-cuff kind—I often do so out of fear. Fear that my rhetorical commonplaces—the commonplaces that lie on my hands, sprint in my eyes, or sit nestled in empty sounds—will bring you shame. Fear that my ways of communicating will be branded as pathology, as aberrant, as not being communication at all. Fear that I will lose my job. Fear that I will lose your friendship, guidance, or interest in me. Fear that I'll be institutionalized. Fear that I will be infantilized. Fear that I'll be seen as less than human.

This isn't to say that my use of your language is always a product of fear. There are times when I genuinely want to use it, understand it, and learn about and from it. I understand that speaking is how you prefer to communicate. I understand that speaking is how you best learn and interact. I understand that you take great joy in speaking and listening to others speak. And I do, I really do want to share in that joy.

But the burden can't always rest on me. I have a language too, one that I take joy in, one that I want to share. And when you deny me that—when you identify my silence as a personality flaw, a detriment, a symptom, a form of selfishness, a matter in need of behavioral therapy or "scripting" lessons—when you do these things, you hurt me. You hurt me deeply. You deny me that which I need in order to find my way through this confusing, oppressive, neurotypical world.

My silence isn't your silence. My silence is rich and meaningful. My silence is reflection, meditation, and processing. My silence is trust and comfort. My silence is a sensory carnival. My silence is brimming with the things and people around me—and only in that silence can I really know them, appreciate them, "speak" to them, and learn from them.

Speaking is an unnatural process for me. When socializing through speech, I will almost always be awkward, and I am OK with that awkwardness. In fact, I am learning to *embrace* that awkwardness, learning to *reclaim* and *redefine* that awkwardness. I am sorry you're not OK with that, sorry that you feel I need to practice, or take anti-psychotics, or frequent the university hospital's psych ward. I'm sorry that you won't appreciate me for who I am and how I operate in the world. I'm sorry that I can no longer consider you an ally, confidante, or friend.

(A version of this essay previously appeared on aspie rhetor on October 24th, 2011.)

Are You Listening?

by Bev Harp

I very much appreciate all of the comments on my last couple of communication themed posts. It seems that a lot of us have similar issues with speech, which is not too surprising. Today, I will talk about a few of the things I have found to help. I am going to try to stick mostly to my own experience, though I may refer to other autistic people I know personally and what they have told me. This is not an attempt to speak for anyone else. If you can use this window into my mind to help you understand an autistic person in your life, you are more than welcome to do so.

The most important thing to keep in mind is that speech is not the same thing as language, and that communication is a much larger concept still. Listening is at least half of the work. When I am not speaking, I am still communicating; most of the time, I am using some form of language. *If you do not try to see what I am already offering, why would you expect me to try harder to give more?*

As I have mentioned before, writing is easy for me. I can tell you much more in an e-mail than I can in person. Telephone calls are the hardest method of communication. I would love to see some of the money collected in the name of autism awareness go toward purchasing keyboards for autistic people who don't have access to them.

I carry a small notebook with me, primarily for drawing squares, but I have also used it to help get my words together. I appreciate people who do not roll their eyes when I write something down before saying it out loud.

Drawing squares is a great way for me to listen. I've encountered people who have let me know they see this as rude (for some reason they view it as flagrant inattention when it's really quite the opposite!). Drawing during a conversation helps me to relax and I can focus on what the other person is saying if I am not forced to look at him/her or the surroundings. Other stims can be useful, too, but a visually oriented repetitive task works best for me. I am much more likely to talk if I am doing these things that help me listen.

I have always used metaphorical language to communicate, especially where emotion or feelings are involved. Sometimes this is in the form of stored scripts, other times it emerges along with the particular situation. This can be a problem for people who feel they are being expected to guess what I am talking about. For that reason, I use it far less than I did in the past, and this is always reserved for ongoing relationships and the necessity to communicate something for which I don't have access to the proper words.

Often, the things I do to communicate are seen as pure silliness. Using gestures instead of words is one that nearly always evokes this response. For some reason, if a person can use speech most of the time, it is assumed that she should always use it. This is somewhat like asking a person who can speak fluent English and passable French to always and only speak in French. At work or school, we usually have to speak the dominant language. Accommodations in these areas might increase the productivity of autistic students and employees considerably. Certainly, with friends and family, we would like to be able to relax and communicate in the ways that come most naturally.

When someone allows me to use these techniques—writing, drawing, metaphor and gesture—*without criticism*, I feel valued and accepted. When another person actually participates in some of them with me, trust is more easily established. I recently passed a two hour car trip with a brother-in-law by saying sentences backward the whole way. It began quite spontaneously and relieved the tension of having to be in the car with another person. In this case, the playing field of conversation was leveled by each of us having to think as hard as the other before saying a sentence.

Beyond respecting these self-created accommodations, what can a person do to help make speech easier?

~Consider whether or not this is the best time for a conversation. First thing in the morning is never good for me. As soon as I walk in the door isn't good. Pick a time when we are both relaxed and have some time to spare. If you know I didn't get enough sleep last night or have had a bad day, save this conversation for later.

~Turn off the TV! This goes for stereos, too. I can't process more than one voice at a time.

~Talk to me about things you know I am interested in. I don't know how to "talk about the weather."

~If you are telling a long story, allow ample space for me to comment. I will always have trouble "breaking in" to a conversation, even on a day when my speech is fairly good. If you can pause once in awhile, but without expectation I will say anything, this is best.

~If you are asking questions, please ask only one at a time. Double barreled questions—Would you like to go to the store, and then to visit Kate?—can be very confusing, and can contribute to speech shutdown.

~Allow for opportunities to say "Me, too!" I have had times when I could not ask for something simple, like a glass of water. But I could agree that I wanted one also, if someone said it first.

~Don't make a big deal about eye contact. The autistic person may hear more of what you are saying if you don't insist on this or try to force it.

~Don't jump to conclusions based on body language. I have often had people interpret my posture or facial expressions to mean something far from what I was thinking or feeling. If you know someone is autistic, be aware that that person's face or body may be speaking a foreign language. Nothing kills a conversation faster for me than having someone tell me what I am thinking. Don't assume.

~ Don't take my silence personally. If you attribute ill will to my not speaking, this will only make talking more difficult. Nobody wants to work extra hard to please someone who has already decided she is hostile!

Other autistic people who read this may disagree with some points. We are all different. Please feel free to add your own suggestions in the comments.

(A version of this essay appeared previously on aspergersquare8.blogspot.com on November 21st, 2007.)

Advocacy: Everyone Can Do It

by Kassiane Sibley

This story happened a long, long time ago, almost 10 years now. It's still exactly what I think of when people tell me about their kid who will "never" self advocate.

I worked for a few years with a boy who we will call C. C was about 9 when I met him. He was nonverbal, really hated typing on the computer, knew a few signs, and had a PECS book. He had experienced many years of ABA therapy, which is very much therapist directed, and he was growing increasingly frustrated with how things in his life were going. His frustration was pretty clear—he was angry a lot of the time and he was lashing out physically when a lot of demands (or unpleasant demands) were made. His PECS book often didn't have what he wanted to communicate in it, so that added further to his communication challenges. What he was left with was behavior as communication.

I'm pretty sure C's parents weren't exactly looking for self-advocacy teaching, at least not what I do. They had the whole "autism as tragedy" thing going on, were into quackery, kind of seemed to resent C for existing (ok, so very much resented C for existing) and wanted compliance and normalcy, not what I was offering. But C and I hit it off right away and I wasn't completely horrified by his expression of his anger. I avoided getting hit, obviously, but I wasn't going to restrain him or, nearly as bad, throw more and more demands in his face when he was upset. That's silly. It does not work. Typicality is not a realistic goal, but being able to express wants and needs is, and it was quite likely that C could learn a more expedient way to make his wishes known.

When I started working with C, I had a rule for his ABA therapists and parents: if C makes clear a want or a need, *he gets it.* If he indicates that he doesn't want to do same with same or whatever, he doesn't do same with same. If he indicates that he is not ready to leave an activity, he doesn't have to leave yet. He needed to learn that he had some agency after so many years of following other people's agendas.

What's the first thing little kids tend to learn to take power over their lives in small ways? The word "no", right? I wanted C to learn that he could ask for things and get them, and that he could say he didn't want to do things and get that. A lot of our time was spent playing and him indicating he wanted or didn't want things, and me putting into words, "No, don't take your block? Alright!" or whatever when he indicated in any way that he didn't like what I was about to do or did like or want something. Showing him that adults do take his wishes into account.

Then I took C swimming one day. This was something his ABA therapists didn't like to do very much because apparently it's a battle to get him out of the pool, he liked swimming in the deep end even though he wasn't an awesome swimmer, and keeping him in the shallow end could be meltdown inducing—he could swim, but needed an adult right there. Not a battle I wanted to fight, but I'm not a fan of the Adult As God paradigm. I liked swimming and I liked C, so it was a good time.

We did some laps, we (well, C) splashed around in the shallow end, and 15 minutes before we actually had to leave I asked C if he was ready to get out.

"NO!"

Clear as day, emphatic, and with feeling.

Yeah, we didn't get out of the pool for another 10 minutes. C indicated no, he was enjoying himself, he did not want to leave. And he did it in a way that no one could deny—no is an important concept in making one's needs known, and everyone knows what it means.

He used the word NO a whole lot—they made him do a lot of inane things (Touch nose? Really???) and he didn't want to. I don't blame him; touch nose is not exactly a meaningful activity. He started indicating preferred activities and even started helping make a schedule of stuff he'd do during his sessions (or what toys we'd play with and such...interactive toys for demonstrating "I don't want to" or "don't do that" are pretty great).

Then he stopped and started biting again. Being bitten hurts. Biting wasn't getting him what he wanted. "What. Did. You. DO?" was my question to the ABA people.

"Oh, he didn't want to do (some meaningless task) and I hand over handed it."

"...what the hell is wrong with you?" (Insert about 15 minutes of full volume yelling about how it was his body and he had a right to not be touched and he had a right to determine his activities, and she owed him one hell of an apology, and he was going to get that apology. Where C could hear it. And where C's parents could hear it, because they were in the same county).

She thought I was kidding. I wasn't. She quit shortly after—apparently apologizing to a just turned 10 year old was beneath her, or to an autistic kid, or being told to by an autistic adult, I dunno.

And C started saying NO! again. Then we started fixing his book and set up a dynavox, but that's a whole other story....

(A version of this essay previously appeared on timetolisten.blogspot.com on October 27th, 2011.)

Pedagogy Of The Confused

by Zoe Gross

I became politically aware when I learned how to say "I don't understand." This didn't happen until I was 20 years old.

There are some things that are harder for me to understand than others. My confusion peaked in freshman year of college, when my Women's Studies class moved from "101" material into more abstract, jargon-heavy content. Words seemed to fly through the air without being anchored to anything so mundane as a stable definition. At the same time, I realized that what I had been taught in high school about writing thesis statements no longer applied to college: I was going to have to relearn the definition of a thesis. This would have been fine, except for the fact that I didn't understand any of the definitions that people were giving me.

I was filled with shame about this. What kind of college student didn't know what a thesis was? How had an introductory Women's Studies class got so beyond me? Did I really deserve to be at college? So if I had to ask for clarification, I often pretended to "get it" after a cursory explanation, when really I was still confused.

My problem with admitting confusion was that I had internalized the idea that my worth as a student was based on my ability to understand things within the same timeframe that others did. I did not feel entitled to ask for clarification when I was confused, because this would be admitting to having failed in my duty to understand. I wanted to tell the truth about what I was thinking, so that I could learn more thoroughly. But I was afraid of being thought of as unfit to be at college, because I had internalized the idea that good students didn't get as confused as I do.

This semester, we read *Pedagogy of the Oppressed* in my Education class. The author, Paulo Freire, talks about the process through which an oppressed person learns about their oppression, a process he calls "conscientization." I underwent this process in my freshman year, and it happened because I was so very confused. After I started hitting cognitive dead ends in my classes, I got online and started reading. I learned about privilege, ableism, disability rights. I became conscious of my oppression as a disabled person. And I began to see that the ideas about what a student *should* be – the ideas that had caused me so much shame – were not inherent in the universe. They were a product of prejudice.

Becoming politically aware meant that I no longer felt so terrible about not fitting into society's idea of what a student should be. I started to think that perhaps society should widen its idea of a student enough to include me. I started to think that I deserved to understand the material, even if my process was slower than that of some of my classmates. Learning about disability rights has empowered me to be in control of my education, to ask questions without shame, to sometimes try to change my environment instead of always trying to change myself. And I have learned to utter the words "I don't understand," without apology and in a loud, clear voice.

(A version of this essay previously appeared on navigatingcollege.org on October 25th, 2011.)

The Meaning Of Self-Advocacy

by Amanda Baggs

Too often people define self-advocacy in narrow terms. They define it in terms of formal groups like People First or Autism Network International. They define it in terms of the ability to use standard language in a specific set of ways. They define it in terms of a specific method of going through the legal system, or other usual channels, to get specific kinds of things done. These are all valid kinds of self-advocacy, but they set people up to believe that only certain kinds of people could ever become self-advocates.

When one inmate in an institution fights back against the staff in defense of another inmate who is being brutalized, this is self-advocacy. I have only seen this happen once. She was brave and heroic in the genuine senses of the words, and she paid the price for trying to protect me.

When an autistic teen without a standard means of expressive communication suddenly sits down and refuses to do something he's done day after day, this is self-advocacy. When his initial peaceful methods are ignored in favor of restraining him and violently shoving him into a car so that staff can meet their schedules rather than listen to him, his decision to bite the driver is self-advocacy. I was there in the car with him.

When an autistic person who has been told both overtly and otherwise that she has no future and no personhood reacts by attempting in any way possible to attack the place in which she's been imprisoned and the people who keep her there, this is self-advocacy. That was me and too many others I knew.

When inmates of institutions (both traditional and those that masquerade as community), including those who are said to have no communication, devise covert means of maintaining communication and friendship in spite of staff's attempts to stamp it out, this is self-advocacy.

When people generally said to be incapable of communication find ways of making clear what they do and don't want through means other than words, this is self-advocacy.

When inmates and "clients" devise both small and big ways of sabotaging staff's attempts to control our lives, this is self-advocacy.

In the book *First Contact,* Dave Hingsburger describes how people with significant developmental disabilities, normally believed to be incapable of self-advocacy, can and do engage in it:

> Helen is her own self-advocate in that her "self" "advocates" that we adapt the world for how she experiences it. This is self advocacy at the grandest level. Why? Because it is immediately apparent that if Helen's personhood can liberate her—our understanding of the personhood of people with disabilities should do the same. Her statement of joy, of self awareness, shows that people who think that she would be better off dead—are simply bigots who choose not to know her. Helen is a radical person. Her message is about radical acceptance. Her life is radically her own. For those labeled "profoundly retarded," emphasize the word "profound."[1]

Then there's the question of things that get called self-advocacy, but aren't.

When a non-disabled person gets full of ideas about what disabled people should be saying and thinking about our lives, and holds us lockstep in his control while pretending to teach us all these revolutionary ideas, that is not self-advocacy. Nor is it self-advocacy when someone is constantly telling us that our existing methods of advocating for ourselves are wrong, that we need to ask permission to have a voice, and that self-advocacy can only be accomplished once we learn to behave and go through "appropriate" channels. Or when an institution sets up a "self-advocacy group" that it keeps busy doing meaningless work to siphon off the frustrations of inmates and prove to others that they're really about "empowerment." These things often get passed off as self-advocacy, though. Real self-advocacy involves respect and listening to us.

When a disabled person decides to disenfranchise entire categories of disabled people on the basis that they're not as worthy or capable of self-advocacy as *her* kind of disabled people, that is not self-advocacy. When people run around saying "I can make decisions of my own, but 'retarded' people shouldn't," "People with developmental disabilities shouldn't live in institutions, but can you please tell me how to lock up my crazy brother?" or even "It's perfectly natural for people like me to hate ourselves, that's just how we are..." that's more like oppression than self-advocacy.

There's also a common practice of getting a bunch of disabled people together for a recreation program and calling it a self-advocacy activity. Real self-advocacy involves getting the tools for real power— not bite-sized pieces of power, but the real thing—in the hands of disabled people. Too often people in these 'programs' are punished as showing inappropriate behavior if we engage in real self-advocacy.

Self-advocacy doesn't always look good on paper. It doesn't always stay within the sensibilities of people who want everything neat, orderly, pretty, and civil. People who declare a certain category of person to be uniformly incapable of self-advocacy are usually the same people who view that category of people as people who must be controlled rather than listened to. Self-advocacy doesn't mean staff get to pat us on the head, use the right buzzwords, tell us what wonderful little self-advocates we are, and then chastise us or put us on a behavior program when we get angry at them about *their* controlling behavior.

Self-advocacy is fundamentally about *true* equality, respect, and power, and about recognizing and changing the current imbalances in all of those things. Whether it is going through the legal system to close an institution, fighting back physically against intolerable surroundings, talking back to staff, sabotaging the power of staff over the lives of disabled people, being listened to when we communicate in non-standard ways, learning that it's okay to have a voice and make decisions, or passively resisting the dominance of others over our lives, real self-advocacy will always upset the status quo in some way.

No matter how legal and proper it is, self-advocacy won't be comfortable and cushioned. It will not give the people who are used to having power over us a warm fuzzy feeling of helping us, nor will their viewpoints on what we *should* be doing be able to dominate us and speak through us. They will not be able to pretend away the power inequalities between us and live in fairyland where everyone's the same and that's what counts. It will frighten them and force them to examine themselves. This will be true not only for non-disabled people, but to disabled people who are used to feeling superior to other kinds of disabled people.

I was once told by a surprisingly renowned "parent-advocate" that I only have a voice because Gunnar Dybwad gave me one, and that I should sit back and let parents and professionals do all the work towards closing institutions in my state. I beg to differ. Self-advocacy was not born with Gunnar Dybwad, no matter how much of an ally he was. It was born the first time a suspected changeling tried to run away before anyone could kill him. And the first time an inmate of an institution resisted staff power. The first time someone without a standard system of communication devised one of her own and tried to communicate basic things to other people.

Self-advocacy has been and is still often labeled intransigence, non-compliance, treatment resistance, *lack* of motivation, behavior issues, violence, manipulation, game-playing, attention-seeking, bad attitude, bad influence, babbling nonsense, self-injurious behavior, inappropriate behavior, disrespect, disruption of the milieu, catatonic behavior, social withdrawal, delusions, septal rage syndrome, and even seizures or reflex activity. Self-advocates have been tortured, intimidated, locked up, separated from our friends and lovers, and killed for our actions since before any organized movements existed. To say that the parent-advocacy movement or any other group of people *created* our voices is arrogant and shows *real* disrespect for the price many of us have paid for using our voices. We have always had these voices, in many forms. It is others who have shut us out, shut us up, and refused to listen.

(A version of this essay previously appeared on autistics.org in 2005.)

Autism, Speech, and Assistive Technology

by Amanda Baggs

I walked into the autism center at my university, hoping that they would be able to help me with many of the pressing problems in my life at the time—many of which ultimately kept me from being able to attend university as it's currently set up, and still keep me from living without assistance. I carried a keyboard, which I had obtained recently for the purpose of communication, because I often have trouble with speech.

I can't remember if that was the day I spoke or the day I used the keyboard, but I do remember one statement made by the local Autism Expert ™: "Maybe we can help you reduce anxiety so you won't have to rely on your keyboard." That's when any remaining ideas in my mind that this person was a real expert on autism fell apart.

I like my keyboard. I've spent my whole life struggling with speech, and I like to have an alternative means of communication. I often feel more comfortable when I use my keyboard, because it does not involve the painful and complicated process of speech in addition to language. My friends even tell me I'm more spontaneous and expressive when I don't speak. And here was someone, supposed to be an expert in the field of autism (I've since learned what autism "expert" means) telling me that if I reduced "anxiety," I wouldn't have to "rely" on this wonderful device so much.

(As a note: my speech problems have little to do with anxiety. I have problems with speech and with expressive language in general. Some are intermittent, while others are constant. This is different from anxiety, although stress and anxiety certainly don't help any—particularly, I might add, stress that comes from dealing with autism "experts" who want to take away my keyboard.)

I'm reminded here of people who use wheelchairs to get around. Many get upset if you refer to them as "confined" to a wheelchair. To those people, a wheelchair is freedom. And to me, my keyboard means freedom. I don't "rely" on it—I use it so I don't have to rely on my limited speaking abilities.

I'm trying to picture someone who had a condition that made it painful to walk all their life, but who managed to walk places for limited distances but never enjoy it, finally being offered a wheelchair to get around as an adult. They could now go out and it would no longer be a painful chore, but something they could maybe even begin to enjoy. In their place, I would be *glad* to have that new freedom. That's how I feel being offered assistive communications technology (i.e. my keyboard). I can enjoy things I could never fully enjoy before, because of the emphasis on speech. (I even more enjoy, a lot of the time, being in a language-free environment, but so far I have no way of applying that to everyday communication situations.) The point is, I am now *more free* than I was before—I am no longer dependent or reliant on a voice that works sporadically and often painfully. And I *enjoy* that freedom.

And here, again, was someone trying to take this freedom away from me, under the assumption that if I could speak sometimes that I must always be able to speak, and that the only thing that could prevent me from speaking would be anxiety. Not only that, but it assumed that speech must be my goal, that I could not be happy without speaking, that I was comfortable when I did speak. Since I have never been particularly happy speaking, I find it difficult to imagine that concept. But there it is.

Why is speech supposed to be the ultimate goal of so many autism therapies? Because it is ingrained into so many neurotypicals that speech and language are necessary to be whole, alive, and functioning as a human being. I have attended so many psychology and linguistics classes which put forth speech and language as the only way to be a truly thinking being. I must not be a truly thinking being then, according to them, because I don't use language in my head.

(When I point this out, of course, I am told that since I am using language to communicate I am talking nonsense, or else that I am some kind of "exception" who doesn't deserve mention in the class—or in the definition of "thinking being" for that matter.)

So language is extremely valuable to most neurotypicals, and speech in particular. Other modes of communication, when used by autistic people, are still not usually "good enough" for such neurotypicals. An autistic woman making her needs known through ways other than speech, rather than being congratulated on her ingenuity, is worried about by her teachers—because she may not learn any new words if she can already communicate. Autistics successfully using pictures to communicate are also considered "not good enough," and speech and language are emphasized. Autistics using written, typed, or signed language are urged to speak, because speaking is somehow considered "better" (I note this occurs a lot with deaf people too). Autistics who can speak sometimes but not others are urged to speak all the time, and if they have difficulty when they do speak, that is ignored.

In some cases, an autistic person may want to speak. If that's so, then they should be given every opportunity to learn. However, a lot of us have other ways of communicating. With a keyboard to type on, I feel a lot more free than I do talking or being expected to talk when I can't communicate adequately that way. There are other times when I can't use language at all, and I am having a really hard time finding assistive technology to deal with that. But the fact that I am having a hard time finding that technology doesn't mean I shouldn't.

I have a right to communicate in whatever means is possible for me to communicate (within the bounds of not hitting or throwing things at people, although I've often had urges to do that to autism "experts"). And not only do I have that right, but I have the right to *choose* what means of communication is appropriate for me. If I am unable to speak, I should certainly be given other options.

But also (and this is what a lot of people, even those who get that first part, miss) if I am able to speak but it is painful, difficult, and draining, I should also be given and allowed those other options. People have a right not to just be alive, but be able, to paraphrase a famous document, to pursue their own happiness. That is, people have a right to not only have enough assistance to stay alive and function minimally in the world, but to enjoy being alive as well.

I have rarely, if ever, been unhappy directly because of trouble speaking. I have quite often been unhappy because of not having those other options for communication (not being able to communicate can *definitely* be frustrating!), and because of all the assumptions that caused that not to happen for so long. And I am still unhappy to see that the first order of business for "helping" an autistic is so often to attempt to take those options away.

(A version of this essay appeared previously on autistics.org in 2000)

Untitled

by Amanda Baggs

The world is thick with sensation. A blue as dark as night with stars that shine both outside and inside. Pressed on my cheek is fur attached to the face of a cat covered in layers of purpose and understanding. She buries her face in mine and holds it there, her purr vibrating through my body.

My hand flutters. And so does hers, three thousand miles away. Our eyes see each other on the screens of our laptops, but our bones call to each other in a more fundamental way. When I am in pain, she feels it. When she is shutting down from working too much, I feel it. We help each other monitor their own bodies.

But it's more than that. We know each other's emotions. The surface ones. The ones we wish we felt. The ones we hide. And most especially, deep down, the feelings that have no names. The ones so specific to a situation that nobody has ever named them.

In every flick of the hand, wobble of the head, the fine detail of our bodies rocking, we each discern the other's environment. But also their understanding of it, their reactions to it. Not just the sensory components of outer environment. There is also the feel of it, the way the space between everything flows and moves and changes color. Objects are alive to us and interact with us as much as we interact with each other.

We have mapped all these things together so much that we don't need words. Words could never come close, anyway. This all happens at a level below words, below concepts, all the way down close to the experience of the world. And there are so many details, so many forms and sensations, that move through our bodies, shaping our movements, which we are aware of in each other, which translates back to the original perception. This happens without effort or intent. Because this is our language.

This is the language we already spoke fluently before we learned that words existed. When we hadn't discovered that language was more than one more set of sounds, that our bodies were attached to us, that the barrage of sensory information had meaning. We found meaning in other places, in other ways. And even after we learned words, this other language remained our strongest means of relating to the world.

The people I know who speak this language the best, grew up with intermittent language comprehension at the most. Understand I am talking about our experiences deep down. Our apparent level of *expressive* language can vary from none to good. That's on the surface. What's going on beneath the surface is another story.

People have tried to tell me that this whole experience is a compensation for poor comprehension skills. People like to think that when disabled people are unable to do one thing, another skill comes in to compensate. This is why people were so puzzled when blind people's senses of smell were shown to be no more acute than anyone else's.

What I think is really happening is this: In a forest, there are trees that cannot grow because they are under the shade of taller trees with spreading branches. Go somewhere without these taller trees, though, and the smaller ones flourish. They're not there to compensate for a lack of taller trees. They're there because the taller trees had made it impossible for them to live.

Our way of experiencing the world is like that. To understand words and ideas, you have to use thought processes that inhibit these abilities and experiences. But take away those thought processes for long enough, and a person can grow quite good at putting together patterns that are invisible to most people.

People have asked me before to "teach them this language." Some of them have expected it to be like symbolic languages: every movement matches a concept. But it's not, so I wouldn't know where to begin to teach it. It's not even as straightforward as body language. It requires intimate, prolonged knowledge of a way of experiencing the world that most people aren't aware of.

I should also be clear: It's not unique to autistic people, nor is it universal among us. Autistic people are probably the ones most likely to experience it, but I've also encountered it more rarely among people who are epileptic or intellectually disabled. My guess is it requires prolonged periods where understanding of language and concepts is, at most, faintly recognized or intermittent. That seems the formula most likely to create it among autistic people. I've spoken to several autistic people who used to understand it but it faded with learning to understand language. Some didn't mind the tradeoff, others missed it so much that they would throw away everything to get back to it, but can't. There are also people where it is faded with time but not gone completely.

I can't account for who loses it and who keeps it with time, after learning language. My only guess—don't take it as fact—is that it has something to do with those of us whose skills fluctuate a good deal, and those whose skills remain stable. Many whose skills fluctuate seem to do so because we can only spend a certain amount of time understanding language, and then we have to go back to where it is lesser, if not gone. It may also have to do with *how* we relate to receptive language. I don't know the answer.

Also keep in mind that when I say receptive language problems, I am not talking about just having trouble making out words due to auditory processing problems. I'm talking about a state where a person can hear a word perfectly but it's just noise, and same with reading. Because it's at a deeper, conceptual level, where even the ideas behind words don't compute. Or don't compute well. This is why a person's apparent level of expressive language barely matters. There are people who can't speak who understand language perfectly. There are people who can, through mimicry and patterns, speak well enough to fool people, but understand little to none of what they're saying. Or who have to go back to a no-language state often enough that they don't lose the skills that go away when language shows up.

There are also people whose language skills look like they're not very good, in terms of vocabulary size and things like that. But if their minds are stably in language or concept mode, they will not experience this either. This is more about how stable a person's ability to use language and concepts is, as well as how far a person is into the world of language and concepts. Rather than about the size of vocabulary or the kind of grammar.

Autistic people who are stable in language or concepts have formed many of their own communities. While I've participated in these communities, they've never felt quite right. People like me seem to be outnumbered there, although plenty of us eventually find each other and form our own connections. When I read people describing the norms in such communities, or generalizing about autistic people based on these communities, it makes it obvious to me *why* we feel less at home here. Some of the things they usually say about themselves:

For communicating with each other, they prefer language to all other forms of communication. Even if they think in pictures or something, it's still easier for them to translate it into language and communicate with each other that way than to try to deal with body language or something. And even when they think in pictures or something else that isn't words, it's still some form of symbolic, conceptual thought.

They prefer text-based communication on the Internet. There's no body language and tone of voice to figure out, and they don't have to deal with speaking and trying to comprehend speech. The language they prefer is literal. They don't like metaphors, implied meaning, or having to read between the lines. They are extremely logical thinkers, and get uncomfortable or even sometimes contemptuous about anything that lies outside the realm of logic. If their thought deals with patterns at all, it's patterns of ideas, intellectual or mathematical patterns. In communication, persuasion, and many other areas of life, they would rather not deal with things that are emotional. It's confusing and distracting, and they would rather focus on logic and intellect. Their own emotions can feel almost nonexistent or fairly strong, but either way, it's unpleasant to have to factor them in when they are trying to think about the world in other terms. It's also hard to pick up on the emotions of other people. Except, in some cases, each other. And, while many of them don't even think to include this, their abilities tend to be stable from one day to the next, except while experiencing some form of temporary shutdown.

These are generalizations, and they only apply to certain parts of the autistic community. Even people who feel at home in those parts won't always match them all the way. But time and time again, when I see people in Internet autism communities trying to sum up their commonalities, it will be similar to what I just said. And because this is so common, many of them will say things like that when trying to sum up the minds of autistic people in general.

But this is not the only sort of mind autistic people can have. There are many others. And when the others find each other, we figure out our own commonalities. Sometimes we have a few things in common with them, but we will have a lot of traits that are different, even the opposite sometimes. Often the different groups have some overlap with each other, rather than being easily separated. And I want to be clear that when I describe people like me, I am only describing one group out of many who find we don't fit the most common mold.

Our best—and for some people, only—way of thinking is pre-conceptual and pre-verbal. This means it is hard to translate into language. Often impossible. The ways we communicate outside of language are many, and are not always even intended as communication. We may pick up on the meaning of each other's movements. Movements that are in response to certain perceptions. In seeing the pattern of movement, we pick up on the awareness of perception as well. We resonate with each other, and with things in our surroundings, from core to core, rather than based on outsides. One of us may arrange objects so that the pattern the objects form point back to who she is. Someone else will see the objects, and will perceive the pattern and know the other person in a way no words could convey. One person's pattern of walking will alter slightly because she has seen someone else, and the other person's hands will move a little differently because he has seen her see him. And they will each understand the other even though no deliberate communication has happened.

Far from finding that understanding words is easier than understanding tone of voice, many of us find that we understand tone more easily than words. Many such things are a matter of only being able to understand one thing at a time, but the people who only understand the words are the ones more likely to be able to speak of their experience so theirs is the one people hear about. In general, we will find just about *anything* easier than understanding language.

Sometimes we find communicating through text easier because it's less overloading. But we never find it easier to understand. We can pull some extra information from the patterns in between people's words. But it's still not the same amount of information we can get without text. What we get in normal environments is not just the way bodies move and the music of voices, but also the sound of their footfalls, the way their breath comes out, and even their smell. Even when we get things from body language and tone of voice, they're not always the same things most people perceive through it. And we generally do best at understanding people like ourselves.

These days, autistic people are known for a literal use of language. But as far back as 1946, Leo Kanner described some autistic people as using an unusual form of metaphor in order to communicate. Instead of the figures of speech known to most people, autistic people would invent our own, that had to do with experiences specific to each of us. When I was young, for instance, my brother barked at me out of a closet and I got a horrible startled feeling in my stomach. Ever since then, I referred to that feeling as "the dog." Many people like me end up with an entire language of metaphors like that, more comfortable with that kind of language than literal language. This isn't because of being better at abstraction, quite the opposite. Our metaphors deal with connecting one direct experience to another. Some autistic people even find that their own metaphors are similar to each other's. I once encountered a small group of autistic people who discovered they could communicate with each other easily that way. They referred to it as "the autistic language."

If we can deal with logic at all, it is as an uncomfortable, secondary way of thinking. Logic requires conceptual thought. Our native mode of thinking is so pre-conceptual that some of us can't see it as thinking at all. It's a way of directly experiencing things, in a sensory and pre-sensory way. When we find patterns, it is not the abstract patterns of mathematics, but rather a concrete form of patterns based on direct experiences of the world. This experience connected to that experience and the next experience. Not involving ideas at all. Some of us are never able to much enter the realm of ideas and logic. Others of us can enter it for a certain period of time, before having to return to what is normal for us. We can become uncomfortable, or left out altogether, in discussions where logical thinking reigns supreme.

When it comes to emotions, we usually experience them intensely. Far from not being able to pick up on the emotions of others, we pick them up so easily that they overwhelm us. Sometimes we confuse them with our own. Our own emotions can be equally intense.

Our abilities are rarely stable. Especially the abilities that take us out of our familiar realm of pre-conceptual experience, and into the realm of ideas and words. I liken it to climbing a cliff. If our baseline skills are on the ground, we have to climb up the cliff to get to other abilities. So we climb up to be able to talk or understand language, and the moment we get distracted we fall back down to where words don't exist, and have to climb up again, if we can. Because of this, our abilities are constantly shifting around and changing. We can never be sure those abilities will be there when they are needed. Some of us can climb high before we have to go back to the ground. So, temporarily, we may be quite good at something even if it doesn't come naturally. We may also experience something similar with learning. We can learn something, lose it entirely, learn it again, and lose it entirely. Sometimes we may get there, but it's never clear whether learning will be permanent or temporary. To people who are only familiar with the most common ideas about autism, it may be confusing how people with these experiences of the world can still be called autistic. But really people with these experiences of autism have always existed among those who get called autistic. And since autistic people have described our experiences, we've always been among them. But fewer of us can describe our experiences, so fewer people are aware of them. We're out there though. In all of the autistic communities. We find each other even if our experiences are rarely the dominant ones in a given community.

Before I found others, though, things were difficult. I felt as if there was a chasm between me and other people. Other people didn't make it any easier. It felt like everywhere I went, people told me, "You don't exist." In big ways and small. The world of people didn't seem to have a place for me.

It was like this even after I found the autistic community. At first I didn't find people that much like me. Still, I found people more like me than I had before. And I talked to them a lot.

At this time, I lived in a redwood forest. And when I'd had enough of the world of people, I'd turn off the Internet and go outside. My cat, Fey, often followed me out. There were rocks, redwood trees, banana slugs, dirt, mushrooms, and other fungi.

I'd fill my pockets with rocks. Or sit on the ground and stack rocks all over my body. And the rocks would tell me about my own solidity. They'd tell me about being part of mountains. And avalanches and mudslides. And volcanoes. And all the other things rocks know about. A small piece of granite in my hand would tell me about the smell of sun on a granite mountainside.

They told me I was part of the world too. Of the larger world. Many people say the world when they really mean the social world of human beings. The world is so much bigger than that. They told me that even if no human being told me this in my lifetime, that I do have a place in the world. A very small, particular place just for me. They said that everyone has a place like that. And that when I am done with my place in the human world, I will turn into all the animals and fungi and plants and microbes that will likely eat my remains. And then I will have other places in the world entirely. I may yet be a redwood tree when I grow up, just like some rocks turn into sand in the ocean. They made it beautiful, not morbid.

Until now, I've never been able to fully express what all those rocks and stuff did for me. It was a surreal period of time. When I was online or with people, the main message I got was I didn't exist. And even when the people weren't around, their general behavior patterns followed me telling me I was a worthless, unreal waste of space. Then I'd go out to the rocks, in my driveway and elsewhere, and suddenly I had a place in the world and everything made sense.
They didn't tell me all these things in words. They told me through the patterns of what they were and where they'd been and what connections they had to other things. It's hard to translate it into words or ideas, and harder still to translate into the dead,

disconnected world that the mainstream culture wanted me to believe in.

Years later, I began to find people more like me. We learned about ourselves by learning about each other. We found that the reasons we felt separate from the mainstream autistic community were similar, only through beginning to know each other. Other people might not have been able to find much commonality between us, because on the surface we often looked different. But if you looked deep into our perceptions of the world, they were very much akin. The more we began to articulate these similarities, the more people like us came out of the woodwork. And it was like watching something we expected to be two-dimensional, and finding three dimensions instead.

And then something happened that, deep down, I'd expected for years. I met someone so much like me that I almost didn't believe it. But it was real. Communication has always been hard. So hard that it falls out of my grasp many times a day. With her, it's almost effortless. When we both observe the same thing, the same colors and textures flow through our minds. It's unheard of in my life for something like this to be real.

It allows a level of intimacy that I'd never imagined. Not romantic intimacy. But the same kind of intimacy you have with yourself. And the same kind of quiet as being alone. But with another person. We spend most of our life making connections with other people that take so much work even at the basic level. It's nice to have one place where that part's easy. Where we can communicate about things that we can nowhere else, because they require so much background information. Where we can relax and the easy stuff happens without even trying.

A cat jumps onto her lap. His fur is black, but *he* looks like a deep orange, glowing piece of amber, warming everything around him. His head rolls to the side as he flips onto his back in a curl of fuzzy catness. She looks down and her hand wiggles side to side with love and glee. My fingers wiggle back.

Our hands are loud. They are loud because, if you know what to look for, you can read in them everything about us and our surroundings. Some of us wait lifetimes to meet people who speak our language. It's worth the wait.

Run Forest Run: About Movement and Love

by Amanda Forest Vivian

The summer after my freshman year of college I took all these pictures and posted them in the Asperger's LiveJournal community.

I took these pictures because I didn't know what I looked like when I was stimming and I assumed it probably looked scary. As soon as I started taking them, I realized it looked sort of cool, at least in pictures, so I took a lot more.

Before, I didn't have an image of what a person who stimmed could look like. I'm not saying I was raised to feel terrible about stimming because I wasn't really cracked down on by teachers and parents like some people are. But it was sort of similar to how I felt about being queer—I either heard vague negative stuff, or silence.* I saw people on the Internet saying it was okay but I had trouble applying that to my real life.

The next summer, I wrote this piece: Functional Stimming. It was mostly a reaction to anti-stimming attitudes at the school, but I tried to approach the issue of stimming in an objective and accessible way. I took pictures of myself stimming and described how I felt about stimming, and I talked about two people I knew who stimmed, and included pictures of them.

Towards the end, I said:

I don't feel great about the way I stim. I wish I could stim the way Clayton does; it seems so natural and unselfconscious, just an intense expression of his feelings. I feel like I have a stimming habit, like I binge on stimming. It feels like an explosion and I feel worn out afterwards.

I remember other kids making fun of me for shaking my knees back and forth in class and compulsively touching my nose while I was reading. I don't know if that's how my stimming got driven underground. I just very much wish that instead of being this giant, dramatic, embarrassing thing, stimming could just be part of my life...

I just went and walked in circles for a few minutes trying to get my thoughts together. That was really nice. That's the kind of stimming I would like to do--calm. Something that makes my thoughts make more sense instead of ratcheting them up to fever pitch.

One night I got stuck in the city with a headache and some general spaced-out-ness and was really screwed in terms of finding a quick subway train back to Grand Central. Last summer was the first time I really started understanding subways at all, and I'm still not very good. So I ended up riding around a lot and it was really late at night and I remember being really proud because I knew I would eventually get home even though it was hard, but I also was feeling unpleasant in other ways because it was loud and hot and I had a headache. I was thinking about Danny because I was seeing him every day and he loved subways. Thinking about Danny always made me think about passing and stimming, so I started stimming while I was waiting for the subway and it made me feel better.

And I had a horrible year in general and I became much more conscious of times when I needed to flap my hand by my side or scrape my palms along the edges of tables or step my feet around in circles. It was weird because things were so awful and in many ways I felt scared because I was letting go of many standards for being normal that I'd previously held and I think I worried that if I wasn't holding myself in place, I would somehow wake up one morning and be nonverbal or something like that.

At the same time, when I went back and read Functional Stimming, it seemed that all the problems I'd had were a lot better. Stimming had become something wholly neutral or positive. It wasn't always this full-body thing that exploded out of me unconsciously when I was alone, and hyped me up more than I wanted. It was just a tool and a joy.

I'd also started to feel differently about the way I hold myself. I think it's called posturing because when I say I move stiffly I don't mean I *am* stiff, or something, but that I find it nice to stick out my arms and legs and hands.

This is an overdramatic version of what I mean, because I'm doing it on purpose, but you get the idea. It especially affects the way I walk when I'm really at all excited or at all nervous. I just move my legs very stiffly, which probably is hard on my feet or something, but it feels really nice. If I try not to look different, it gets even worse because I'm nervous, and it ends up just being in the legs which are moving really mechanically. (One time Amanda Baggs wrote a post which in part was a description of how she notices ASD people based on how they walk. Some of this explains well what I'm trying to talk about.)

I guess this spring it occurred to me that I'm not the only person in the world to ever hold my hands differently and I started thinking about what I was afraid of looking like. There was obviously something I was freaking out about and trying to avoid but when I thought about it I realized it just looked like the way some people with ID and ASD walk and hold themselves all the time, and it also looked like some people with cerebral palsy. Once I started thinking of it that way, it didn't seem like a bad way to hold myself, because I associated it with other people and not just me being different by myself.

Now instead of trying to walk normally and then occasionally walking really stiffly, and also having these huge full-body stim explosions when I'm by myself, I just walk in a way that is more uneven and "posture"-y and I tend to kind of burst into a run more and sort of have stiff legs and move them around in a jumpy way. Not that I don't jump around on my own sometimes when I'm excited, but it doesn't feel like a huge problem that takes up a lot of energy, it just happens from time to time. And I don't feel bad about holding my hands in a stiff/curled-up way that feels good.

Of course I have criticisms of the camp where I worked this summer because you should always be aware of flaws, but it was in many ways very cool and very different from The School, because we weren't encouraged to think of ourselves as socially separate from and superior to the campers. Staff got involved in campers' interests and senses of humor; we weren't trying to get them to copy us. To the extent that we were trying to do stuff, we were trying to make sure they liked us and had a good time with us.

This was apparent before the campers even got there, just from the tone of our training. I was already feeling pretty happy and safe a few days into orientation, when we were going back to our cabins for a break. I felt excited and as often happens I ended up running for no discernible reason. Another counselor saw me and said, "Run Forrest run!"

I have had people make shitty comments about the way I run, and although this person was being friendly I can still imagine that I might have felt embarrassed and angry to have been "caught" doing something like that. But I guess since Forrest Gump is in fact disabled, even though she probably wasn't trying to make a comment about me looking disabled, I just processed it calmly in my head: "Forrest Gump is disabled and I'm disabled and I reminded someone of Forrest Gump. That makes sense." In the moment it made me feel good.

I also just remember dancing a lot (I had never danced before) and being excited and squealing and posturing and tripping over things because I was running around so much, the whole time I was at camp. It wasn't anything to be ashamed of because I was doing my job properly, and there were lots of awesome people around who also squealed and ran around a lot and flapped and made motorboat noises. There was a moment when I remember being really excited and happy in a really disabled-looking way in front of the whole camp, and I felt sort of transcendent and like I was going to cry. It was a weird sensory experience too, and just in a lot of ways one of the best moments of my life.

One time in seventh grade, I remember walking around with my shoes untied and not caring what other kids said until one girl said, "You look like a boy with your shoes untied." Then I immediately tied my shoes. Since then I've gone through periods of really really wanting to look like a boy, and even though I don't feel that way anymore I generally would find it cool to be told that something about my appearance looks like a boy. I tie my shoes now, because I would probably trip over myself when I start RFRing, but I'd like to think I own the possibility of looking like a boy. And I want to also own the possibility of looking disabled.

This is a pretty nice thing actually. I don't enjoy passing. Just kidding, I love passing. Just kidding, I hate passing. I mean I don't know. I am likely to think people who are visibly disabled have it worse, but I sometimes really wish I was visibly disabled and sometimes I feel like the fact that I'm not is what has caused basically all my anxiety/dissociation problems.

I have a lot of what I think are probably normal issues for women my age--basically, thinking that I'm horrible-looking and combing Facebook for pictures of myself and even if it's just a picture of my arm totally flipping out about how my arm looks horrible. Or maybe I have it on a level that isn't normal. I just look at pictures and think *I'm smiling differently from everyone else in the picture. My face is bigger or smaller than theirs. I'm holding my legs differently. My hands look stiff. No one in the picture looks like they're my friends. I look like I'm just lurking in the background.*

I just engaged in a bunch of this yesterday so I'm certainly not claiming that I feel great about myself now but I think that my feeling shitty about myself has been reduced to a more standard level. I also feel like I have something to move towards the way other people do when I think about how I'd like to look or how I'd like to be. Because I have images of people who look like me.

This is the reason I have trouble identifying as just Autistic instead of developmentally disabled, just because lots of the people who have led to me feeling okay, and feeling like a kind of person instead of just something unclassifiable, have been people with ID and other disabilities. I've talked about this a lot. But I just realized the other day that things are feeling so much better so I wanted to tell you some more.

*I'm sure my parents would take issue with this, especially in terms of queer stuff. I know that most people have it much worse but the thing is that most of the messages I got about queerness and DD were either mildly negative, acted like it didn't exist, or were very long-sufferingly tolerant (like my high school). Which isn't terrible but does make it hard for you to actually form into an adult because you feel uncomfortable/depressed about a lot of the things that you are.

(A version of this essay previously appeared on adeepercountry.blogspot.com on August 27th, 2010.)

342

On Being Articulate

by Julia Bascom

They say I'm articulate.

(I think about all the words that stay locked in my throat, and I give a small and terrified smile and look over their shoulder and into nothing at all.)

I'm really quite lucky I have such a command of language.

(There are maybe five people in the whole wide world I can talk to face-to-face without wanting to die, without having a panic attack, without needing to hurt myself or sleep for hours afterward. Two of them receive speech therapy. None of them obey the usual laws of dialogue. I know that, really, I'm lucky to have anyone at all.)

My verbal agility is a sign of something, they're sure.

(When I'm trapped into a conversation in the kitchen of someone else's home, I stare at the table and see nothing at all, and my throat closes and my ears ring and the world is small and distant and hot and I am agile because adrenaline alters our capabilities.)

I'm really quite social.

(If I am asked *how are you* I will always say fine. If you ask me anything at all I will throw as many words as I can in your general direction. I can have quiet hands but the loudest mouth, I'm very advanced, and for my next trick I'll even ask what's up with you.)

I can answer every question you might ever have.

(Except for *what do you need* or *how do you feel* or *do you want anything* or *is this okay*.)

I can request independently and answer yes-no questions reliably.

(I can request independently because I never make requests, which means independence, which means I must not have to but I could if I did, right? But if you ask me if I need help I will say *no*, and if you ask, as my hands fly around my ears and my shoulders go tight and small, if I'm okay, I will say *yes* because I can't say *no* and if I could it would mean more talking and less space and I will say anything at all to get you to go away until my brain is my own again.)

I am verbose and prosaic in my speech.

(I am as helpless to stay silent when you speak to me as I am to move when I need to do laundry. I freeze, staring at my dirty clothes, and every cognitive break I own clamps down because I *can't*, because there are too many steps, because this has been the Summer Of Laundry Wars and I have *lost*. But there are no steps at all in unhinging my jaw and going somewhere very far away and echoing, echoing, reciting and remixing scripts about Why I'm Not In School and What I Did This Summer and Why We Deserve Human Rights until the tape runs out.)

I have such a good grip on the English language.

(And such a poor grip on reality, going somewhere still and quiet and out of my head while my mouth turns tricks for you.)

———

I'm never told I'm impolite or out of place or off script.

(Bad, too serious, perseverative, disconnected, hateful, boring, too enthusiastic, dogmatic, of course. All of those. And that's just for talking about a show I like, without even stepping on anyone's toes. For being happy, for getting excited about something, for trying to *share*. For saying something that wasn't an answer to a question. But everything's fine, and I'm very polite, I'm very well trained.)

I can say whatever you ask of me.

(I'm very obedient.)

I'm an Acceptable Autistic.

(I never disagree with you to your face, and you'll probably never hear about it because the gore in my stomach when you tell me I must be very high-functioning gets pulled down by the fear of *quiet hands* and *you must not understand* and *I know putting yourself in other people's shoes is hard for you*.)

I'm a Forgettable Autistic.

(As a child, I didn't cry when I broke my wrist, which meant I didn't feel pain. I read about social skills when I was bullied, so I wasn't mistreated. I didn't cry when I was abused, so it wasn't abuse. Now, I tell you it's fine and I walk away, and maybe I sat in a hallway for two hours the other week, unable to remember how to stand, but I can tell you I'm fine so I must be.)

I'm articulate.

(So you don't have to listen.)

Loud Hands: I Speak Up With My Fingers

By Amy Sequenzia

I have loud hands. I must, since I use my hands to communicate. I type what I want to say.

But that's not the only reason why I have loud hands. It is because I finally learned that I cannot be silenced, I will not be silenced.

Being a non-speaking autistic once meant, to me, accepting what people decided I wanted, felt, thought.

It is the way many autistic people are treated. In my case, it got to a point where people said I did not feel pain. After a burning accident, with second-degree burns on my arm, some people decided that I wasn't feeling anything, that I should go on with my day as they had planned it. The same thing happened after I broke my nose. Nobody thought or bothered to ask me how I felt. They silenced my hands, and because my face doesn't always show my emotions, they silenced my voice.

I am autistic. For too long this statement, so real and true, was something I was told to be sorry about. I was expected to be grateful that people pitied me; that they were forgiving of the "weird" ways I behaved; that they would make decisions for me because I did "not understand anything." The word "proud" was not expected to accompany the word "autistic." So I kept my hands quiet.

I use my very loud hands today to say: I am a proud autistic woman.

Loud hands can have many meanings. It has, in my life. It meant, when I was young, to learn how to type. I had not been successful in using sign language. Typing helped me be able to choose my favorite food, my favorite color. It also allowed me to tell my parents things that, up to that point, I could only get out through crying, smiling or screaming.

I had found a voice but it wasn't my voice. My parents believed in me but they were alone. I looked, and still do, very disabled. I also have other disabilities. The things I was typing then were not what I felt. Instead I was trying to apologize for being me. I was accepting the assumptions about myself that were the assumptions of many, if not most, neurotypical people. I was typing what I thought to be the truth about myself. I was ashamed of being autistic, like most people believed autistic kids, and all autistics, should be. I was seen, and saw myself, as a burden and an "unfortunate event."

Because of my other disabilities I was not able to communicate for a long time. I was having too many seizures and spent many days in hospitals. After that I was numb from the medication. Between the terror in my brain and all the medications trials I lost some years of learning how to speak up. I wasn't strong enough. It took a long while for me to relearn too many lost skills. When I started typing again I began to feel like I deserved to be heard.

It has been a long and slow process. My self-esteem has been severely damaged by years of listening to people talking about me in front of me, calling me names, labeling me "severe" and "retarded," even saying I did not have human dignity (I heard about that later, not as it was said).

Despite this sad reality, I would no longer have "quiet hands." It all started with small poems. I was speaking up about my life and some people started to pay attention.

Typing about my life was not easy. Through poems, I began to show how similar in our dreams and expectations of being heard and respected we all are, autistic and neurotypical alike. I will call this phase the second step in my loud hands process. At this time, I also became aware of other autistics who were also speaking up for the right to be respected, the right to be heard. They were, and still are, an inspiration.

I like to think that my coming out with autistic pride helped me gather the support from some neurotypical friends. This is very important to me because I need a lot of help with everything I do. They respect me, understand my difficulties and allow me to be myself. Having these friends' support allows me to continue to type my thoughts. Their help with my safety and general care allows me to focus on speaking out. If I had to focus on things like, for example, eating without making a mess, this would take a lot of energy from me (besides, the cerebral palsy interferes with my coordination). I prefer to use my energy on things I believe are more important to my life, and things that I can try to change and have a greater impact.

But my process wasn't finished. To have really loud hands I needed to speak out and state it clear that I am autistic and proud of it. I had to overcome the anxiety of exposing myself and the echo of old voices in my head, the voices of teachers and "experts" who said so many times that I was nothing.

So I started by typing letters on disabilities advocacy; I went places and challenged people's misconceptions about me; I wrote an essay. The final phase of my process: I now have loud hands.

But being proud of being autistic is not enough to end stereotypes. We are part of a large spectrum and each one of us has very specific challenges. The many labels given to us by neurotypical "experts" make our struggles towards inclusion more difficult.

Autistics with a "high functioning" label might also have hidden disabilities that make others deny the accommodations necessary for them to thrive. They are expected to overcome their autistic related anxieties and fit in, "get over it."

Autistics with the label "low functioning" are not expected to succeed, ever. Unless, maybe, after many years, they can look and act a little more like a "normal" person. They are the "hopeless" ones, the ones who need to be "fixed." Their stories become "tragedies" and their real self, ignored. Most neurotypical people refuse or never think about trying to understand their language or allow them to express themselves. They are segregated, bullied, pitied but never heard, never listened to. There is still very little interest in trying new approaches to address the usually extreme anxiety and sensory issues that are manifested in what is, again, labeled "odd behavior." The favorite approach still is to "fix" the autistic, children and adults. The children might be lucky with a sensible early intervention that values who they are and make sure their abilities are valued too. The adults are usually ignored, isolated from community living or, almost always, treated like children, chastised for their "wrong behavior."

Non-speaking autistics are also labeled "low functioning." That's me. There still is a misconception that if you don't speak you can't understand, think or even hear. People talk about you, not to you; they ask questions not to you, but direct the conversation towards a third person, even when you can communicate through signs or other augmentative communication devices; or they talk to you by yelling, as if a loud voice will make us "understand better."

Despite many non-speaking autistics coming out as self-advocates, there still is great bias and suspicion about their abilities. In some cases, these autistic individuals communicate through facilitated communication (FC) – I am one of them. Because of many years of being labeled "low functioning," "severe," "difficult," and despite a very complete set of guidelines intended to assure the FC user authorship, we are often looked at with suspicion, as frauds. The fact that many have been validated in several studies and others now type independently is conveniently ignored.

Is it because of the way we look? Is it because some of us need breaks to recharge, calm down or just do a little flapping between lines? We still want to be respected as we are, with the whole set of things we do to manage better our responses to outside stimuli. Even though we might have found a way to communicate and show expressive intelligence, we still have to fight for the right to be ourselves.

I personally can tell that it is very frustrating when I am so misunderstood. When I decide to type, it can take days or even weeks for me to finish an essay. Then I have to review it, line by line. I need breaks, my arms get stiff. If I have a bad seizure, I might need more than a day to recover. But sometimes I type quickly and without breaks. Every time, I get very tired from the brainwork, trying to organize thoughts in an intelligible way. And then, when I meet people, I might be completely overwhelmed and unable to type or focus on anything. That's when I most need to do the things I do to be able to focus again. Or I need to be left alone. It is also when I am dismissed as "too severe." It is as if I am only worthy if I behave in a certain way that the neurotypicals find acceptable.

Hidden abilities created the myth of "low functioning" autistics, like hidden disabilities created the myth of "high functioning" autistics. It doesn't really matter to our lives and how we live what label we are given. We still fight misconceptions, from all sides. It seems that the great majority of neurotypicals want us to be more like them, talk like them, and not do things, when we speak, that they don't do when they speak. That's one important reason for the neurodiversity movement. That's why having loud hands is so imperative. We are who we are and we are not ashamed of it.

When I started typing essays and reading articles by other autistic self-advocates, I saw that we all want the same things, no matter where in the spectrum or where in our personal lives we find ourselves. We want to be respected for who we are, autistics that flap, spin, twirl, fidget; autistics that communicate not only by talking but by any other way; we want to be included for the things we can do, the way we can do these things; we want to be supported so we can be ourselves and reach our potential, at our own time and in our own terms.

We have loud hands and we want to be heard.

Accepting MY Normal

by Kimberly Gerry Tucker

Growing up, I never bothered looking at people long enough to see them as anything other than blurry models out of Matisse paintings; jumbled but interesting. I especially hated pictures of relatives hanging on walls. You could never ever avoid their staring eyes. I'd have to dash past them. I also couldn't sit in vinyl chairs, eat mushy things, flush the toilet when I was stressed, step on the black parts of the linoleum, wear noisy "click-clack" shoes or take showers (as opposed to baths). For seven years straight I had the same thing for lunch: One jelly sandwich, Fritos, and pudding hot in the thermos, with milk. I changed things up in high school and for the next few years had one orange, chocolate milk, and a cheese sandwich for lunch. I was proud of myself for it proved I could be flexible and make a change!

I did like the academic side of schooling. But balls would bounce off my face in gym. Not once did I ever consider it as a place to acquire friends. In fact, the others held their hands in front of my face, "Yoo-hoo? Is anyone in there?" There was a girl in my grade school class who would kick me till I was black and blue because I did not speak. She couldn't figure me out, so she lashed out. In addition to Aspergers, I've got a dual diagnosis of selective mutism. This means my oral speech takes a freefall down my throat like a runaway elevator. Every time that girl walked down the aisle by my desk, she kicked my leg, hard. After a while, I began sticking my other leg in the aisle too. You see I wanted both legs to get bruised evenly. I was telling my mother I was clumsy, falling down a lot, falling off my bike. She would never believe I was only falling down on one side.

When I was diagnosed with Aspergers thirteen years ago at the age of 34, I was told by a peer that I would "feel a kinship, a belonging such as I had never known, with others that have Aspergers, and also with even the most severely affected on the autistic spectrum." This statement is true! Long distance communication through snail mail pen pals has been a big part of my life (with other Aspergians). It's also easier than face to face. I came to know a little girl at the age of five (she moved away when she was 12) who had never had oral speech. She knew a few signs, and if you paid attention, she "spoke" in many, many ways; if you listened. She liked to lean back on a slide and look up at trees holding hands, the way I used to do (still do!), with the sun shining through the branches.

My interest in writing started young. My Grandma was hearing impaired. She was a fragile woman with a playful air about her and she always had a sly wink for me. Unfortunately, she could read everyone's lips but mine. I didn't speak up, they said. I didn't enunciate, they said. No matter, because we found our own way to communicate. I found a way to have a voice. I wrote her long sprawling notes in my little kid scrawl and she read every single word silently to herself, answering me aloud afterward.

Last year, when I saw the movie "The King's Speech" I was near tears throughout it, as I could identify with the humility, anger, frustration, embarrassment, sadness and all the other mixed emotions that impaired communication can bring. What's more important to acknowledge however is the perseverance, the strength needed to face every day, the pep talks one gives one's self, the importance of accepting help when one is by nature a true loner.

I admire fluent oral speakers, but I remind myself that they too possess fears and foibles. Speaking is an art. When I was 12, I thought drinking a bottle of vodka would make me a chatty Kathy. It put me in a coma and I nearly died. My attempt to change my natural inclination toward silence nearly silenced me forever. I had to learn to accept my 'biological make-up.' I wanted to sit on a rock in the woods and stare at the lacy tree canopy in its shades of emerald, celery, and pea green...above my head, rather than join the kids in their boisterous and noisy games on the cul de sac. Now I know that that was MY normal, and that's okay. I connect with nature. With paints, with grout when I do mosaics, with cats, dogs, trees! My hands are never still. Maybe my vocal cords have not been used as much as other people's throughout my lifetime, but my hands have been loud! All this time they've been making murals. There's that one I helped paint on the school's concrete wall for the bicentennial in sixth grade. And the one at the day center in 2007, and then there's all those paintings I've sold! That's a form of communication.

Communication connects, soothes, reaches multitudes, teaches, moves, inspires, and more. Anxiety is a cruel slayer of spoken word, of expression. Not having words makes you so vulnerable. But alas! Through the arts of writing and painting, I find expression easiest of all. With autism, people need to listen with their eyes! Look with their ears! There are loud hands all around, busily communicating if your heart listens. Whoever said autistic people don't use body language? Pay attention. I am a student, a mother, a person who has tried to turn my natural strengths (writing, painting, researching, nurturing) into sustaining and rewarding activities. Through the arts the uninterrupted flow of expression is a means to say simply, 'Here I am. I exist.'

By the way, I'm strong enough now to take less crap from people. If someone kicked me, I wouldn't kick back (that would be stooping to their level) but I would definitely find a way to communicate my displeasure!

Moving Forward

Autism Awareness is Not Enough: Here's How to Change the World

By Steve Silberman

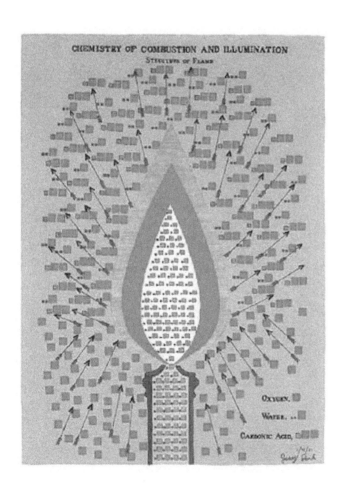

"The Structure of Flame" by autistic artist Jessica Park. Courtesy of Pure Vision Arts: http://purevisionarts.org

In 2007, the United Nations passed a resolution declaring April 2 World Autism Awareness Day — an annual opportunity for fundraising organizations to bring public attention to a condition considered rare just a decade ago.

Now society is coming to understand that the broad spectrum of autism — as it's currently defined, which will change next year with the publication of the DSM-5 – isn't rare after all. In fact, "autism is common," said Thomas Frieden, Director of the U.S. Centers for Disease Control and Prevention, last week in a press conference. The subject of the conference was a new CDC report, based on 2008 data, that raised the official estimate of autism prevalence among children in the United States from 1 in 110 to 1 in 88.

The CDC's announcement brought out the usual range of conflicting responses and disputes about causes and cures. Mark Roithmayr, president of the fundraising organization Autism Speaks, immediately branded the report proof of an "epidemic," though Frieden and other experts were careful to point out that the apparent increase was likely "the result of better detection," rather than a true spike in the population of autistic kids.

That theory is bolstered by two recent studies in South Korea and the United Kingdom, which suggest that autism prevalence has always been much higher than the estimated 1-in-10,000 when the diagnostic criteria were much more narrow and exclusionary. What's changed now is that — in addition to the radical broadening of the spectrum following the introduction of diagnostic subcategories like Asperger's syndrome and PDD-NOS — clinicians, teachers, and parents have gotten much better at recognizing autism, particularly in very young children. That's actually good news, because by identifying a child early, parents can engage the supports, therapies, modes of learning, and assistive technology that can help a kid express the fullest potential of their unique atypical mind.

No matter where you stand on the rising numbers, there is one undeniably shocking thing about them. Once that 1-in-88 kid grows to adulthood, our society offers little to enable him or her to live a healthy, secure, independent, and productive life in their own community. When kids on the spectrum graduate from high school, they and their families are often cut adrift — left to fend for themselves in the face of dwindling social services and even less than the meager level of accommodations available to those with other disabilities.

Meanwhile, the lion's share of the money raised by star-studded "awareness" campaigns goes into researching potential genetic and environmental risk factors — not to improving the quality of life for the millions of autistic adults who are already here, struggling to get by. At the extreme end of the risks they face daily is bullying, abuse, and violence, even in their own homes.

On March 6, a handsome, friendly, 22-year-old athlete in Sunnyvale, California named George Hodgins was shot by his mother Elizabeth, who then turned the gun on herself. The bodies were found by George's father Lester, a Bay Area park ranger. The horrific crime became a *cause célèbre* in the media and the special-needs blogosphere — one that focused primarily on speculation about the kind of suffering that could have driven a mother to such a desperate act. George was posthumously diagnosed in the news as "low functioning and high maintenance," and sometimes his name wasn't even mentioned in the ensuing discussion, as if the young man was a bystander at his own murder.

Vigil for George Hodgins, Sunnyvale CA

In response, an autistic self-advocate in California named Zoe Gross organized a vigil on March 16 for disabled victims of family violence like George. Holding candles aloft under a tent pitched at Sunnyvale City Hall, autistic men and women of all ages — along with parents and allies from the disability-rights community — read the names of those who had been killed, with a poignant eulogy for the disabled victims of the Nazi eugenics campaigns that paved the way for the Holocaust. As drizzling rain fell around the warmly-lit tent, George's former teachers at the Morgan Autism Center shared vivid memories of an energetic boy who loved listening to music and getting in the pool to swim. Instead of painting him as little more than a source of anguish and grief for his mother, who was struggling with her own psychological issues, they recalled him as a sweet, cheerful, engaged, and enthusiastic student who used assistive technology to communicate.

For autistic activists like Gross and Paula C. Durbin-Westby, a professional book indexer and choirmaster at her Episcopal church in Virginia, Autism Awareness Day is not a cause for celebration. In their eyes, the dire messaging designed to frighten wealthy donors into opening their wallets every April 2 — such as the infamous 2009 "I Am Autism" video, which framed the condition as a terminator of marriages that works "faster than pediatric AIDS, cancer, and diabetes combined" — reinforces dangerous negative stereotypes and increases the stigma faced by autistic adults, most of whom don't wake up in the morning yearning for a cure or wishing that their peers on the spectrum had never been born. Instead, members of groups like the Autistic Self-Advocacy Network look forward to an era when their community no longer faces violence at home or discrimination in the workplace, in housing, in education, in the legal system, in health care, and in society at large.

Two years ago, Durbin-Westby proposed that autistic people and their families and friends recast April 2 as an occasion for promoting acceptance and understanding rather than vague "awareness," and reclaim the day as an annual opportunity to celebrate their community's diversity and vitality. "I started Autism Acceptance Day as a corrective to the ubiquitous negative images we see every April," she recalls:

> The first World Autism Awareness Day referred to autism as an 'equal destroyer.' From videos that talk about autism as some sort of soul-sucking, demonic persona, to 150 empty strollers signifying that autism has robbed parents of their toddlers, navigating April for many Autistics has been like walking through a field of (stroller-shaped) land mines. No more! Autism Acceptance Day takes back April and puts it where it belongs — into the hands of Autistic people, supportive family members, friends, and communities.

Durbin-Westby's notion of rebranding April 2 in a more positive and proactive light is catching on with local autism advocacy groups worldwide. The Autism Society of Northern Virginia recently declared April to be Autism Acceptance Month, and other groups are getting onboard via social networks like Facebook and Twitter.

Obviously, even a month of acceptance will not be enough to dramatically improve the lives of people on the spectrum. What could be done to make the world a more comfortable, respectful, and nurturing place for millions of autistic kids and adults — now, starting today?

That's the question I posed to a group of self-advocates, parents, and teachers that included Nick Walker, an autistic aikido master who founded his own dojo in Berkeley; the first openly autistic White House appointee, Ari Ne'eman; Emily Willingham, one of the sharpest science writers in the blogosphere; Lydia Brown, a prolifically articulate and thoughtful 18-year-old self-advocate at Georgetown University; Todd Drezner, director of *Loving Lampposts*, a groundbreaking documentary on autism and neurodiversity from a father's perspective; and the editors of *Thinking Person's Guide to Autism*, which is my personal recommendation for parents to read after their son's or daughter's diagnosis.

The ideas generously offered here — from outlines for education and public-policy reform, to calls for more 24-hour businesses and innovative assistive technology, to persuasive arguments from the trenches for transformations of attitude — are a road map to a more equitable neurodiverse society that will help all 88 out of 88 kids maximize their creative potential.

Lydia Brown

Lydia Brown is an Autistic student at Georgetown University who interns for the Autistic Self Advocacy Network. She blogs at Autistic Hoya.

1. **Accept us**. Autism is a part of who we are. As sure as skin color or sexual orientation, we cannot change being Autistic. Acceptance starts by understanding that we are not broken, defective, or diseased. We do not need to be fixed or cured. There is nothing wrong with us. Yes, autism is a disability, and yes, some Autistic people are very severely disabled. Accepting our autism does not mean ignoring or denying disability; it means accepting us for who we are, as we are.

2. **Respect us**. We are people, fellow human beings. We deserve to be treated with the same respect afforded to our non-Autistic peers. Respect starts by understanding that we are full and complete human beings, with individual personalities, life experiences, goals, and preferences. We deserve an education, access to communication, and a place in society as we become adults. We deserve to live without fear of being abused, manipulated, or hurt. We are not less than.

3. **Support us**. Because we are disabled to varying degrees and in multiple ways, we need support, services, and accommodations to successfully navigate a world not made for us. Supporting us starts by

understanding that we are usually the people who can best define what types of support and services we need, especially once we become adults. Some of us may need services throughout school and/or higher education. Some of us need help with seeking and keeping employment. Some of us need help with living independently or semi-independently, or with activities of daily life. Without appropriate supports, we will not have equal access and opportunity.

4. **Include us**. We deserve equal access and opportunity throughout the community and throughout our lifespans. Inclusion starts by understanding that we are part of the community and deserve to be included in it. As children, we may not be ready immediately for full inclusion, but full inclusion should be the ultimate goal for every Autistic child. Full integration into the community means living outside institutional or segregated settings and working outside a segregated setting. If we need accommodations or support to fully participate in the community, then provide those accommodations. We need to belong.

5. **Listen to us**. Too many conversations about us and issues that affect our lives take place without any of us present. Listening starts by recognizing that we have valid, legitimate, and important things to say about our lives and about the issues that affect us collectively. Like any group of people, we are not homogeneous in opinion or ideology, and this diversity is part of the Autistic community. Yet we must be included in any conversation about us, because decisions made by policymakers, school administrators, and grant reviewers often impact our daily lives and our future outlook. We can speak (or write or sign or type) for ourselves, and it's time to listen.

Shannon and Leo Rosa

Shannon Des Roches Rosa *is the mother of an autistic son and an editor of* Thinking Person's Guide to Autism. *She blogs at* Squidalicious.

1. **Watch movies about real autistic people.** We need to uproot and replace the Rain Man as a cultural stereotype. Most autistics are not savants — and most autistics are not like most other autistics. I recommend Todd Drezner's *Loving Lampposts* as the autism movie that everyone should see; it showcases the wide-ranging and complex abilities of people on the autism spectrum.

2. **Be a role model of autism understanding in everyday life**. Autistic behaviors like flapping and humming may not make sense to strangers, but they almost always have a function for an autistic person. If you see a person like my son behaving quirkily in a public place, it's OK to smile and nod — especially to model that understanding and acceptance for kids. (We will move on if our behaviors become disruptive!)

3. **Welcome us**. Many autistics and autism families feel isolated, even within their extended families and immediate communities. If you aren't sure what we need or how to include us, ask! We would so much

rather be asked — even if we need special arrangements, even if we might have to leave early, even if we have to say no — than never get included at all.

4. **Seek autism-friendly autism education resources**. When looking for autism education resources, ask yourself: Does this agency, book, or website support and respect autistic people and their families? If the answer is "no," then go elsewhere — no matter how well-established, funded, reviewed, or popular the resource is. I direct people to The Autistic Self-Advocacy Network, Rethinking Autism, Wrong Planet, and Thinking Person's Guide to Autism as starting points.

5. **Demand support for autistic adults transitioning out of school**. Autistic people, like anyone else, deserve the best possible quality of life — yet there is no comprehensive infrastructure to support their transition out of school and into the real world; not at my home state of California's level, not at the federal level. The transition can be especially harrowing for autistics who need significant day-to-day support. My son and his peers deserve better.

Carol and Arren Greenburg

Carol Greenburg is an autistic self-advocate, a consultant for families of kids with special needs, and mother of an autistic son.

1. **Respectful autism awareness cards** widely available commercially so I don't have to keep reinventing this wheel for the material I hand people introducing my son or myself. Nothing long-winded or rude, but a teaching moment should not have to start with an apology for autistic behavior.

2. **Whatever your own neurostatus, put yourself on a 30-second pause before you react** to somebody whose public behavior you find off-putting.

3. **Require autism awareness training with the input of autistic self-advocates** for every single educator in the US, not just special ed teachers. I've heard this is done in Japan, why can't other countries follow suit?

4. **More retailer sensitivity toward customers with sensory issues.** It would be nice if the staff in restaurants and stores would show greater willingness to dim lights and turn down music. Sensory seekers like my son can find loud environments and control their personal music volume. Sensory avoiders like me can't go inside many public venues.

Paula C. Durbin-Westby, founder of Autism Acceptance Day

Paula C. Durbin-Westby is an autistic self-advocate who blogs at paulacdurbinwestbyautisticblog.blogspot.com.

1. **Think of autism as a disability and a difference, not a depersonalized "disorder."** When a person has a disability, that person is still a human being. That person with a disability has a body, a mind, interests, dreams, and goals, even if you can't discern them. Only people have rights under the Developmental Disabilities Act and other protective legislation. A disorder can be "combatted," "cured," "prevented," and "eradicated" in any manner (including questionable goals, treatments, or interventions) that researchers and others see fit. A person with a disability has the right to be who they are and to be accepted for who they are, without the need for a "fix" or "cure."

2. **Realize that not all behavior is intentional communication.** What we call "behavior" is what can be observed. Many behaviors cannot be observed; they are internal, and are as important as any outward activity. Do not assume you know the reason for or function of a behavior, especially if you are making the assumption based on why you think a non-autistic person would be doing that same behavior. Behaviors are tied to ways of navigating the world. Where behaviors are simply "odd" or different, there is no need to expend energy on doing anything other than supporting the person and working to end discrimination based on harmless behavioral characteristics. Education should focus on the strengths of Autistic people, not on making us "indistinguishable from our peers." By the way, our peers are other Autistic people.

3. **Augmentative and alternative communication for all!** Communication takes more than one person. A communication device is not communication. Research priorities and dollars should refocus on communication needs. A variety of communication systems may be needed, even for a single individual, depending on circumstances. AAC can benefit Autistics who do have speaking capability as well as those who do not use speech to communicate.

4. **Eliminate the use of restraints and aversives**. Not every "challenging behavior" needs a take-down response. Consult Autistic adults, who have insights into strategies that can be used to replace the dangerous and trauma-inducing use of these aggressive techniques. Do not automatically restrain people who are self-injuring — use pillows or other soft objects to deflect self-injurious movements. Learn de-escalation techniques. Do not automatically restrain someone who is kicking a piece of furniture. Let them calm down. Help them calm down. Find something for them to kick that is cheaper or less concerning. Restraint is meeting aggression with aggression. What does it teach? Think about that.

5. **Teach children to respect and accept differences, including disability**. This suggestion has ramifications far beyond the disability world. A general acceptance of others who are different from us is a necessity in a world that is becoming more globalized. Disabilities are no exception. Pretending to have a disability for a day is not enough. Children without disabilities need to meet and engage with those who have disabilities, with someone acting as a facilitator of those encounters where necessary. Children (and all people) need to learn that people with disabilities are both very different from and very similar to them. Find common ground as well as nurturing and appreciating differences, even differences that are considered "difficult."

Emily Willingham

Emily Willingham is a writer, scientist, partner, and parent. She manages the Double X Science site and blogs at The Biology Files. *"Life is easy to chronicle but bewildering to practice."* — E.M. Forster, novelist

1. **Practice perspective taking**. It's ironic that autistic people are expected to have trouble with insight into others when so many people have trouble with insight into autistics. Everyone should try on the other person's shoes and walk around in them for a while.

2. **Practice not judging**. It's hard not to judge. We make countless judgments big and small, every day. But before you judge another person, remind yourself that behavior is communication. Rather than judging, ask yourself, "What is that person's behavior saying that will help me understand better?"

3. **Practice compassion**. It's a corollary to the first two, and it's not easy. That's why it takes practice.

4. **Practice being yourself**. The best possible way to understand how hard anyone's personal battles can be is to understand how much you fight yours every day. What are your obstacles to just being You? Everyone has them. Behind every social facade is the deeper reality of who we are as individuals. If you find yourself in there and accept that person, you may find it more natural to accept the deeper reality of others, as well.

5. **Practice courage**. It takes courage to do any of these things. Being the one who takes perspective, works not to judge, practices compassion, and embraces personal individuality is a courageous act that can separate you from social norms and make you stand out, sometimes uncomfortably. Autistic people do it every day, purposely or otherwise. You can, too. Bring your courage, and acceptance easily follows.

Kassiane Sibley

Kassiane Sibley is an autistic activist and gymnastics coach. She blogs at Time to Listen.

1. **Stop killing us, and stop glorifying our killers**. Every time an autistic person is murdered, people fall over themselves to feel sorry for the killer. That's pretty terrifying if, like me, you are actually autistic right this minute. Stop. You are not supposed to side with killers, empathy does not work that way.

2. **24-hour EVERYTHING**. A lot of us hate crowds. A lot of us are stuck with mass transit. A lot of us are just not daytime people. If things were open 24 hours, not only would we create jobs, but those of us who are at our worst during normal business hours would have the energy to get way more done for ourselves.

3. **Turn the volume and the lights down**. Just in general. Nothing needs to be as loud or as bright as it is. Save some energy — and save everyone's processing energy, not just mine.

4. **Listen and look more for substance than style**. Sometimes it's hard enough to make what we mean clear, especially if we struggle

with language. Please take what I say as what I meant, rather than deciding that I am mean or rude or inconsiderate or whatever for not wrapping it in bubble wrap first. What I said is far more important to comprehension than how I said it — I promise.

5. **Tolerance and awareness are nowhere near enough. Teach acceptance, early and often.** Little kids take their cues from the adults around them, mostly. Teach them, from a very young age, that some people are not like them and this is AWESOME. Tolerance says, "Well, I have to put up with you." Awareness says, "I know you have a problem and are working earnestly to fix it." Acceptance says, "You are amazing because you are you, and not despite your differences, but because of them." That rocks. Make that the norm.

Jennifer Myers and her son Jack

Jennifer Byde Myers is co-founder of Thinking Person's Guide to Autism *and director of the Myers-Rosa Foundation.*

1. **Change the word "talk" to "communicate."** When my son was younger, therapists just wanted him to talk. They still call it speech therapy. Talking is overrated. We don't care if he "talks," we want him to be able to communicate his needs effectively so he can lead the life he wants to live, not the one we think he wants to live.

2. **Invest in education**. Train the aides that work with people with autism. Fund the supports that are federally mandated in the schools yet remain unfunded by the feds. And invest in the education of every American so we can have a future with people who are knowledgeable and able to teach, provide professional services and lead our country in a way that encourages inclusion and equality.

3. **Stop electing bigots**. If a political entity is willing to say that gays, or single mothers, or people of color are less valuable to society, or are less worthy to receive respect and fair treatment under the law, how likely is it that a minority that is as diverse as the autism community will receive respect and needed services. Vote for the changes you want to see.

4. **Put fences around parks, or at least part of the park**. It's not that I am too lazy to keep an eye on my son, but really, if I mess up for even a minute, he could end up as a hood ornament. I do not take him to parks that don't have at least three sides blocked from traffic, and consequently he has missed out on a lot of parks. Recreation should be enjoyable for everyone on the outing, and safety is paramount.

5. **Create an Autism Corps, like the Peace Corps**. Train a generation of young men and women to work with autistics who need support with daily living skills like grocery shopping, or getting to work. Give parents and caretakers respite by providing free or very reduced rate childcare. A trained support network could provide an infrastructure for autistics to lead more independent and fulfilling lives.

Stephen Shore and Leo Rosa

Stephen Shore *is an autistic self advocate, author of* Beyond the Wall *and* Understanding Autism for Dummies, *and professor at Adelphi University.*

1. **Move the conversation from tolerance and acceptance of individuals on the autism spectrum to understanding and appreciation**. ("Tolerance and acceptance" give a sense of *putting up with* something, whereas "understanding and appreciation" suggests valuing the contributions that individuals with autism bring to humanity.)

2. **Know that if everyone were the same, the world would be a very boring place**.

3. **Understand that often the most important thing to a person on the autism spectrum about employment** is making sure the job is done right. (Suggests that quality of workmanship is often the primary motivator of completing a task.)

4. **Recognize that autism *is***. (Autism is neither good nor bad. It just exists, and it's up to us to make as much good from the condition as possible).

5. **Empower others to lead fulfilling and productive lives**. That's the greatest gift we can give to an individual on the autism spectrum, and to the rest of humanity. (That way, the individual on the autism spectrum will be fulfilled and productive, and society will receive the great benefits of that person reaching their highest potential.)

Garret Westlake

Garret Westlake is the Director of the Disability Resource Center at Arizona State University's Polytechnic campus. He is also the CEO and Founder of STEM Force Technology, a company that provides coaching and employment services for individuals on the autism spectrum.

1. **Hire someone with autism**. You don't need to look very far to find exceptional people with exceptional talents.

2. **Learn from someone with autism**. You might learn a new skill, a joke, or a fact, but you will definitely gain perspective, understanding, and appreciation for how someone else sees the world.

3. **Abolish average education**. Why do we strive for broad mediocrity in education? Encourage outliers. Create access and accountability in education for student strengths — not weaknesses.

4. **Understand autism as diversity**. If we still struggle with issues of race, gender, and sexual identity, where are we with accepting disability? Disability is diversity too.

5. **Laugh**. Everyone needs more of it. We can all do it together.

Ari Ne'eman

Ari Ne'eman *is the President and co-founder of the Autistic Self Advocacy Network. He currently serves as Policy & Program Evaluation Committee Chair for the National Council on Disability.*

It has often been said that the United States lacks a national disability policy — instead, we have dozens of different disability policies, each developed for a different part and level of government and often conflicting with each other. The story of US disability policy is one of the slow development of different laws, programs and infrastructures, many of which still operate based on outdated and obsolete assumptions regarding the degree to which disabled Americans could be included in society. This reality significantly hinders the full realization of the civil and human rights of Autistic people and other people with disabilities. What would a national disability policy look like if it was aligned with the goals of the Americans with Disabilities Act?

1. **Values-Based Policymaking:** Research and science have always played a large role in disability policymaking, in large part due to a history of disability being viewed mainly as a public health issue. But while science can tell us much about how the world is, it falls to values to tell us how the world should be. When assessing the quality of different forms of service-provision, we should think about both efficacy and ethics.

2. **De-Medicalization:** Over the course of the last forty years, the de-institutionalization movement has made tremendous progress in closing large residential facilities which segregated disabled people from society, shifting funds into more individualized supports in local communities. Although this is an important first step, ensuring that people with disabilities have access to choice and self-determination requires more than just moving from larger to smaller housing. It also requires a real sea change in how we approach disability services. We require a shift from the expectations of institutional life — which presumes a hospital environment, in which medical experts make decisions about patients — to the expectations of home life — where staff providing support to a person with a disability are working for the person and the pursuit of their goals and judgment.

3. **Equal Protection of Law:** Many of the worst injustices faced by people with disabilities would be considered illegal and the source of considerable public outrage were they to occur to a non-disabled person. Federal law allows for people with disabilities to be paid less

than minimum wage. States with bans on corporal punishment nonetheless allow the use of "aversive interventions" — the inflicting of pain as a means of behavior modification for children and adults with disabilities — despite the fact that the two are indistinguishable from each other. When disabled people are killed by family members and caregivers, public sympathy is often with the killer, who will frequently receive a more lenient sentence than if they had murdered a non-disabled person. Only when labor laws, protections from abuse and torture, and other relevant legal rights are applied equally for people with and without disabilities will we move forward as a society.

4. **High Expectations:** Much of our disability policy is predicated on low expectations that can often become self-fulfilling prophecies. Students with disabilities who take the alternative assessment rather than the standard means of assessing student achievement are more likely to be segregated from the general education classroom, less likely to have received any literacy instruction, and frequently lack access to Augmentative and Alternative Communication supports that could help them better perform at their full potential. People on Social Security's two disability income support programs (Supplemental Security Income and Social Security Disability Insurance) face a maze of bureaucratic regulations that often discourage or prevent attempts to return to the workforce or to save in order to develop assets. Changing the expectations our society has for people with disabilities was one of the main goals of the ADA. Now it is past time for the rest of our country's disability policy infrastructure to catch up.

5. **Disability as Diversity:** There is a long history of both the public and private sector working to try to encourage diversity in education, the workforce and elsewhere in society. Unfortunately, people with disabilities are often excluded from these efforts. For example, much of the recent push on the part of the federal government to close disparities in health care outcomes on the basis of race, ethnicity, gender, and sexual orientation excluded people with disabilities as yet another important under-served population. Many private sector affirmative action programs forget to or deliberately do not include

disability, a failure that exists in higher education as well. Fortunately, some progress has been made in this sector, with the Obama Administration making the employment of people with disabilities within the federal workforce and among federal contractors a major priority. More work needs to be done to ensure that whenever we talk about addressing the needs of underserved populations or creating more diverse classrooms and workplaces, people with disabilities are not left out.

Liz Ditz and her grandson

Liz Ditz blogs at I Speak of Dreams.

1. **Universal acceptance of the idea that "human abilities are a constellation, not a linear spectrum."** Universal acceptance of the big idea that different brains come with different strengths and weaknesses, and societies need all kinds of minds to be robustly

healthy. This is big-picture neurodiversity, embracing not only autism, but ADHD and other neurodivergencies now called dyslexia, dyscalculia, and so on.

2. **Radical restructuring of the American pre-K-12 model along these lines**: **Make early childhood education a highly-valued, trained, and compensated profession** (right now, early-childhood teachers make poverty wages and have little training in elements of recognizing neurodiversity and providing appropriate supports to kids who struggle.)

3. **Make high-quality universal early education available to all**, including specialized services and remediation, without having to qualify by testing. We know that there are areas in which autistic people (and other neurodiverse people) struggle, and these areas are often evident in very early childhood. But getting help now requires going through testing, evaluation, and qualifying and continuing to qualify for "services." If we had a highly trained cadre of early childhood educators, some if not all of the helpful services would be available as a matter of course to students who needed them.

4. **Make pre-K-8 teaching a highly valued, highly trained, and highly compensated profession**, adopting some proven elements of the Finnish model:
- All teachers have undergraduate degrees in a field of study other than education.
- All teachers have graduate degrees in education.
- Entry into teacher-training graduate programs is highly selective.
- Teachers have several years of post-graduate mentoring with gradually increasing responsibility (as do physicians, with the progression of medical school > internship > residency before independent practice model.) As a result, teaching is a high-status and high-prestige profession, with a great deal of expertise gathered over years, and with continued professional development over time.

5. Eliminate the "wait to fail" and medical model for children experiencing school difficulties. Step in when pupils start to lag behind.

> A factor contributing to the success of the Finnish system is the use of early and powerful intervention when a student begins to fall behind. Frequent diagnostic testing ('formative testing') at early stages reveals students who need extra help, and the Finns provide it intensively, with one special-needs teacher for every seven special-needs students in some schools. The McKinsey report points out that, in Finland, about a third of students receive remediation. — Patrick Basset, "The Finnish Model"

6. Replace the "medical model" with the "diversity model." It turns out that all kids can learn, given good teachers, early and intensive intervention, and a supportive school and peer culture. U.S. schools need to move from a medical model (learning disabilities) to a diversity model (learning differences), and re-orient themselves to identify, value, and use a student's strengths as "workarounds" and palliatives to weaknesses.

7. Focus on equity rather than competition.

> Since the 1980s, the main driver of Finnish education policy has been the idea that every child should have exactly the same opportunity to learn, regardless of family background, income, or geographic location. Education has been seen first and foremost not as a way to produce star performers, but as an instrument to even out social inequality. In the Finnish view, as Sahlberg describes it, this means that schools should be healthy, safe environments for children. This starts with the basics. Finland offers all pupils free school meals, easy access to health care, psychological counseling, and individualized

student guidance. — Anu Partanenen, What Americans Keep Ignoring about Finland's School Success, *The Atlantic*

Todd and Sam Drezner

Todd Drezner *is the father of an autistic son and director of* Loving Lampposts: Living Autistic.

1. **Anyone who asks "Where are all of the autistic adults?"** must make a donation to the Autistic Self Advocacy Network.

2. **We should no longer describe autistic people as "high functioning" or "low functioning."** Supreme Court Justice Potter Stewart famously defined pornography by saying "I know it when I see it," and many of us feel the same way about defining "low functioning" and "high functioning." But our instant definitions don't hold up under scrutiny.

3. **Every major autism organization in the country (and every minor one for that matter) should have at least three autistic people** on its board.

4. **Parents who receive a new autism diagnosis for their child should immediately be issued a copy of Jim Sinclair's "Don't**

Mourn For Us" and a list of resources to help them. These should include websites like *The Thinking Person's Guide to Autism,* blogs by autistic adults such as *Autistic Hoya*, and blogs by parents of autistic children like *We Go With Him* and *Mom-NOS.* Should there be additional room on the list, it might also include a few resources to avoid.

5. **Fox should immediately cancel "Touch."**

Nick Walker, Sensei

Nick Walker is an autistic educator, author, psychologist, activist, parent, and martial arts master. He holds an M.A. in Somatic Psychology from California Institute of Integral Studies, where he currently teaches in the Interdisciplinary Studies program. He is founder and senior instructor of Aikido Shusekai, an aikido dojo in Berkeley, California.

1. **De-pathologize autism and autistic people**. Autism is a natural form of human neurodiversity. Labeling it as a "mental disorder" or a "disease" has no scientific basis, has no benefit for autistic people or their families, and leads inevitably to stigmatization, shame, and marginalization. Blind people, Deaf people, and many other disabled people get the services and accommodations they need without being labeled as having mental disorders. We don't have to call autism a disorder or a disease to acknowledge that it's a disability that can

require accommodations. Stop worrying about the latest changes to the DSM criteria, and just remove autism from the DSM entirely, like homosexuality was rightly removed years ago.

2. **Use the language of diversity, not the language of pathology**. Language matters. The language that is used in talking about autism and autistic people affects how autistic people are perceived — by themselves, by others, by society – and thus how they are treated. In an autistic-friendly world, anyone speaking of autistics would observe the same linguistic conventions that civilized, non-bigoted people observe when speaking of any other social minority group (e.g., African-Americans or gays). You wouldn't say that an African-American "has negroism" or "suffers from blackness," so don't speak of an autistic person as "having" or "suffering from" autism.

3. **Forget "normal."** Recognize that when it comes to human diversity — including the diversity of minds — "normal" is a highly subjective, culturally-constructed fiction. Recognize that there is no "normal" mind, and that conformity to the local conception of "normal" is in no way synonymous with health, well-being, or personal fulfillment – and is, in fact, often in direct conflict with those things. A healthy, thriving autistic person looks very different from a healthy, thriving non-autistic person. In nurturing the development of autistic individuals, the goal of parents, educators, therapists, etc. should be to produce healthy, thriving, autistic people, rather than autistic people trained to stifle their true selves in order to pass as "normal."

4. **Equal protection under the law, broadly interpreted and strongly enforced**. Recognize autistic people as a social minority group, grant them the same legal protections that are (or should be) extended to ethnic minorities, interpret those protections as broadly as possible, and rigorously enforce them. When an autistic person is abused for acting autistic, prosecute it as a hate crime. Anytime an ABA "therapist" grabs an autistic child's hands to stop her from stimming, prosecute it as criminal assault and as a hate crime. Individuals and organizations that speak of autism as a "disease" or "tragedy," and talk

of "curing" it, should be prosecuted for hate speech and incitement to violence, just as if they were advocating a "Final Solution to the Jewish Problem." Anyone involved in seeking or implementing prenatal tests for autism or any other sort of prenatal prevention of autism should be prosecuted in international court under the Genocide Convention, which classifies as genocide any attempt to prevent births within a targeted group.

5. **Work for global peace and economic justice**. Many non-autistic parents worry that if they don't subject their autistic kids to extensive (and expensive) "treatments" to bring them closer to "normal," the kids will never be able to take care of their own basic survival needs, and will end up in awful institutions or on the streets. This is an entirely legitimate concern. But the reason it's a concern is that we live in a world in which the forces of global capitalism have replaced the true spirit of community with an artificial sense of competition, isolation, and "every man for himself," and in which all but the most wealthy are kept in a constant condition of anxiety and fear of scarcity. This is not the natural state of humanity, and not the way the world has to be. Every disabled person in the U.S. could be supported for life on a fraction of the money that our government spends killing people in the Middle East each year – to say nothing of the funds that would be available if we made giant corporations and the wealthiest 1% of Americans pay their fair share of taxes. Instead of working so hard to change autistic people in the name of helping them survive in a cruel world, why not work to make the world less cruel?

Julia Bascom

Julia Bascom is an autistic self-advocate who blogs at Just Stimming.

Obviously a lot more than these five things needs to be changed — but without these five, the rest won't matter.

1. **Stop killing us**.
2. **Stop abusing us**.
3. **Start recognizing our communication**.
4. **Slow down. Value us**.
5. **Stop killing us**.

Rachel Cohen-Rottenberg

Rachel Cohen-Rottenberg *is a wife, mother, writer, and artist on the autism spectrum. She blogs at* Journeys with Autism *and edits and publishes the site* Autism and Empathy.

1. **Understand that there are many ways to communicate, and that one is not better than another**. I can't read nonverbal signals. I have auditory delays. I need a little extra time to find the words. Sometimes, my words go up over mountains and down through valleys before I know that I've made myself clear. It's not going to change, and my inability to change should not mean social exclusion. Please remember that I have the same need for connection and inclusion as you do.

2. **Slow down when you speak**. I need time to process what I hear and to come up with a proper response. Just as an able-bodied person should give space to someone attempting to board a bus in a wheelchair, or a hearing person should take a moment to write back and forth with a Deaf person ordering food in a restaurant, so a non-autistic person should take a moment to listen to and to communicate with an autistic person.

3. **Remember that talking with a disabled person is not an heroic act**. There is absolutely nothing required in the way of superhuman patience to communicate with a person with a disability, and stopping to listen to someone with atypical communication, far from being a charitable act, is an act of bringing a fellow human being into human community. Social inclusion and interaction, when someone desires them, are basic human rights that no disabled person should have to request, and that no able-bodied person with an ounce of ethical understanding should refuse.

4. **Go outside your comfort zone**. However uncomfortable, awkward, or annoying it may feel to deal with someone who puts out unexpected nonverbal signals (or none at all), or who speaks in an atypical manner (or not at all), it doesn't hold a candle to how excruciating it is to go through the world isolated because people just feel too uncomfortable, awkward, or annoyed to deal with you. The discomfort, awkwardness, and annoyance of able-bodied people may only last a minute, or a half hour, or an hour, and then they go back to their regularly scheduled lives. Please imagine how it feels to keep meeting up with a world full of people who turn away, every day, because their discomfort trumps our longing.

5. **Put yourself in our shoes**. It is vital that able-bodied people consider how soul-wearying it is to keep trying until one finds those people who simply accept the awkwardness — my awkwardness, their awkwardness, our awkwardness — and make a connection. It hurts the heart to keep going out and trying. Ask yourself: What is keeping you from extending a word, a listen, a desire for connection to us? And

how does your failure to use your social skills to bring other human beings into community translate into a social disability located in autistic people, rather than in the able-bodied world?

(A version of this essay appeared previously on http://blogs.plos.org/neurotribes on April 2nd, 2012.)

To My Beloved Autistic Community On Autism Acceptance Day 2012

by Paula C. Durbin-Westby

It's the beginning of Autism Acceptance Month. (Autism Acceptance Day is officially April 2.)

Acceptance means accepting yourself as you are, even in the face of persistent attempts throughout your life to get you to be what you are not. Especially in the face of persistent attempts throughout your life to get you to be what you are not. The best you can be is Autistic. Let me explain. "The best you can be is Autistic" means that you are at your best when you are being fully who you are, able to express yourself and move through the world in ways that are right for you, comfortable for your body. "The best you can be is Autistic" does not imply impairments, "less than," "can only do so much." On the contrary, it means that you are who you are—your pervasive Autistic self (which actually includes those parts that observers might think are "typical" just because they can't see anything that looks unusual to them), and that encompasses *all* of who you are, not just the parts that have been "permitted," and not just the stuff that the DSM of the moment says are your deficits.

You have the right, *or should*, to grow in ways that are good for you, that *you* think are good for you. You have the right to make changes in your life that *you* think are the correct ones for you. If stimming helps you get through the day, you have the right to do it. If making eye contact is a goal of yours, go for it! *You get to choose.* When others choose for you (in the case of children or in some support roles) let it be not in the vain attempt to "normalize" you, but to help you be your best Autistic self. This is no different (speaking in my parental role) from helping *any* child learn and grow to be the best person possible. This is no different (speaking as an Autistic adult and former Autistic child) from learning at a pace that is both challenging and not way outside the "envelope" of what works for you.

Autism Acceptance Day is for Autistic people reading this blog, Autistic people who can't read this blog, Autistic people who will never read this blog but whose lives might be impacted by those around them learning to embrace and cherish *all* of who they are. Autism Acceptance Day is not limited to acceptance for the "high end" (whatever that is) of the spectrum. Autism Acceptance Day is for the Autistic children in the JRC (and let's not forget other children who are there as well). Autism Acceptance Day is for the Autistic adults (and others with disabilities) in institutions and for their family members who are working for the change that will allow them to live in their communities with appropriate supports. Since it always gets brought up, Autism Acceptance Day is for adults who wear diapers, don't speak, and smear feces. Autism Acceptance Day is for the children who get put into restraint and seclusion when school should be safe. Autism Acceptance Day is for the kids who get bullied, and it's for the toddlers whose parents are already trying to prevent them from showing any Autistic characteristics. Autism Acceptance Day is for kids who spend 25-40 hours a week doing ABA instead of getting some time off to be *kids.* Autism Acceptance Day is even for Autistics who don't want to be Autistic (they need feel no pressure to celebrate the day!)

Autism Acceptance Day is for the Autistic activists who work hard to bring a gleam of understanding to beleaguered parents who have heard one too many versions of the "horrible news" story. Autism Acceptance Day is for Autistic parents who are raising our children (Autistic or not) in the face of other people's doubts and our challenges. Autism Acceptance Day is for our non-autistic allies, remembering that we and we alone get to determine who our allies are, who support our right to be the Autistic people we actually are and always will be. Autism Acceptance Day is for non-autistic parents who try to understand their children, even if they don't really, and strive to make the world a better, accepting, place for them.

Autism Acceptance Day is for Autistic children, and Autistic adults, who might be: sad, afraid, confused, worried, anxious, happy, ecstatic, joyous, and every other condition that is part and parcel of the life and world of any human being.

Happy Autism Acceptance Day!

(A version of this essay appeared previously on autismacceptanceday.blogspot.com on March 31st, 2012.)

What I Want To Say To Fellow Autistics

by Kaijaii Gomez Wick

There is so much I want to say. I want to communicate with you. I want to know the way you smile when you drink lemonade made from powder, and your favorite episode of *Supernatural*, and your favorite gifs. I want to see what you look like when someone compliments you, blushing. I want to know you, not the bullshit small talky kind of way, the way that makes me feel I'm touching your soul. I want to meet you on the street and flash secret glances and let our gazes cross for an intimate second. I want to go somewhere with you that you like, a movie theater on a mid-Tuesday with scant arcade players, and I want to stuff my ears with napkins alongside you and laugh at the ketchup-for-blood drama. I want you to know that I kind of love you and I really just want to meet you.

I want to tell you this right now, right here, so even if we never meet I can touch your heart and sew together crushed muscle if you want my help.

It's okay to be wrong.

It's okay to not understand.

It's okay to be confused.

It's okay to not be able to do normal or basic or simple things.

It's okay to be messy and complicated and difficult.

It's okay to not have everything figured out.

It's okay to get things wrong and fuck up.

It's okay to be mad at yourself and not be perfectly self-loving.

It's okay to be prickly and bitter and sharp at the edges others shattered into you.

It's okay to be passive and not be able to say yes or no because even a question mark is an order.

It's okay to have bad memories and freak out and panic.

It's okay to fail.

It's okay. Maybe we'll be lunching somewhere and playfully debating the correct pronunciation of 'ether' and maybe I'll be cooking something odd but delicious (and odd just means something that hasn't been done to death anyhoo) and we'll know it's okay. Because we'll be good enough and know we're good enough, and

you

are

good

enough.

Okay?

Moving Forward: What's Next For The Loud Hands Project

by Julia Bascom

The Loud Hands Project is a transmedia project by and for autistic people, dedicated to the radical notion that autistic people have things to say.

Transmedia means that we embrace multiple media platforms and forms of communication in our various component projects—web-based, text-based, video-based, and more. The Loud Hands Project is an ambitious endeavor with a broad scope, recognizing that there are many different facets, components, and ways to fulfill our very specific focus on autistic people, speaking.

What Does The Loud Hands Project Do?

The Loud Hands Project is a constantly expanding directory of resources, films, transmedia publications, and writings on and for:

- autism acceptance
- disability pride
- history of the autistic and disability rights movements and communities
- neurodiversity
- inclusion & self-advocacy

- survivors of anti-autistic bullying and abuse

and is actively engaged in the creation, maintenance, and recognition of autistic culture and resilience. The Loud Hands Project supports resilience among autistic people by creating and supporting specific grassroots and creative autistic culture, anti-bullying, and disability pride programs by and for the autistic community. Some of the component projects the Loud Hands Project is currently developing include:

- Loudhandsproject.com
- Videos made in conjunction with Alternative Assessment production company
- "Welcome to the autistic community" materials for the newly diagnosed
- Future anthologies on a variety of topics
- and more!

Loudhandsproject.com

The Loud Hands Project website serves as a library and celebration of Autistic history, culture, and community. To this end, it offers:

- A virtual library of critical documents in Autistic culture and history
- An interactive, introductory guide to neurodiversity
- An exciting new feature known as *Community Conversations*, to be discussed below
- A directory to other cross-disability history resources online

The virtual library of Autistic culture and history will be carefully built, organized, and maintained over the coming years, a project that will last and need revision and expansion for as long as our community continues to grow. The interactive introduction to neurodiversity will be ready upon the launch of loudhandsproject.com, as will the directory to other cross-disability history resources available online. The first of many *Community Conversations* will begin; these will be twice-annual conversations hosted and archived on loudhandsproject.com, in which the autistic community will be invited to share their thoughts via multiple forms of media regarding autistic culture, identity, experiences, and community. The results of each six-month conversation will be archived and added to the Loud Hands Project library of autistic culture and living history.

Video and Film Projects

A critical element of the Loud Hands Project from its creation has been our use of video and film. Two of the specific projects currently being crafted on this media platform include:

- "About Us, Without Us," a documentary concerning the national conversation around eugenics and prenatal detection of autism, currently happening *without* the voices of the very people who will be directly affected, and how that conversation might change if autistic perspectives were included.
- The development of multiple short videos, eventually culminating in a DVD, incorporating video and written content from across the history of the Autistic community, establishing our historical context.

"Welcome to the Autistic Community"

Using the Loud Hands website as a spring, the Loud Hands Project will commence the creation and distribution of a variety of materials (curricula, picture books, pamphlets, and more) designed for the newly diagnosed of all ages, including late- and adult-diagnosis, children, and classrooms, welcoming them to the community and providing an introduction to autistic culture, self-advocacy, and neurodiversity. Initially, this will take the form of a letter drive, blog carnival, and pamphlet-design competition, with ongoing further refinement and eventual publication of materials.

And More!

The Loud Hands Project, in existence for less than a year, is actively pursuing additional projects and platforms that help advance our goal of reminding the world that autistic people have things to say. To that end, we will continue to present at conferences, develop trainings, materials, and other practical resources, collect footage, and work to expand our virtual libraries and the scope, diversity, visibility, and vitality of our community. If you see an opportunity, please drop by loudhandsproject.com and let us know.

Conclusion

On World Autism Awareness Day

by Anne Foreman

jeremiah was a bullfrog / was a good friend of mine / i never understood a single word he said but i helped him drink his wine

joy to the world / all the boys and girls / joy to the fishes in the deep blue sea / joy to you and me.

It takes a long time to figure out that you're not the reason you aren't real.

I am submerged in a sea of words and they are as accurate as anybody's. Sometimes I wonder, honestly, how people without echolalia think. Now I possess a primordial sludge of words like DNA, an alphabet soup of base pairs that I can line up in whatever way I see fit. Scully sings the song quoted above, and her voice is awful. We reserve the right to have awful voices. I reserve the right to pronoun confusion, to repetition, to tripping and muddied syntax. I reserve the right to type instead of speak.

Other people, other structures are the reason you're not real.

You learn to accept a laugh track. What I remember is a mind emptied of words, and a mouth full of them. Other people shoved them in there. I talked and talked the way I was supposed to and yet the entire time, I was silent. I was tied up in a closet in a small corner of my head.

This is not our fault.

But you were not put here on this earth to be laughed at and obscured. And anything counts as yelling.

After years of silence, drowned in mimicry and others' speech, the first sounds of my own I made were squeaks and whimpers. I also rocked. I rocked and screeched and flapped and I didn't know how to do these movements before. If you move you are already less silent.

Anything counts as yelling. They're going to laugh, and you're going to believe it, but eventually you will need to scream.

You can be a moving twitching ugly alien *thing* and never say what they want you to and never talk at all and this is louder than multiple years of proper parroted jabber. Once you start to collect your own echolalia, their words stop getting in. You start with utter silence and work from there. You eventually excise the lies. They robbed me of sincere serious speech, but I am reclaiming it, slowly.

When they laugh, keep yelling. When they tie your soul up and cut it out and dump it in a corner, keep yelling.

If a(n autistic) shark stops stimming, it will die. Don't stop stimming.

(A version of this essay appeared previously on andromedalogic.tumblr.com on April 2nd, 2012.)

Contributing Authors:

Jim Sinclair • Cal Montgomery • Ari Ne'eman • Corina Becker • Zoe Gross • Amanda Forest Vivian • Julia Bascom • Bev Harp • Amy Sequenzia • Nick Walker• Steve Silberman • Paula Durbin-Westby • Kaijaii Gomez Wick • Amanda Baggs • Kassiane Sibley• Kimberly Gerry Tucker • Melanie Yergeau• Savannah Logsdon-Breakstone • Chloe R. • Anne Foreman • Meg Evans • Shain Numair • Karla Fisher• Elizabeth J. Grace • April Herren • Penni Winter• Alyssa Z. • E • Anonymous

Acknowledgements

This anthology could never have come to press without the support and assistance of countless individuals. The editorial team would like to extend particular and specific thanks to our donor partners and sponsors, who helped us get our foot in the door:

Partners:
Jessica Hatch
Karla Fisher
Autism Storybook Mom

Shareholders:
John Kilcullen
Andrea L Shettle

Our indispensable proofreaders:

Valerie Sobczak
Jessamyn Schnackenberg
Janet Hammond
Jennifer A. Peterson
Allegra Stout
Emily Lawrence
Spencer Hunley

Our pinch-hitters:
Jessica Hatch
Amanda Forrest Vivian

A special thanks to Zoe, Claire, Melody, Shannon, Jennifer, Andrew, Leta, and Savannah, who provided scripts, expertise, reassurance, emotional support, and confidence when it was lacking, and without whom this would have remained the vaguest of ideas.

And lastly, special thanks to Ari Ne'eman, who listened and pushed back and then dared it to happen.

CPSIA information can be obtained
at www.ICGtesting.com
Printed in the USA
LVHW111159190822
726304LV00001B/74